D1751695

# CLAUDIA JONES

Black Lives series

Elvira Basevich, *W. E. B. Du Bois*
Denise Lynn, *Claudia Jones*
Utz McKnight, *Frances E. W. Harper*
Joshua Myers, *Cedric Robinson*

# Claudia Jones

## Visions of a Socialist America

Denise Lynn

polity

Copyright © Denise Lynn 2024

The right of Denise Lynn to be identified as Author of this Work has been asserted in accordance with the UK Copyright, Designs and Patents Act 1988.

First published in 2024 by Polity Press

Polity Press
65 Bridge Street
Cambridge CB2 1UR, UK

Polity Press
111 River Street
Hoboken, NJ 07030, USA

All rights reserved. Except for the quotation of short passages for the purpose of criticism and review, no part of this publication may be reproduced, stored in a retrieval system or transmitted, in any form or by any means, electronic, mechanical, photocopying, recording or otherwise, without the prior permission of the publisher.

ISBN-13: 978-1-5095-4930-6
ISBN-13: 978-1-5095-4931-3 (pb)

A catalogue record for this book is available from the British Library.

Library of Congress Control Number: 2023932869

Typeset in 10.75pt on 14pt Janson by
Cheshire Typesetting Ltd, Cuddington, Cheshire
Printed and bound in Great Britain by TJ Books Ltd, Padstow, Cornwall

The publisher has used its best endeavours to ensure that the URLs for external websites referred to in this book are correct and active at the time of going to press. However, the publisher has no responsibility for the websites and can make no guarantee that a site will remain live or that the content is or will remain appropriate.

Every effort has been made to trace all copyright holders, but if any have been overlooked the publisher will be pleased to include any necessary credits in any subsequent reprint or edition.

For further information on Polity, visit our website:
politybooks.com

# Contents

*Acknowledgments*  vi

Introduction  1

1  Jones's Early Years (1915–1936)  18

2  Communist Party, USA (1936–1946)  36

3  The Early Cold War (1945–1950)  79

4  Anti-Cold War and Deportation (1950–1955)  120

5  London (1955–1964)  164

Conclusion  212

*Notes*  226
*Index*  263

# Acknowledgments

I have admired Claudia Jones for over twenty years now. One of my first graduate school essays was on Jones back in 2001, before much of the great scholarship that has been written on her was produced. This book is part of my small contribution to the study of Jones's life and activism. There is so much more to learn about her and there is a coterie of wonderful scholars who have contributed to this project and the larger understanding of Jones's life. I owe a debt of thanks to those scholars including Carole Boyce Davies, Lydia Lindsey, Erik McDuffie, Dayo Gore, Cheryl Higashida, Ashley Farmer, Marika Sherwood, John Munro, Kennetta Hammond-Perry, Rochelle Rowe, Sarah Dunstan, Patricia Owens, and Bill Mullens. I have also been lucky enough to work closely with other Jones scholars including Charisse Burden-Stelly, Derefe Chavannes, and Zifeng Liu. They have all influenced my thinking on Jones and the radical Black Left, and their scholarship helped me to put together this book. I must single out Zifeng Liu as having been especially helpful with this project: as I took it on during the Covid-19 pandemic that shut down archives and the ability to travel, Zifeng shared with me some of his research on the *West Indian Gazette* and the Camden Sisters' book on Jones.

The reference librarians at the Schomburg Center for Research in Black Culture were immensely helpful. Though the center remained closed for much of the pandemic, they helped to get some of the material I was lacking from the Claudia Jones Memorial Collection. Archivists and librarians at the New York University Tamiment Library archives also helped to get material. After years of researching Jones, I realized that there were several holes in my knowledge which archivists and librarians helped to fill, including those at my institution's library who secured microfilm of several communist newspapers. Librarians and archivists are the beating heart of the history profession and so much of my work is thanks to them!

Historian Keisha Blain deserves an enormous amount of thanks and praise; never have I met another scholar who promotes the work and careers of others as much as she does. I must thank her for recommending me to Polity Press for this project. She is also the reason my scholarship has become so visible in the last several years. As editor of *Black Perspectives*, Blain invited me to become a regular blogger, which put my work out to a larger audience and led to a plethora of invitations for projects.

I'm very thankful to the many people who I have collaborated with over the last few years on projects having nothing to do with Jones; my other scholarship has helped me to understand Jones's life and the people she worked with, lived with, socialized with, and loved. Tony Pecinovsky has been a friend and collaborator on many projects, as has Phil Luke Sinitiere. Vernon Pedersen and the others in the Historians of American Communism (HOAC) have been good friends and colleagues and encouraged me to take on another big project, editorship of the *American Communist History* journal. I'm also thankful for the larger scholarly community at my home institution: the people I see every day and who I can chat with about scholarship, family, politics, and everything else. I'm especially thankful for Cacee Hoyer, Stella Ress, Anya King, Jason Hardgrave, Kelly Kaelin, Kristalyn

Shefveland, Sukanya Gupta, Veronica Huggins, Sandy Davis, Brittney Westbrook, Mary Lyn Stoll, and many others.

My dear friends from graduate school are a constant presence and I've been lucky to have them in my life to keep me grounded in the tumult that is undergraduate instruction – Chocolate Pants (Greg Geddes), Smooch (Gaylynn Welch), Heg (Dee Gillespie), Plasticus (Melissa Wrisley), and Goaterella (Mary Weikum). There are others who remain nearby via social media – Shannon King, Jennifer Cubic, Marian Horan, Sarah Boyle, Melissa Madera, Gulhan Erkaya Balsoy, Meg Engle, and so many more who deserve to be named.

My family has always been partially the one I was born into and mostly the one that I made. Thank you to my parents Jack Lynn and Judi Lynn. My brother Dan, sister-in-law Angie, niece Megan, nephew Ryan, sister Corinne and her partner Erin are only a text away whenever I need something or when we just need a laugh, or, in the case of Erin, to find out what Jones's medical records mean. Losing our dear cuz-bro Andrew left a hole, but we remember him always for the love and laughter he gave and not the pain he suffered. My best friends Ang Reap and wife Jess Bacon-Reap, Danielle Copeland and Jess Amisial, Nicole and Steve Russell, Sue Wee and Mark Hickman are all part of my extended family. Adrian Gentle has been a supportive and caring partner for many years, putting up with me dragging him around the country for research or just a good hike. And of course, my darling daughter Cybele, who is fiercely independent, but always willing to take a trip, especially if I'm covering the bill.

I am grateful to David Horsley of the British Communist Party for arranging a meeting between Tionne Paris, Winston Pinder, and me, on a sunny afternoon in May 2022. An octogenarian, and a local social justice legend, Pinder had kindly agreed to answer our many questions about his memories of Jones. So much has been written about her political life, so it was her personal life we wanted to know about. But for Pinder, Jones was an activist first, always focused on her work, never glorifying herself and never taking credit for her sacrifices. He told us she was a great dancer who talked about her mother frequently, but that she was reticent to open up to people unless they were close friends, and even then, she didn't focus on her troubles or worries, or linger on her poor health; she was wholly devoted to the emancipation of everyone. She was a person he admired and loved, who was taken too soon and who left behind hundreds of political allies and friends. For myself, it felt special to have a personal connection to someone who had known Jones and worked with her. I did not uncover everything I wanted to know about Jones for this project, but I nonetheless submit it as another humble contribution to what has already been written.

# Introduction

*For Claudia Jones*

Just to tell you
that part of us
sailed on with you

To tell you
we'll renew our planting
this bleak and mournful day

We'll change the seasons,
the sun and moon
of man-made years

That soon
our tears will flower
into reason's beauty

And our land
will call you home
to be its heart.[1]
    Edith Segal

Claudia Jones was deported from the United States in 1955 because she was a Black radical communist. As the poem above indicates, she was a loved and respected leader admired by her friends and comrades. She was a devoted antiracist and anti-sexist who advocated peace, demilitarization, and anti-imperialism. She was a leading thinker in the American Communist Party (CPUSA) and a prolific writer whose comrades worked diligently to prevent her deportation. Jones was what US intelligence and legislative leaders deemed an enemy of the state and a national security risk. In violation of the constitution and the Bill of Rights, she was monitored, harassed, arrested, and eventually deported from a country she had spent most of her life in. She was sent far from her family, friends, and comrades to a country she had never lived in before, where she would stay for the remainder of her short life.

Jones was also deeply influential, well-known among both Black and white comrades for her acute theoretical grounding and her activism. She was loved by her family and friends, worked with progressives and liberals to improve the lives of women and people of color, and left a legacy for later Black radical feminists. She remained known and influential among a small group of activists and scholars who mined her written and spoken work and eventually resurrected her for a larger audience of activists. Above all, Jones was a committed communist who not only anticipated the consequences of US militarization and capitalism but also envisioned a socialist future, the eradication of monopoly capitalism, and the achievement of social justice for the oppressed. Her writing and activism continue to offer important lessons for contemporary audiences.

## The Long Life of Claudia Jones

After her premature death in 1964, scholars and fellow communists kept her in remembrance. Some of her friends and comrades lived long lives after her and taught a younger generation of activists about her life and work. The US communist press regularly featured Jones in articles, and in 1968 a group called the Claudia Jones Club was created in Chicago to honor her legacy and continue her work to seek justice. In 1969 the communist *Daily World* honored Black history week (which would become Black history month in 1970) with an homage to Jones and her friends Pettis Perry, James Ford, and W.E.B. Du Bois. In 1974, CPUSA leader and Jones's comrade Henry Winston noted in *World Magazine* that she "was a passionate voice for truth and justice." That same year, Alva Buxenbaum, a leader in the CPUSA's Women's Commission, published an article in the Communist Party of Great Britain's (CPGB) *Daily World* on US communist women and their struggles for women's rights. She listed Jones as one of the CPUSA's significant leaders.[2]

In 1981, the scholar and Party activist Angela Davis wrote about Jones in her book *Women, Race, and Class*, describing her as a leader and "symbol of struggle for Communist women" who had refuted the "usual male-supremacist stereotypes" about women and women's roles. Jones, Davis argued, showed that Black women's leadership had always been essential in people's movements, and would take even her own progressive friends to task for failing to take women's rights and women's roles in the movement seriously. Most important, Jones believed that "socialism held the only promise of liberation for Black women."[3]

In 1985, Buzz Johnson, a Tobago-born activist, compiled a book on Jones titled *"I Think of My Mother": Notes on the Life and Times of Claudia Jones*. Published by his own Karia Press, Johnson's book was put together with the help of Jones's friends and comrades, including Donald Hines and Billy Strachan, who had worked with Jones in London. Johnson credited Jones's long-time friend (and former romantic partner) Abhimanyu Manchanda for encouraging the project. It was the first book on Jones, and it included news clippings and speeches offering a history of her life in her own words. The same year, Johnson wrote an article commemorating what would have been Jones's seventieth birthday. He noted that the importance of his book was that, in all the years since she had passed, no work had been done on the study of her life.[4]

Three years earlier, Buzz and his then partner Yvette Thomas had been involved in founding the Claudia Jones Organization (CJO), set up to address the needs of "African Caribbean women and children." The organization, which still exists today, is based in East London and engages in community outreach and education. Buzz and Yvette's son, Amandla Thomas-Johnson, has talked about Jones's influence on his parents and many others, and how she remained an important presence in London even years after her death. He recalls that as a youth he attended CJO programs including a Saturday school and a summer school. Every year on Jones's birthday the CJO would organize an event at her grave in Highgate cemetery, next to Karl Marx's grave. The group would lay flowers and sing:

> Oh Claudia Jones's birthday, Aye Claudia Jones's Birthday,
> Oh Claudia Jones's Birthday, we celebrate it today.
>
> To Claudia, that female conqueror, in England and America she was a freedom fighter.

The song was written by a Calypso musician to celebrate Jones's life of activism and her commitment to the emancipation of all.[5]

That the first significant look at Jones's life came out of a London publisher is not surprising, given that her legacy in England is linked to the popular Notting Hill Carnival and her work with London's West Indian community. Though she spent most of her life in the United States, her memory was scarred by anticommunism, and the American friends she left behind still operated in its shadows. In 1987, another London group began its own project to document Jones's life. The Camden Black Sisters (CBS) was founded in 1979 by Lee Kane and Yvonne Joseph as an educational and aid organization for Black women. The group sought to create their own space to discuss issues relevant to African/Caribbean women. CBS was based in Kentish town, where Jones had spent many of her London years, so the group decided to create a project to draw attention to her life and work. Jennifer Tyson, a CBS researcher, reached out to the CPUSA for information on Jones. In 1988, the group published *Claudia Jones, 1915–1964: A Woman of Our Times*. The book included a personal and political biography and aimed to bring Jones to a wider audience.[6]

Aside from Angela Davis's earlier work, one of the first scholarly treatments of Jones came from Donna Langston, a professor at the University of Washington. Langston wrote that she first learned about Jones not in the US, where she was virtually unknown except among communists, but from attending a "cross-cultural Black women's studies course" at the University of London. She was told that Jones was the Angela Davis of her time, likened by the actor, singer, and activist Paul Robeson to Sojourner Truth and Harriet Tubman. Langston attributed the silence around Jones in the United States to the narrowing of US political culture during the Cold War. Her name had been forgotten, while others like Robeson or Elizabeth Gurley Flynn were remembered. To remember Jones was to engage with the "history of fascism, sexism, classism, and racism."[7]

In January 1989, Winsome Pinnock, a British playwright whose family was from Jamaica, debuted her play *A Rock in the Water* at London's Chelsea Royal Court theater. Based on Jones's life, the play was performed by the Royal Court Young People's Theater. It told the story of Jones's ejection from the US and her life in England fighting for the rights of Black Britons against "right-wing extremist groups." Given her own years spent in youth theater, Jones would no doubt have appreciated the fact that young actors were playing the roles, but she likely would not have agreed with the description of fighting against "right-wing extremists" since she just as often criticized liberals for their tepid action on securing justice. The play is currently being adapted for film. That same year, Julie Whittaker from BBC Midlands contacted the CPUSA to gather information for a short documentary titled *Claudia Jones: A Woman of Her Time*, which was created with input from some of Jones's American comrades, including James and Esther Cooper Jackson, Marvel Cooke, and Louise Weinstock. Both the BBC documentary and the play speak to how Jones's life in England was more readily remembered outside of communist circles than was her life in the United States.[8]

In the early 1990s, scholar and activist Marika Sherwood was alarmed that so many of the leading West Indian and communist activists who had known Jones were passing. She decided to organize a symposium devoted to Jones's life and work – thirty people responded and the symposium, held in 1996, was recorded. Sherwood decided to undertake further biographical research, and eventually published the symposium transcripts along with contributions from Jones's friends and colleagues, Donald Hind and Colin Prescod, in 1999, under the title *Claudia Jones: A Life in Exile*. This was the most comprehensive biographical work to date focused on Jones's life in London, and it brought her to the attention of an even larger audience. Sherwood later shared her research material with other scholars by depositing it at the Schomburg Center for Research in Black Culture in Harlem, New York, paving the way for work by a new generation of scholars.[9]

In the wake of Sherwood's and Johnson's groundbreaking studies, Jones began to appear more regularly in scholarship among historians of American communism and the Black Diaspora in the 1990s. The growing literature on the CPUSA had largely ignored women, especially Black women, but that now began to change. Toward the end of that decade, there were at least three dissertations that either focused on Jones's life and work or included her in a study of radical Black women. In an article from 1998, Rebecca Hill discussed Jones's work on women's issues within the Party and her keen analysis of the need for different approaches to women's oppression. Kate Weigand devoted a chapter of her 2001 book *Red Feminism* to Jones, examining her most significant and widely known written work, "An End to the Neglect of the Problems of the Negro Woman!" As Weigand explained, Jones was a far more significant presence within the Party than had previously been acknowledged. Not simply a leader, she had been an important thinker when it came to influencing the Party's policy and practice. As Charisse Burden-Stelly notes, Weigand showed that Jones moved Black women "beyond narratives of victimhood," revealing them to be "empowered, progressive, active, and desirable." Weigand's book and Hill's article were important revisions in the largely male-dominated CPUSA histories.[10]

Jones's name increasingly began to appear in scholarship on socialist feminism, the Caribbean, and the Black Freedom Struggle. She was included in the *Encyclopedia of the American Left*, with an essay written by Robin D.G. Kelley. Kelley also discussed Jones in his 2002 book *Freedom Dreams*, where he noted that Jones positioned Black women as the vanguard of liberation movements and had advanced the argument that "the overthrow of class and gender oppression" required the "abolition of racism." John McClendon wrote an entry on Jones for the encyclopedia *Notable Black American Women*, arguing that she was committed to the Leninist notion of Democratic Centralism, which centered authority in the Party's Central Committee but made room for the rank-and-file to debate and critique policy and theory – something Jones excelled at.[11]

There were, however, few scholarly analyses focused primarily on Jones, until 2007, when the most significant study on her life and work was published: Carole Boyce Davies's *Left of Karl Marx*. The book, Boyce Davies noted, was not meant as a "traditional biography" but instead offered an analysis of Jones's life, literature, and activism. While Jones had been written about in relation to communism, Black Nationalism, and feminism, Boyce Davies approached her as an individual thinker and writer whose influence on the movements she engaged in was widespread and significant. As Burden-Stelly argues, this study "made an invaluable conceptual contribution" in its discussion of "radical Black female subjectivity." Boyce Davies positioned Jones as a "radical Black subject," defined as someone who "resists the domination of systems, states, institutions, and organizations" that "maintain oppression, exclusion, exploitation, and docility." The book brought Jones more attention and inspired new generations of scholars and activists to think about how to formulate a politics of liberation. Boyce Davies had also been in contact with Manchanda's ex-wife, Diane Langford, who had carefully preserved Jones's papers. Langford entrusted Boyce Davies to deliver the papers to the Schomburg Center for Research in Black Culture, further increasing the material available to future scholars.[12]

## Claudia Jones Today

The scholarship and activist groups that kept Jones in remembrance influenced later generations, but they also confronted misinterpretations of her legacy. In her lifetime Jones was a target of anticommunism, in the United States and also in Britain. Her memory has either been sanitized, as in England where she is primarily remembered as the founder of Carnival, or ignored entirely – as in the United States – because she was a committed communist, a member of the maligned CPUSA, and an outspoken revolutionary. In the US, anticommunism continues to be used as a tool to circumscribe social justice movements, with right-wing leaders like Donald Trump deploying it against even the most moderate proposals for social justice. But new generations have embraced Jones and her committed activism, and reject anticommunism as a tool of the elites. Jones advocated the destruction of capitalism and militarism, the dissolution of old and new empires, and the advent of a socialist United States. Today, in a period that has been described as late-stage capitalism, and at a time when corporations are literally and knowingly choosing to destroy the planet for profit, Jones's work and activism remain relevant and have begun to resonate with young activists.

In recent years polls have shown that American and British youth have soured on capitalism. Several media outlets have attributed this to the Covid-19 pandemic and the political posturing of government officials who urge young people to stay in their low-paying jobs for the sake of the economy. But even before the pandemic, austerity measures had led to a serious decline in quality of life. Culture wars have obscured the economic ills of others, obfuscated the reality of material decline, and provided cover for devastating cuts to already limited social programs. Although there is an increased interest in socialism on the left of the political spectrum, the right has begun to appeal to young voters. In the absence of a viable political agenda, the right-wing has managed to draw in young white people with racism and rage, directing frustration away from capitalists toward people of color. White nationalists have used racism and white supremacy to deflect attention from capitalist devastation and ensure the perpetuation of economic policies that favor the wealthy.[13] But more and more young people are growing disenchanted with capitalism as it continues to ravage people and the planet, and as policymakers of all political stripes focus on ensuring corporate profits. The rise of Black Lives Matter (BLM), an organization founded in 2013 by three young Black women – Alicia Garza, Patrisse Cullors, and Opal Tometi – was fueled by youth disaffection with institutions that perpetuate oppression, in particular the criminal legal system. Jones would have celebrated BLM's founding, given her commitment to Black women as leaders in resistance struggles. As Lydia Lindsey argues, there is a "traceable arch" between Jones and organizations like BLM that react to the "cycles" of racial capitalism, "nationalism and state-terror." Jones's intellectual and activist work was a "presage" of BLM in terms of how it engages with the Black radical and intellectual tradition and in its understandings of Black women's oppression.[14]

More recently, in the summer of 2020 – with the combined exigencies of the Covid-19 pandemic and a public policy that favored corporate profits over public health – American and British youth took to the streets to express their frustrations. Following the police murder of George Floyd in May 2020, in Minneapolis, Minnesota, protestors came out in unprecedented numbers in both the US and the UK. Some of them demanded a reckoning with history and began tearing down monuments that represented empire and the use of slave labor for wealth accumulation. In July 2020, protestors in Bristol tore down a statue of the slave trader Edward Colston and threw it into the harbor. In the United States, long-contested Confederate statues were removed, and in other locations around the world statues and other racist symbols of empire and capitalism were taken down. In Antwerp, Belgium, for example, a statue of King Leopold was removed.[15] Globally, many are growing disillusioned and angry with capitalism's history of exploitation and destruction, and with the bleak future it offers.

Corporations have answered by trying to commodify socialist heroes like Jones. Corporate virtue signaling is notorious for using civil rights icons to sell products, the most recent example being Dodge Ram's use of a Martin Luther King Jr. speech in one of its truck advertisements. These companies have tried to connect to a younger generation interested in social justice by using famous civil rights figures to link liberation to material accumulation, selling the message that emancipation can be found in personal wealth. Jones has not yet reached that type of notoriety, but on October 14, 2020 she was featured as a Google Doodle. The Doodle's accompanying text commemorated Jones's appearance on a British postal stamp in 2008, in a series on "Women of Distinction," and nodded to her role in founding Carnival, but it provided a half history that only briefly mentioned the fact that she was a communist. As Amandla Thomas-Johnson has noted, the danger with such attempts to mainstream revolutionary figures is that they get "rolled into ... various national projects," their memories become "muted," and their critiques become watered down and de-radicalized.[16]

In 2021, Marika Sherwood's book on Jones was republished by Lawrence & Wishart. In her preface to the new edition, Lola Olufemi argued that although Jones is remembered, her radical politics – including her lifelong devotion to Marxist Leninism, and her commitment to the global liberation of the colonized – have been sanitized. The CPGB never wholly embraced Jones because she "challenged their failure to acknowledge the plight of colonial subjects." Olufemi reasons that it is simpler for British communists to ignore Jones than to acknowledge that some of their own membership were racist. Her memory in Britain focuses on an apolitical depiction of her as the founder of Carnival, rather than as a committed liberationist who challenged the capitalist, imperialist state. Jones did not found Carnival as just a celebration – it was a response to white supremacist violence that targeted London's West Indian community. Jones also used it to introduce white Londoners to Caribbean culture, celebrate Black beauty, and radicalize the oppressed to stand up for their communities. Olufemi notes that Jones's lifelong struggle with her health is also an essential part of her memory. She operated in a world that was "determined to kill her," and which took her life as she became a leading figure in global liberation movements. What could have been we will never know, because she lived in a world that operated (and continues to operate) to kill "prematurely" those who threaten the social order.[17]

While the remembrance of Jones in Britain contains important elisions, in the United States her memory remained in anticommunism's shadow. She and her generation have, at best, been marginalized in the history of the Black Freedom

Struggle or, at worst, been seen as radical agitators, treasonous in intent and practice. Activists in the US and UK have found other ways to commemorate her. In 2008, a blue plaque was unveiled in Notting Hill remembering Jones for her role in the Carnival celebration. The plaque was the work of the Nubian Jak Community Trust, an organization devoted to commemorating the significant impact of Black Britons; its unveiling, organized by the Carnival committee, was attended by the High Commissioner for Trinidad and Tobago. In 2010, the filmmaker Nia Reynolds produced a fifty-minute documentary on Claudia Jones's life titled *Looking for Claudia Jones*. English Heritage, a non-profit that manages historic sites, announced in 2023 that a blue plaque will be placed in Vauxhall, South London at one of Jones's former residences. The go-ahead for the plaque was secured by an activist, as a commemoration of Jones's life, influence, and activism during her London years.[18]

In 2020, Steve McQueen, son of a Grenadian mother and Trinidadian father, featured Jones in an episode of *Small Axe*, a series of five films that takes its name from a proverb: "If you are the big tree, we are the small axe." The films aired on the BBC in the UK and on Amazon Prime in the United States, and showed the challenges faced by Black Britons from the 1960s to the 1980s. McQueen said that the series was meant as both entertainment and education. He noted that most people do not know who Claudia Jones is, but hoped that after watching the episode they "will go out and find out."[19]

In the United States, the Claudia Jones School for Political Education, based in Washington, DC, has taken inspiration from Jones. The organization is devoted to political causes like labor organizing as well as educating the public on Jones's life and work. It maintains an online archive of some of her most significant publications and invites scholars and activists to discuss her influence, her work and the work of her comrades, and her continuing relevance to contemporary struggles. The group is also partnered with other activist organizations focused on anti-imperialist and anti-poverty struggles that continue to plague the US and the former colonies. It is an organization that takes Jones's anti-racism, anti-sexism, anti-imperialism, and peace activism as a foundation for its own work.

## Claudia Jones's Life's Work

Coupled with the growing research into her life, scholars and activists have looked to Jones as a model for how to face some of the myriad challenges in the twenty-first century. Her ideas were foundational in the Black Freedom Struggle, but are also useful in contemplating the problems she faced and that continue to exist. As an influential communist, immigrant, and women's rights advocate, her life's work focused on theorizing an emancipatory ethos that centered the most exploited. Jones's contributions to freedom struggles include her criticisms of the fascist policy manifested in militarism and policing, her focus on the threat of monopoly capitalism and its role in the oppression of people of color, women, the colonized, and the working masses, and her insistence that the most oppressed (Black women) should take the reins in liberation struggles. She argued that by recognizing the most oppressed and working toward their liberation we could ultimately achieve the liberation of all people.

Above all, Jones was a Marxist. She offered a prescient and still relevant critique of monopoly capitalism. It was capitalists who benefited from war, poverty, racism, and sexism. Oppression was not a byproduct of capitalism; rather, capitalism thrived on and required oppression. Capitalists operated with the state to ensure profit at the expense of any real commitment to democracy. Jones believed that only with the destruction of capitalism could liberation be achieved. She did not, however, limit herself to traditional Marxist thought. Jones believed that Marxism fell short in its understanding of both racism and sexism. A class-only theory did not account for oppression within and among working people. In the United States, for example, class status was linked to race and gender, and the most exploited workers were Black women handicapped by racism, sexism, and class oppression. As Lola Olufemi has noted, Jones pointed to "race as a modality in which class is lived." The white working class were often collaborators with capitalism, and even among left-progressives racism and sexism meant that white activists did not see people of color as their peers. Women were also excluded and marginalized in the labor movement. This viewpoint remains a challenge today, as some on the left continue to mute how sexism and racism operate with class oppression.[20]

Focusing on Black women's triple oppression, Jones argued that they represented the most oppressed and exploited group. She believed that in order to secure emancipation, Black women had to take the lead among the global proletariat. Much of Jones's written work took her fellow communists and left-progressives to task for ignoring Black women. What progress could anyone hope to make by ignoring the most exploited? Organizing workers for their liberation meant organizing ALL workers – including domestics, housekeepers, childcare workers, teachers, etc. In this way Jones helped to redefine labor in the Marxist cosmology: while the male shopfloor worker was important, Black women's leadership, she argued, would be central to the liberation movement. Jones also believed that labor unions were important tools in cultivating class solidarity.

Today labor unions have been defanged and are beholden to the goodwill of political parties. This process began during Jones's lifetime as the unions fell prey to internal and external redbaiting. But Jones was convinced that interracial cooperation among workers would succeed in usurping corporate power. The same youth who have soured on capitalism today have begun leading unionization efforts across the United States and Britain in a united front against capitalist power.

Jones was an internationalist, anti-imperialist, and anti-colonialist. She did not define liberation narrowly, restricting it within the confines of the Western nations; as a colonized citizen, she understood that imperialism and colonialism strengthened the capitalist states and impoverished the colonized. She worked with activists around the world to address the privations of colonialism and imperialist exploitation. In the post-World War II years, as liberation movements secured independence, she was wary of corporate and military power as imperialism began to take on a seemingly benign image. The formerly colonized found that independence left them beholden to the imperial might of their former colonizers, and to the growing military behemoth of the United States. Liberation, therefore, required peace and demilitarization.

Jones was a peace activist. Peace was more than just the absence of war; it meant destroying the institutions that perpetuated inequality. Jones was alarmed that the end of World War II was leading to an endless conflict between the Soviet Union and the United States. She believed that militarism and war harmed women and children the most and that the United States was creating a permanent war economy. During the Cold War, imperialism took the form of a corporate colonialism upheld by American militarism. War also operated as an excuse for the violation of civil liberties and the suppression of liberatory struggles. Any challenge to the status quo became treasonous during times of conflict, and in the militarized United States there was (is) no other time but wartime. Jones saw what the United States would become – a country in a forever war focused on policing the world, while the American people are left fighting over the leftovers.

Perhaps Jones's most important quality was that she was not a pessimist – she did not lose hope in the face of what often felt like insurmountable barriers. She retained hope in the people, the colonized, the marginalized, and, just as important, their allies. She always believed it would be socialism that ushered in an equitable future. Activists today face the largest concentration of wealth in recent memory, neo-colonial extractive politics in the former colonies, and a climate crisis that remains largely unaddressed because capitalists are unwilling to forge a future in which the planet comes first. The military behemoth that Jones and her comrades predicted has evolved into the largest and most expensive military-industrial complex in the world, a complex that sustains US capitalism and continues the exploitation of postcolonial states. Jones's life and work offer a path forward to understanding how to achieve an equitable future. Capitalism and freedom do not coexist, democratic institutions cannot be wedded to the marketplace, and freedom will not be gifted by politicians beholden to corporations. For Jones, only with the destruction of capitalist and militarist institutions and states can the people secure justice. She advocated that the path forward required socialism.

# 1

# Jones's Early Years (1915–1936)

*Change the Mind of Man*

Against the corruption of centuries
Of feudal, bourgeois, capitalist ideas
The fusion of courage and clarity
Of polemic against misleaders
Who sought compromise with the enemy
*These* were the pre-requisites of victory.

No idle dreamers these –
And yet they dared to dream
The dream long planned
Holds in socialist China.

From Yenan, cradle of the revolution;
Of their dreams, their fight
Their organization, their heroism
Yenan – proud monument to man's will
To transform nature, and, so doing
Transform society, and man himself!

                          Claudia Jones[1]

It was a cold New York winter day when Claudia Cumberbatch and her three sisters and aunt landed in New York Harbor on February 9, 1924. Leaving their home in Port-of-Spain, Trinidad, where the average temperatures in February could reach 26 Celsius, Jones and her sisters faced a snowy, 1-degree winter day and an nighttime low of −10 degrees. Jones would later write that her parents had hoped the United States would provide them with economic opportunity and a welcoming place to raise their daughters. What they found instead was a country on the verge of an economic crisis, racial inequality, dangerous working conditions, and a constant struggle for survival. Trinidad, a British colony, faced poverty resulting from imperialist mandates; this, it turned out, was not unlike the Black experience in the United States, where official policy perpetuated racism and poverty.[2]

Jones's parents, Charles and Minnie Cumberbatch, had arrived two years earlier hoping to settle in their new country, secure jobs, and bring their daughters to the US. Their fortunes were tied to the colonial economy, and a drop in the cocoa trade throughout the Caribbean led to economic turmoil and migration for thousands of West Indian families to the United States and elsewhere. Claudia's arrival in the United States marked the beginning of her radicalization. The bleak conditions for Black Americans, and her own family's experience with poverty and racism, were what made her a communist. She would draw on her youthful experiences in Harlem to inspire her critique of monopoly capitalism, her faith in Black women's political leadership, and her commitment to socialism. As the poem quoted above shows, Jones became committed to changing the "minds of men," getting them to recognize that emancipating the most oppressed would emancipate everyone.[3]

## Trinidad and Tobago

Christopher Columbus landed on Trinidad in 1498, on his third trip to the Western Hemisphere; there he came upon the indigenous Arawak and Kalinago Indians. Columbus claimed the island for Spain, but the Spanish took nearly 100 years to settle it and the nearby Tobago island. In 1592, they created a capital named San José de Oruña in North Trinidad. In 1757 the governor moved to Port-of-Spain, followed by the Cabildo (town council) in 1787, making it the capital. In 1783, the Spanish and French created a plan to "develop Trinidad economically," and they started by inviting white settlers into the area. By agreement, the French and Spanish encouraged primarily Catholic settlement. Settlers were drawn by offers of free land, and many of the French who came from surrounding islands brought enslaved people with them. They were also given additional land for each newly imported enslaved person. The Haitian revolution, which led to the displacement of French slaveholders, increased the island's population.[4]

As scholars of racial capitalism have shown, the European industrial powers were founded on the racialized labor of the African diaspora. Racial capitalism, as defined by Charisse Burden-Stelly, refers to the "mutually constitutive nature of racialization and capitalism." Hilary McD. Beckles argues that European interests in the Caribbean led to competition over control of the region's resources and indigenous and enslaved labor. In the sixteenth and seventeenth centuries, the British, French, and Dutch attacked the Spanish colonial economy. Their goal was to "achieve maximum wealth extraction" in this new landscape. The Caribbean economy was deliberately created for a "singular purpose" as an "external economic engine" for "national economic growth."

As the European powers competed with one another to seize land and labor, they created an "immoral entrepreneurial order" that was "beyond the accountability of civilization." Far away from their own legal and social orders, European settlers ushered in an era of extreme cruelty against the native and enslaved populations.[5]

As Trinidad and Tobago's first Prime Minister Eric Williams explained in his book *History of the People of Trinidad and Tobago*, the Spanish were interested in little else but gold and silver. They forced the native population to work in mines looking for precious metals the islands did not have. In seeking to extract resources and labor from the indigenous populations, the Europeans were forced to negotiate as the native groups resisted the colonizers' encroachment. What followed was a series of treaties that led to a "web of relations" between the indigenous, the Europeans, and the Africans. This web was an "entanglement" that led to "resistance and tension."[6] Williams argued that the Spanish obsession with gold meant that Trinidad and Tobago were left undeveloped, with the Spanish often shipping indigenous people to their other colonies for labor. When this exploitation thinned the indigenous population, enslaved people from Africa were forcibly brought to the islands. For a time, tobacco was the basis of the islands' economy, until cocoa trees were planted. Once French planters arrived, they introduced sugar; there was also a healthy trade in coffee and cotton.[7]

In 1797, Spain "surrendered" Trinidad and Tobago to the British, though it was not formally ceded until 1802. Britain abolished the slave trade in 1807, which ended African importation into the islands, but slavery itself was not formally abolished until 1838. Even after abolition, Britain "worked hard" to maintain the "extractive model" it had developed in its colonial administration. Trinidad and Tobago joined other Caribbean islands in what was called the "British West Indies" (BWI), which formalized the islands as part of the British Empire. That name would be abandoned in the post-World War II period of decolonization, in favor of the "Commonwealth Caribbean."[8]

Finding it difficult to secure a cheap labor force locally, sugar planters in Trinidad began importing Indian indentured servants, a practice that did not end until 1917. As McD. Beckles argues, the intention behind importing laborers was to "prolong wealth creation and appropriation" similar to slavery. What followed was a "long century of British colonial brutality" until rebellions across the Caribbean "discredited the colonial state." But the British military ferociously suppressed the rebellions and engaged in massacres. Even as West Indians rose up against the colonial regime, "political oppression" was deployed to "maintain maximum wealth extraction."[9] By the beginning of the twentieth century, the imperial powers were busy cleaving away at the African continent, and the United States had transformed the Caribbean Sea into a "de facto American lake." Some of the "older" British colonies in the BWI began to experience economic hardship, while islands like Trinidad emerged as more successful in the sugar industry. This led to the migration of people to other islands as well as to the United States. These early migrants came primarily from Jamaica and Barbados. Eventually Trinidad would face a similar decline in its economic circumstances.[10]

As Jones later wrote, her family's migration was prompted by the decline in the cocoa trade, but Trinidad at the start of the twentieth century faced several problems. Planters insisted that they needed to continue the importation of Indian indentures because of a shortage of laborers, even though Jamaicans and Barbadians were migrating in search of jobs and local workers were also available. A Trinidadian lawyer named Prudhomme David accused the cocoa and sugar planters of preferring indentures because they were cheap, easily exploitable, and could be kept in a state of "semi-servitude."[11]

As part of the empire, the citizens of Trinidad and Tobago were socialized and educated to be good colonials. As Williams put it, schools taught students to "be British," with an "un-West Indian" education. Buzz Johnson had a similar experience in primary school until independence in 1962, when he entered high school. The young were taught that they were part of the empire and that the Queen was the ultimate authority. It was an assimilationist education similar to the "uplift" ideology in the United States – its message was that behaving as a white person would lead to integration and equality. The reality was that so many of the West Indians who came into contact with the British were treated with contempt and faced racism and discrimination regardless of their behavior.[12]

The outbreak of World War I in Europe caused other problems in the colonies. A significant number of men from the BWI volunteered to fight for Britain, but faced hostility, segregation, and violence from white British soldiers. The men who served in the British West Indian regiment had a disproportionately higher disease rate than other regiments, were often refused service at the British forces canteens, and faced racist verbal abuse. Aware that this treatment might provoke discontent, the Colonial Office persuaded the War Office to give the regiment a raise that had previously been denied. On returning home to Trinidad, ex-servicemen took part in labor protests which "shook the colonial structure to its very foundation." Price gouging was common during the war with prices increasing "145 percent" in Trinidad and "126 percent" in Port-of-Spain where the Cumberbatch family lived; wages remained low, adding to the general discontent. Resistance to the price-gouging and low wages was fueled further by the veteran's inability to secure work. A 1919 strike in Port-of-Spain, led by ex-servicemen, was imbued with a "nationalist . . . racial, and ideological" demand for a "Black world controlled and governed by Black people." Meanwhile, cocoa production was in decline and the Great Depression that would soon reverberate across the globe prevented the crop from ever "recovering its former position" as a leader in Trinidadian agriculture.[13]

It was this tumultuous environment that led Jones's parents to seek opportunities elsewhere. Jones's father, Charles Bertrand Cumberbatch, was born in Trinidad on January 15, 1884 to a family of hotel workers. Her mother Sybil Logan (Minnie Magdalene) was born September 4, 1890 to Thomas Logan and Catherine Eustache. The Logan family were landowners and part of the middle class. Charles and Sybil married in Port-of-Spain on November 26, 1913. Their first daughter, Sylvia, is listed as having been born the following fall, on October 16, 1914. Claudia's birth certificate, located by Carol Boyce Davies, confirms her birthday as February 21, 1915, raising doubts about the authenticity of her older sister's official birthdate. Sylvia's naturalization form gave her age as thirty-two in April 1946, which suggests that Minnie was likely pregnant when she married Charles. Because she was Catholic, they may have listed Sylvia's birth as occurring later than it did to cover up the fact of premarital sex, a common practice. Jones's sisters Yvonne and Lindsay followed in 1917 and 1919. Claudia's birth certificate lists her birthplace as Cazabon Lane, Belmont, a suburb of Port-of-Spain, but as Boyce Davies notes, Jones later gave her birthplace as Woodbrook, a newer suburb of the city built on the remains of an old plantation, suggesting that the family moved there later.[14]

## United States

Like so many other Caribbean immigrants faced with declining economic conditions, Charles and Minnie decided to try their luck in the United States. The two traveled there in the spring of 1922 on the *SS Vaughn*, arriving in New York on May 1. They chose the US in the hope of improving their children's situation and finding freedom. Jones would later write that they were quickly "disabused" of this hope, facing as they did poverty and the "scourge of Jim Crow."[15]

The family moved to Harlem, New York, during the age of the Harlem Renaissance in art, literature, music, and politics. As historians Stephen Robertson, Shane White, Stephen Garton, and Graham White have noted, histories of this renaissance have obscured the fact that the neighborhood was for most Harlemites a "tragic slum." A large influx of immigrants expanded the neighborhood with settlement north to 160th Street and as far south as 110th Street. The Harlem population was over 200,000, one-fifth of whom were from the Caribbean. Limited housing stock led to overcrowded apartments, while manufacturing jobs were dominated by whites, leaving largely underpaid and exploited service jobs for Black residents. The crowding, poor work conditions, and lack of access to health care led to a disproportionate amount of illness in the community. As Robertson et al. argue, these conditions meant many had recourse to gambling as a means of supplementing their low incomes. Its popularity meant that residents were vulnerable to police harassment and white gangsters, and it tainted Harlem with the stereotype of criminality.[16]

Harlemites set up institutions and organizations that helped them to negotiate the poor conditions and to face off against white racism. These institutions could include card games or meetings with friends, as well as fraternal orders like the Prince Hall Masons and the Elks. There were local branches of the National Association for the Advancement of Colored People (NAACP), and the CPUSA would eventually also set up its own Harlem branch. But as Robertson et al. explain, one of the most significant organizations was Marcus Garvey's United Negro Improvement Association (UNIA), the Pan-African group that was devoted to "racial unity and uplift." Between 1920 and 1926, 24,000 West Indian immigrants, including the Cumberbatch family, moved to Harlem, and would become the "base" of radical groups like the UNIA. It is not clear if the Cumberbatch family were involved in the Garvey movement, but Trinidad had the largest non-US UNIA branch at the time, so it is likely they had at least heard of it.[17]

Charles and Minnie spent just under two years trying to create a life in Harlem before sending for their four daughters. The girls arrived in February 1924 accompanied by their aunt Alice Glasgow and a cousin named Meta who was a year older than Claudia. The family lived at 404 St. Nicholas Avenue in Central Harlem, a few blocks away from the famous Apollo theater. The apartment building the Cumberbatch family lived in housed other West Indian immigrants, as did the surrounding apartment buildings. Charles Cumberbatch worked as a furrier and Minnie as a dressmaker. The girls attended school at PS 4, today called PS 4 Duke Ellington, located on 160th Street.[18]

New York City public schools were integrated in 1900, nevertheless, Jones and her sisters were taunted for being West Indian. By junior high school, she had "integrated" into the community, as she would describe it, and had many friends. The popular Jones decided to run for school government. The student-body government mirrored that of the city administration and Jones ran for mayor with a Chinese student. Even though teachers tried to convince Jones to choose another running mate, the two were elected with an overwhelming majority.[19]

The Cumberbatch family suffered a great misfortune in November 1928, when Minnie Cumberbatch died from spinal meningitis at her place of employment at 2089 Madison Avenue. Spinal meningitis can be transmitted in different ways, but it most often occurs as a virus that, if left untreated, can have devastating effects within twenty-four to forty-eight hours, including brain damage and death. As Dr. Joseph Doane wrote in 1927, there were cases of spinal meningitis in every city, usually "brought about by crowding, improper food and faulty living conditions," and it could spread in schools and workplaces. Today it would be treated with antibiotics that were not available in 1928. Doane described the onset of the disease as "sudden and stormy," since someone who was well could exhibit severe symptoms – headache, a chill, high fever, dizziness, nausea, vomiting, a slow pulse, and a stiff neck – within three to five days of infection. Sometimes the stiffness would travel throughout the body. Where Minnie picked up the infection is unknown, but it seems to have struck her quickly since she was at work when she died. This event would prove to be formative for the young Claudia.[20]

In a 1952 speech Jones stated that, when thinking about injustice, "I think of my mother." She noted that in a country that claimed to be a beacon of democracy, her mother had died at work at the age of thirty-seven, exhausted, overworked, and sick. Jones said that it was then, at only fourteen, that she understood the suffering of Black people. It was racism and class exploitation that took her mother from her and left her father to raise four girls. Her mother died having been disappointed by the promises of immigration, the mythology of the "American dream," and the fact that success remained out of reach for families such as hers.[21]

Charles Cumberbatch became the girls' sole parent. Jones and her father would disagree on politics later in life, but he remained influential in her political evolution. According to Jones, her father was politically astute and identified with the African diaspora. After taking charge of his daughters' care, Cumberbatch lost his job as a furrier and went to work as an editor for the *West Indian American News*, where he worked on African freedom campaigns. Jones credited her father with infusing in her and her sisters a pride in their "African heritage." She remembered him discussing African freedom movements and the struggle for equality in the United States. Her father's politics, her mother's early death, and the Jim Crow conditions in a city without formal segregation influenced Jones's political awakening at a young age.[22]

Cumberbatch started his editing job just as the Great Depression struck the country. Needing to take on additional work to supplement the family's income, he became the maintenance supervisor of their apartment building, although this did not significantly improve the family's finances. When Jones was about to graduate from Harriet Beecher Stowe Junior High, her father was unable to afford her commencement clothes, so she could not attend the ceremony. Her absence would have been noticed since she was the class mayor and was graduating with honors as well as receiving a good citizenship award. She cried for days after the ceremony. It was a humiliation that stayed with her.[23]

The only high school available to Harlem's girls was Wadleigh, the first public high school for girls in the city. Though Jones had attended integrated schools before, the girls from Harlem made up only 25 percent of the school intake. At Wadleigh she thus encountered a much larger white student body and regularly experienced the sting of anti-Black racism from her fellow students. White students would ask her for her notes and then ignore her after school. White teachers would ask Black students if they wanted to make extra money by cleaning the teachers' homes, and they would have them read poems using Black dialect. These experiences fueled Jones's growing political awareness: she later wrote that even as a teenager she questioned whether the Bill of Rights ever actually applied in the United States.[24]

The discrimination and harassment at school led to her involvement in the Junior NAACP and the Urban League. Harlem had been a focal point of political activity for years, but during the Great Depression there was a growing youth movement spurred on by the declining economic conditions throughout the city and the country. Both the NAACP and the Urban League set up youth groups that were more activist-oriented than the larger organizations. Jones would cut her activist teeth in these youth groups and, as her friends recall, it was here that her politicization began. But she was also a typical teenager who was involved in other extracurricular activities. She studied drama with the Urban League and performed throughout the city. She was also President of the Spartan Tennis and Social Club.[25]

Before Jones's senior year of high school, she had her second bout of tuberculosis. She blamed this on the conditions in the building where the family lived, reporting that open sewage was a problem and that the moisture in the apartment had likely made her sick. Jones was "sick practically all of her life." As a youth she contracted malaria. When she was sixteen years old she contracted "tuberculosis of both lungs" for the first time and was treated at Harlem hospital. Her condition was serious, but not rare in Depression-era New York City. Overcrowding, poor housing, and, for some residents, poor diets made controlling tuberculosis in the city difficult. In 1897, the authorities had made tuberculosis reporting mandatory, but several doctors still refused to report cases on confidentiality grounds, and some were still not convinced that the infection was passed between people, instead blaming "miasmas." City control was boosted in the 1930s when a Tuberculosis Bureau was created within the health department. It mandated a three-pronged approach to control: "screening of at-risk populations, supervised therapy, and the forced detention of infectious patients." City officials were aware that the disease was especially infectious in poorer neighborhoods; by 1930 the death rate among Black New Yorkers was more than three times that among white residents. The health department partnered with the local Urban League in the 1920s to create the Harlem Tuberculosis and Health Committee. Despite these efforts, several health officials were critical of the city's program for Black patients, and as late as the 1940s there still were no Black doctors at the city's tuberculosis hospitals. The main treatment at the time was "bed rest and nutritional support," with surgery for some of the worst cases. Compliance was difficult since few could afford to take time off work for lengthy rest periods. The biggest problem was that little or no effort was made to improve the conditions in Black and poor neighborhoods that led to higher numbers of patients and deaths in the first place.[26]

Patients were sent to one of the roughly twenty-five sanitoriums in the city or on its outskirts for treatment. Jones was sent to Seaview sanitorium, a facility built in 1913 on Staten Island. She would spend the next year of her life there. The building was designed to maximize the patients' view of the sea and included sunrooms and balconies where they could get fresh air and sunshine. Over the years it had had several extensions to accommodate more patients. By the time Jones arrived the balconies had been enclosed and cottages added.[27]

Jones spent her time at the hospital reading and learning. She also reflected on her mother's Catholic faith, eventually deciding to reject it and its "hierarchical" teachings. The business director of the Spartan Tennis and Social Club, Irma Offord, organized letters to be sent to her while she convalesced. Because the facility was integrated, Jones was not insulated from racist treatment. In one memorable incident she volunteered to give blood to a fellow patient, an Italian woman with whom she shared a blood type. Other patients told the woman that if she accepted Jones's blood she might turn Black. A Jewish doctor tried to educate them on the "inviolability of blood types" in relation to race, but they remained unconvinced. Despite the other patients' discouragement, the woman who Jones donated blood to was so grateful it embarrassed her.[28]

After a year of care Jones was released from the sanitorium and went on to complete her last year of high school. Though she eventually recovered well enough to leave Seaview, her illnesses later in life and her premature death at age forty-nine suggest that her youthful experience of illness had long-term consequences. In 1952, a Dr. Louis Miller reported on Jones's illnesses. She had told him that she suffered at least six colds per year with bronchitis, and had contracted pneumonia several times. She also reported "severe headaches" on a weekly basis, which the doctor described as the "migraine type." A chest X-ray showed "extensive tubercular pathology" "far greater" than was usual in tuberculosis patients. The doctor noted that there was barely any healthy tissue in her lungs. Her long-term illnesses were linked to the conditions in the housing that she grew up in; like her mother, Jones faced severe (and avoidable) illness that would eventually take her life at a young age.[29]

Despite her poor health, Jones still had to contribute to the "family larder," so after school she went in search of work, because "college was not an option." Her first job was in a laundry. Here she witnessed the overwork and "speed up" that were required of the workers. In addition, the summer heat led many women to faint. She left the laundry for a factory job that required her to use toothpick and glue to set a nail head. Finding this boring, and earning only $14 per week from it, she secured a job as a salesgirl at a Harlem millinery and lingerie store, where she worked for two years.[30]

Her father, meanwhile, found work in the Works Progress Administration (WPA) Federal Writers' Project (FWP) in 1936 as the editor of the "negro material of the Racial Minorities division" for the New York City guidebook. The group was tasked with compiling a book to be titled *Negroes of New York*, and Cumberbatch's job was to collect information on the "contribution" of Black writers to the "culture and development" of the city. In this role, he would experience something akin to what his daughter would face years later. The editorial staff were redbaited, and it was alleged that they were "re-writing" the entire text to give it a "revolutionary slant." In October 1938, Baxter R. Leach, a journalist who worked on the project and contributed a piece on Black Americans in radio broadcasting, published a two-part article in the *New York Age* newspaper attacking Cumberbatch and his fellow editors.[31]

In the first article, Leach wrote that the "Negro division" of the FWP was a "hot bed of agitation," a "haven for incompetence," and a refuge for "Trotskyites, Stalinists, and Marxists." He claimed that anyone who objected to this "unholy alliance" was immediately removed from the project. He believed that many "competent" people had been dismissed on various pretexts, while others had been kept on because of their political persuasion. Writer and radical activist Claude McKay and historian J.A. Rogers – who Leach described as "Exhibits A and B" when it came to communist influence – were working on the project. Several prominent individuals were attached to the project: W.E.B. Du Bois helped compile a bibliography, and Arthur Schomburg (the historian for whom the Schomburg Center for Research in Black Culture is named) had provided guidance before his death in June of that year. Leach complained that all that work, presumably including his own work, was now "piled high" somewhere on a dusty shelf, while four white writers were "holding forth in the division." In other words, he claimed that the white writers were doing all the work.[32]

In his second article, Leach identified Jones's father as one of the leading culprits in the scheme. He accused Cumberbatch – along with Charles Alexander (the "high priest" of the group), Roi Ottley, and Everett Beans – of "re-writing" the entire project. Leach claimed that Alexander was one of the most "active agitators" in the CPUSA, and that he had been the lead organizer of protests against the FWP in New York in May 1937, when nearly 10,000 people employed in WPA projects, including the FWP, went on strike against proposed cuts to the payroll. If Alexander had led the protests, this was not reported on in the press. Roi Ottley, formerly of the Black newspaper *Amsterdam News*, was another of the rogue editors Leach identified. He claimed that Ottley had never written a book or edited a newspaper, citing this as evidence of his alleged incompetence.[33]

What Leach held against Jones's father was that he had been an editor at the "tabloid" *West Indian American News*. He wrote that all four men were handing out ridiculous assignments (such as identifying all the pool rooms in Harlem), and that the project was bankrolled by the US Treasury Department. All told, Leach claimed that there were forty Black writers involved, only nine of whom were assigned to write for the book, while seven communist whites dominated the writing projects. Leach's accusations of communism were neither new nor original. Since its inception, the New York FWP and other parts of the WPA operating in New York and elsewhere were accused of being "Red Nests." In 1936, the Republican National Committee labeled the FWP a "festering sore of communism," and individuals working within the project had to defend themselves against the accusations.[34]

A month after Leach's articles, Representative Martin Dies (who led the House Dies Committee, the precursor to the House Un-American Activities Committee) claimed that the state FWPs were producing propaganda which, he argued, contained appeals for "class hatred." He wanted this removed from all the WPA's proposed books (there were many projects ongoing at the time, though ultimately few of the books were published). Unidentified witnesses told the Dies Committee, in secret hearings, that the books contained accusations against "business and industry." One witness claimed that the books "build up the case for the Negro," that case being the "oppression of the Negro everywhere." Others claimed the books included propaganda that supported the labor movement. As scholars of anticommunism have noted, anti-Blackness and anti-labor were (and remain) an essential part of anticommunism. Black activists, writers, and artists were often dismissed by anticommunists, and just as often by liberals like Leach.[35] Cumberbatch was never a communist and he and his daughter frequently disagreed about politics, but as both would later learn, anticommunism has never required evidence to make a charge stick, nor does it even require communists.

Cumberbatch's contribution to the project included one submission on "Negro Actors, Past and Present," written in 1936 – well before Leach accused him and the others of hijacking the project. In it, Cumberbatch wrote that Black people had appeared on stage as early as the sixteenth century, but in Harlem the first production came in 1914 with *The Old Man's Boy*. He went on to describe several other productions featuring Black actors, including *Emperor Jones*, which originally starred Charles Gilpin. Eventually the role was taken up by Paul Robeson, Jones's future friend and political comrade. *Negroes of New York* would not be published in Cumberbatch's lifetime – the WPA and the FWP were dissolved in 1943, leaving several volumes unpublished. The book was eventually published in 1967, after both he and Jones had passed. Cumberbatch was let go from his job even before the WPA was shut down; by 1942 he was fifty-eight years old and unemployed.[36]

By that time, Jones had been a member of the Communist Party for over five years and the federal authorities were starting to take notice. As the poem at the start of this chapter indicates, the youthful Jones had become aware that capitalism was exploitative, and she was devoted to usurping its power and convincing others that solidarity could emancipate the oppressed. Jones's parents were an important influence in her radicalization; her mother's early death remained an inspiration she would invoke throughout her life, and her father's work on African Liberation campaigns and writing and editing were projects she would also take up. Jones found her political home in the CPUSA, alongside comrades who understood that racist oppression could not simply be integrated into the class struggle. She would commit herself to interracial solidarity, but she would also push her white comrades to understand that sexism and racism infected the lives of working people and were barriers to progress. As with her father before her, anticommunism would close in, but for Jones the consequences would be more severe.

# 2

# Communist Party, USA (1936–1946)

*Clay Sculpture*

Molecules long hidden lay
In earth, rich aged with time
Dust of the ancients stamp the way
Of peoples, rich in rhyme.

I've held in hand unmolded piece
Unformed and pliant blob
And wondered as I rolled and ceased
What form would start to throb.

I've marveled how its contents rare
Are snared in secret lime
How nature hid in tablets here
Past history in its prime.

But most of all when turning round by hand this property
I turn the lock on all mankind's recorded history
For hear lies proof supremely clear that bold humanity
Can storm all doors through toil and will – if they but see!

                                                  Claudia Jones[1]

Jones was clear about why she joined the Communist Party. She was early on "disabused" of the promises of freedom and equality in the United States, as her family faced the poverty, poor working conditions, substandard housing, segregation, and bigotry which led to her mother's premature death. Jones was radicalized by her lived experience as a Black woman in the United States, and the CPUSA became her outlet to seek radical change. The Party was at its height in the 1930s, as capitalism failed during the Great Depression, the myth of meritocracy was damaged (for a time) by economic turmoil, and the growth of fascism abroad worried progressives and radicals. Jones would join the Party when its influence was widespread and when liberal progressives were still willing to work openly with communists.[2]

Erik McDuffie argues that Jones and other Black radicals joined the CPUSA not to be part of "a conspiratorial movement" or to act as spies, but as a "vehicle for advancing racial equality" as well as women's rights, labor rights, and anti-imperialism. McDuffie identifies Jones as one of a second generation of Black women to join the Party. The first generation included radicals like Grace Campbell and Maude White. These women laid the groundwork for challenging the Party's assumptions about gender, race, and class. Though they did not use the language Jones and her colleagues did to describe "triple oppression," McDuffie argues that these women nevertheless had a keen sense of Black women's "superexploitation," which they wrote about and discussed in Party circles. It was the second generation that would name it.[3]

In the 1930s the Party recognized that European fascism was not distinct from policy and practice in the United States. It was in that decade that the communist politics of antifascism and antiwar were forged. Before the rise of Hitler, American communists watched with concern as

Benito Mussolini's government in Italy imprisoned anarchists, socialists, communists, and others critical of his regime. Much like the current rise in fascism in the United States, Hungary and other countries, authoritarians in the 1930s targeted left-wing movements and constructed them as a threat to the status quo. While back then the interracial Communist Party was singled out as a threat, today it is Black Lives Matter activists and their allies who are dismissed as Marxist agitators. Then, as now, fascists engaged in anti-Black racism and misogyny, and weaponized demands for equality by dismissing them as treasonous.

As Alberto Toscano has argued, a Black radical critique of "right-wing authoritarianism" has moved understandings of fascism in the United States "beyond analogy." For Black Americans, describing US laws and its criminal punishment system as fascistic is not a metaphor. Black Americans do not have to look far to find fascists; it suffices simply to look at local law enforcement to see the agents of social control in action. Toscano defines fascism as "a set of repressive tactics" and a "political and ideological process" that targets "racialised and subaltern populations" differently than it does others. The "very existence and sociality" of these populations is seen as a threat. Part of this process – which, he argues, underlies capitalism – is "contempt for the oppressed" as a "survival process" of fascists or those who enact fascism. Long the targets of policing and punishment systems, Black Americans have lived under a racial fascism which, Toscano contends, is not fixed but represents an evolving system. It is what he calls a "counter-revolution" working in conjunction with the "persistent pattern" of the "racialization of class."[4] Bill Mullen and Christopher Vials have argued that the difference between fascism and "racialized rightlessness" is insignificant given the realities of racist oppression. In the 1930s, the Party and its members, including Jones, offered an analysis of fascism as something enacted in the Western nations against people of color globally. They argued that this was not an aberration in the United States – fascist fault lines had long existed there in the form of state terrorism, control, and the persistence of oppressive institutions. This was an analysis Jones and her Party comrades would use as the foundation of their activism. The rise of an authoritarian like Donald Trump should not have been unexpected given the long history of fascist oppression in the United States.[5]

## Joining the Party

McDuffie's second generation followed their earlier counterparts in rejecting the mainstream Black Freedom Struggle's respectability politics and sexual mores that demanded behavior acceptable to white supremacist culture. Jones also resented and rejected the masculine culture of Black Nationalist movements. In 1935, before she joined the Party, she was a member of the Federated Youth Clubs of Harlem, and wrote a weekly column for its newspaper called "Claudia's Comments." She described her column as writing a "precis" of the relevant editorials at the time on the 1935 Italian invasion of Ethiopia. Ethiopia was symbolic for Black Nationalists because the country had retained its independence when most of its neighbors had been colonized. Italy sought to subjugate the country and combine its African empire – Ethiopia lay between its two colonies of Eritrea and Somalia. Jones attended one of the group's meetings and witnessed her boss reading out her precis to great acclaim without giving her credit. This was one incentive to leave the organization behind.[6]

Jones was also attracted to the Party's analysis of the "Negro Question" (as it was then called). In 1928, the Party adopted the Black Belt Thesis, which recognized Black Americans in the Black Belt (the south) as an oppressed nation with the right to self-determination, and Black people in the north as a "national minority" with the "right to full integration." It stated that a portion of the southern states be allowed to secede to create a Black homeland. The Party's concept of self-determination was different from that of radical Black activists, especially those in the nationalist and socialist African Blood Brotherhood (ABB), a group that preceded the Party. Lydia Lindsey argues that Grace Campbell, one of the first generation of Black women in the CPUSA, forged her socialism in the ABB and believed that self-determination came from within Black communities. Campbell became a communist because she saw the Party as the leader in the working-class struggle. She was a "prime mover" in establishing its Harlem branch, which would become Jones's home branch.[7]

The Black Belt Thesis seemed contrary to the class unity the CPUSA advocated and would be a topic of debate for years. But it was also a policy that appealed to young activists like Jones who saw the Party as combining Black Nationalist sentiments with class unity. Campbell wrote an early analysis of the "Negro Question" the year the Thesis was released; in it she argued that Black people were the vanguard of the class movement. She rejected the idea of a separate Black republic and advocated instead "winning equality and economic opportunity." But she did note that if freed people had been given land as promised after the US Civil War, they would have been able to "advance Black freedom." Jones's own analysis written years later would agree with Campbell, arguing that "decades of capitalist development" in the south had not got rid of the "remnants" of slavery, thereby preventing the development of "popular democracy."[8]

Another criticism of the Black Belt Thesis was that it focused on race and "occluded" issues of gender (or "sex" as that generation called it), centering the liberation struggle on an imagined masculine Black community and eliding the struggles of Black women. Maude White, who attended Moscow University in the Soviet Union with nationalist heroes like Ho Chi Minh and Jomo Kenyatta, witnessed the debates at the 6th World Congress of the Communist International (Comintern) where the Thesis was approved. The Comintern, based in Moscow, was the organizing body for international communism. As Cheryl Higashida argues, the Thesis solidified White's determination to fight racism "relentlessly," but like many of the first generation of Black Party women, she was critical of the exclusion of gender. White confronted Party leaders when she was told that the needs of white and Black women in unions would not be considered separate. She insisted on the recognition of Black women's oppression while also pushing for "interracial solidarity." Though the Thesis would raise questions among Party members and lead to heated debates, Lindsey argues that it put the CPUSA ahead of other organizations, like the Socialist Party, that saw racism as a "remnant" of class struggle and insisted that socialism would usher in equality. While the Party rank-and-file did not always adopt the policy that race had to be considered as a separate class identity, Black women pushed their comrades to reject a class-only analysis of oppression.[9]

Perhaps more than the Black Belt Thesis, it was the Party's organized efforts on behalf of the Scottsboro Boys that attracted Black members – and Jones certainly cited this as one of her inspirations. It also evidenced fascism in practice, as law enforcement colluded with the criminal legal system to circumscribe the rights of the Black youths involved in the case. In March 1931, nine youths were arrested in Scottsboro,

Alabama for the rape of two white girls on a train. Within sixteen days of their arrest, eight were tried, convicted, and sentenced to death, while the ninth, Roy Wright, was released because of his young age. The trials were hasty, the defendants had inadequate counsel, and the community was fully prepared to lynch them either through the courts or directly. This case would come to define the CPUSA's Depression-era antiracism and antifascism, as it was one of the first visible cases of what Party members called lynch law. Police, courts, and prosecutors became the new lynch mobs, and the criminal legal system was seen as an instrument of capitalist and racist oppression. The Party adopted a mass organization strategy to publicize the case, targeted public officials with letter-writing campaigns, and raised money to hire attorneys for the defense in the subsequent appeal trials. The case dragged on throughout the decade, but the Party remained committed, and its members were active in raising awareness and support for the defendants.[10]

Jones heard about the Scottsboro Boys from the street-corner speakers who operated throughout Harlem. Some of them were communists, others were nationalists, but the Scottsboro case was on their minds. Jones was "impressed by the Communist speakers" who saw the "heinous frameup" as akin to the imperialist invasion of Ethiopia. For them, the oppression of the Ethiopians by a European power was not qualitatively different than the US oppression of Black Americans. Some Party members who knew Jones noticed her interest, so they began to talk to her about the CPUSA and its work. Her disillusionment with the nationalists pushed her to join the Party in 1936.[11]

Jones was assigned to the Harlem section of the Young Communist League (YCL), where she participated in rallies and made speeches in the Scottsboro Boys' defense. Louise Thompson (later Thompson Patterson), another second generation communist, was an essential organizer in the defense and would become one of Jones's Party colleagues and collaborators. Thompson Patterson began working for the International Labor Defense (ILD) in 1932, and focused her work on the case. Committed to defending working-class defendants, the ILD arranged the Scottsboro Boys' defense, raised funds, and organized rallies and letter-writing campaigns. Thompson Patterson became a friend of some of the Scottsboro Boys' mothers. She also befriended Ruby Bates, one of the two white girls that had accused the boys of rape, but who had recanted her testimony and become an active figure in the campaign. Thompson Patterson organized marches and rallies, and traveled the country with the mothers and Bates to raise awareness.[12]

Audley Moore was another young activist drawn to the Party through the case. Moore has been described as a "powerful" speaker and an important organizer in the Scottsboro and anti-segregation campaigns. She had been active in the United Negro Improvement Association (UNIA) in her native Louisiana before moving to Harlem with her sisters in the 1930s. Marcus Garvey, the UNIA founder and leader, had been deported in 1927 and the group fractured; new Black Nationalist organizations emerged, and the CPUSA became a political home for many. Ashley Farmer argues that Moore appreciated the CPUSA because of its Black Belt Thesis, which made "Black Nationalism and Black self-determination" central to its "organization's agenda." Both the Thesis and the Scottsboro campaign positioned the CPUSA as a leading organization in the Black Freedom Struggle. Its Harlem branch was home to influential organizers and activists like Moore and Jones. In the 1950s, Moore left the CPUSA because of "frustration" with the group's "disregard" for self-determination, but she and Jones helped the Party to draw in Black members and challenge white supremacist thinking among white members. McDuffie argues that together these women laid a foundation for Black Left feminism.[13]

Jones's comrade Pettis Perry remembered the Scottsboro case as essential in his own radicalization. Perry was living in Los Angeles and working at a mill when a communist coworker approached him and mentioned that there was going to be a "revolution one of these days." He gave Perry copies of the communist newspaper *Daily Worker*, which contained stories about the Scottsboro Boys. Perry would describe this as a "political awakening" after which he became "alive" for the first time. He began to develop a "nationalist consciousness" and joined the Party after seeing how white comrades stood up for Black comrades. But it was the Scottsboro case that prompted his awareness and his radicalization. The Party's leadership in the case drew in Black members like Jones, Moore, and Perry, who would become leading figures in the Black Freedom Struggle and, in the case of Jones and Perry, CPUSA leaders.[14]

The Party's antifascism was also central to its appeal. Jones joined the Party in the wake of the 1935 declaration of a Popular Front against fascism at the Comintern's 7th Congress. The Popular Front policy opened the Party up to working with people and organizations it once dismissed as social fascists: liberals and progressives. McDuffie and Mary Helen Washington argue that the second generation of Black communist women forged their politics in the antifascism of the Popular Front, which would later inspire a Black Popular Front during the Cold War. The Black Popular Front engaged in an "anti-colonial, anti-fascist, and anti-racist politics" at a time when the European empires were in decline and the United States was seeking global military hegemony and neo-colonial control in newly independent states. The Popular Front held that US Cold War policy was fascistic due to its anti-Black racism, its targeted suppression of radical activism, and its attack on hard-fought union rights. In other words, the US had taken on aspects of the fascist states that had come to power in the 1920s and 1930s.[15]

The Italian invasion of Ethiopia and the Spanish Civil War were central to radicalizing Jones and her peers, including Esther Cooper, who also joined the Party around the same time. During the Ethiopian war, the Party sought to demonstrate its anti-imperialist credentials as well as its ability to unify working people behind a single cause. It created the Provisional Committee for the Defense of Ethiopia, but rejected plans to picket Italian-owned businesses and instead focused on the potential for unity between Black and Italian workers. The Party was unable to rally large numbers behind the campaign, partly due to logistical issues like getting aid and people into Africa, but also because of conflicts with Black Nationalists who rejected the Party's interpretation of the invasion.[16]

In 1936, civil war broke out in Spain between fascist forces under Francisco Franco and the democratically elected Popular Front government. The CPUSA's attention shifted to the war in Spain, where hundreds of American communists and radicals traveled to fight in support of the Spanish government. Among them was Jones's friend Louise Thompson Patterson, who traveled to Spain as a witness to the conflict and the brutality of Spanish fascists. While there she broadcast her observations on the radio. The growing fascist encroachment across Europe fed Party fears that the United States, with its own fascist tendencies, could be the next to fall.[17]

Jones joined the Party along with this second-generation cohort of women who would remain influential both in its ranks and more generally for the twentieth-century Black left. Some became close friends and working colleagues, and many of them helped influence Jones's thinking on race, gender, and class exploitation. Jones herself would be one of the most influential Black women within the Party, and from the beginning she took the Popular Front antifascist mandate seriously. She worked with Party members and fellow travelers along with other non-affiliated activists who would also make a mark in the Black Freedom Struggle.[18]

## Party Work

One of the individuals Jones met was Ella Baker. In 1935, Baker was working for the Works Progress Administration, but she would later go on to work in civil rights organizations including the NAACP and the Southern Christian Leadership Conference (SCLC), and to help found the Student Nonviolent Coordinating Committee (SNCC). At the time though, Jones, who likely met Baker through her father, was interested in Black women's labor. In 1935 Baker teamed up with communist Marvel Cooke to publish an article titled "The Bronx Slave Market" in the NAACP's *Crisis* magazine. The article exposed the street-corner "slave markets" in Bronx, New York, where Black women went daily to try to secure domestic work. The system was rife with problems, including the abuse and exploitation of Black women workers.[19]

Lindsey argues that Baker and Cooke's article, together with Louise Thompson Patterson's April 1936 article "Toward a Brighter Dawn," informed Jones's thinking on Black women's "tripartite" oppression. Patterson's article focused on Black women's labor in domestic work, but for Lindsey it pioneered a new understanding of domestic work under capitalism. It also featured the first use of the phrase "triple exploitation" – the idea that Jones would later articulate and, as McDuffie notes, "popularize." Patterson wrote that the Bronx slave market was a "graphic monument" to the most exploited worker in the US: "the Negro woman." Black women faced "triple exploitation – as workers, as women, as Negroes" on a daily basis and without the benefit of union representation or inclusion in New Deal legislative protections. This paradigm challenged the Party's traditional focus on the industrial shopfloor as the site of exploitation and potential revolution.[20]

Under her surname Cumberbatch, Jones herself would write about the need to organize domestic workers in unions in a 1936 *Daily Worker* article. After Jones was assigned to the YCL, she was offered a job with the *Daily Worker*; it was not well paid and she had turned down a much more lucrative offer from the WPA, but she was becoming a committed communist. The article was about the National Negro Congress's (NNC) Harlem youth section and its work organizing Harlem's domestic workers. The NNC was an important Popular Front coalition of Black labor leaders, activists, and communists advocating for equality, unionization, and the recruitment of youth into the movement. It is a brief article that highlights what "The Bronx Slave Market" had articulated the year before – that Black women's exploitation in white homes left them to "eke" out a living on "starvation wages." Jones argued that the women needed to be organized to demand better conditions and wages. The article also foreshadows some of Jones's later work in which she would identify Black women as the most exploited and ignored demographic among working people. She argued that organizing Black women would be a step toward the emancipation of all workers. The following year Jones stopped publishing under her surname and began using the pen name Claudia Jones. The author of an article published after Jones's first arrest claimed that she took on the pen name when she became a regular contributor to the *Daily Worker*. Carole Boyce Davies suggests that she might have adopted it to avoid legal issues. Whatever the reason, it would eventually hold off the authorities for years.[21]

In 1937, Jones spent six months at the CPUSA's National Training School in upstate New York. When she returned to Harlem, she began working with the YCL and other youth organizations affiliated with the Party. That year she was featured in a pamphlet written by her YCL colleague and friend Henry Winston. The pamphlet focused on the young Black leaders in the Party and included a smiling photo of a young Jones. Barely a year into her Party membership, she was already making an impression. The pamphlet reprinted a speech Winston had made at the NNC second annual meeting in October about youth organizing.[22] A native Mississippian, Winston had moved with his family to St. Louis, Missouri during the Great Depression in search of work. There he came across the Unemployed Councils, a CPUSA-adjacent group that organized unemployed workers to demand relief – both unemployment and housing. He became an important organizer and was sent to New York for training. Winston stayed in New York and by 1936, the year Jones joined the Party, he was the YCL's National Organization Secretary and a member of the Party's Central Committee. Winston's and Jones's CPUSA careers paralleled each other as they both rose to leadership positions and faced legal harassment as a result. In their early Party years both became central YCL leaders and visible Black Party members.[23]

Also included in the pamphlet was Angelo Herndon. Herndon had become well known after his 1932 arrest under an old slave insurrection law in Atlanta, Georgia. He was planning a march on the state capital to protest the removal of thousands of people from the relief rolls meant to provide financial aid to the unemployed. He was arrested and detained and the communist literature in his boarding room was used against him in his trial. Herndon was found guilty and sentenced to eighteen to twenty years on a chain gang. The ILD defended him, and he was eventually exonerated in 1937. That same year Herndon published an account of his trial, prison time, and conviction in his book *Let Me Live*, one of the first examples of prison literature in the United States.[24]

In 1938, Jones was elected to the YCL's National Committee. She also worked with the Southern Negro Youth Congress (SNYC), where her colleagues James Jackson and Esther Cooper, who would later marry, were leaders. The SNYC was created in 1937 out of frustration at the Roosevelt administration's failure to "challenge the southern Jim Crow system," the eviction of Black sharecroppers and tenant farmers from land, and the racial discrimination in payment and benefits. The organization led a campaign for "civil rights and economic justice," and held its first conference in February 1937. Jones wrote an article urging young agricultural workers to attend the conference and hundreds of NNC delegates from its youth section did so. The SNYC was devoted to interracial organizing, so both Black and white youth were encouraged to join. Jones appeared in the organization's "first recruiting brochure," and she met Sallye Davis, Angela Davis's mother, at an SNYC conference held in Alabama.[25]

The NAACP Youth Council sent its best wishes to the SNYC, as did several other organizations. The 1930s saw an uptick in campus activism and youth organizing, especially for civil rights, and the SNYC drew in several interested young people who faced poor economic conditions and limited opportunities. While the NAACP had its conflicts with the CPUSA, open relationships between the two groups were not yet the liability they would become.[26] Jonetta Richards argues that though most civil rights organizations "welcomed" the SNYC's creation, the NAACP remained "somewhat ambivalent" because communists were openly involved in it. But Jones and the Jacksons, who became active CPUSA members, remained committed to their work and were encouraged by their collaboration with liberals. Jones was enthusiastic about the SNYC's work and reported in 1938 that the organization was committed to the "economic, social, and cultural desires" of southerners, both Black and white. It focused its campaigns on citizenship rights, including eliminating poll taxes and "anti-suffrage laws," securing Black people on juries, educational opportunities for Black people, and the release of the Scottsboro Boys. Esther Cooper Jackson "prioritized" the rights of Black women, and in its 1937 platform the SNYC articulated its commitment to the "future" of Black "womanhood in the south." The organization thus encompassed many of Jones's priorities – linking economic struggle to the struggle for Black and women's liberation.[27]

Jones's early journalism for the Party included her reports on youth organizing; she also appeared throughout the *Daily Worker* as an important organizer bringing together youth for anti-lynching rallies, interracial meetings, YCL conferences, and significant Party business including the drafting of its constitution. In her first year as a member she shared the stage with National Chairman Earl Browder at the Party's eighteenth anniversary celebration. Jones was also part of an effort to bring together Black YCL members with an Italian YCL affiliate to build interracial unity. Jones said of the meeting that it represented a "good beginning" in the attempt to "break down all divisions" between Black and white youth. When an article about the meeting was published in 1939, the YCL members discussed working together, but no one questioned why there were segregated branches or why the branches were organized around segregated communities. This was just one indication of the challenges of organizing white radicals for Black rights; while ideologically committed, the group seemed to struggle with changing ingrained prejudices.[28]

## From Antifascism to Antiwar

One of the Party's biggest challenges would come in 1939 when it made a controversial move that hurt not only its organizing but also its credibility and its appeal to outsiders (as well as some of its own members). Throughout the 1930s the CPUSA had become an important voice in antifascism, and the Party was critical of the US government's committed neutrality. But when in August 1939 the Soviet Union signed a non-aggression pact with Nazi Germany, the CPUSA adopted the Soviet antiwar policy and shifted to backing US neutrality. For many, this confirmed that the Party was just the US branch of Soviet communism and that it took its orders from Moscow. Even before the pact, the show trials and purges in the USSR had begun to disillusion many former Marxists, who came to believe not just that the violence in the Soviet Union was the fault of a madman, but that communism itself was a mad ideology.[29]

Gerald Horne has argued that it "overstates the case" to claim that the pact did untold damage to the CPUSA, since there was already an antiwar sentiment among many members, with some seeing another war between the European empires as an imperialist contest to preserve their colonies, much like World War I. Alliances with the British and French, given their treatment of people in Africa and the Caribbean, were considered intolerable. Some members also pointed to the ability of the two main US political parties (Republican and Democrat) to change position without being accused of being collaborators. And some argued that even if the CPUSA officially supported the pact, this was not the position of all members. For Jones and her fellow Black comrades, it would be impossible to fight fascism with a segregated military; segregation was, after all, a manifestation of racial fascism.[30]

During these internal conflicts, and into the war years, Jones's contributions to the Party went beyond organizing, as she began to make her mark as a writer and thinker. In 1938 she contributed an article to the YCL's *Weekly Review* on youth organizing, and also sat on the paper's board. By 1940 she was a regular contributor; in 1942 she became associate editor, and by 1943 she was the *Review*'s editor-in-chief. Her writing would continue to appear in the *Daily Worker*, and she also began authoring pamphlets. In July 1940 she published the antiwar pamphlet *Jim Crow in Uniform*, which articulated the Party's antiwar stance and opposition to the segregated US military. She raised the question: Why should Black Americans fight for a country that does not protect their citizenship rights?

Jones appeared at antiwar rallies throughout the twenty-two-month period that the Nazi-Soviet non-aggression pact lasted. At these rallies she and others articulated the Party's opposition to the war, demanding the welfare of soldiers and their families, job training for work and not war, and the dismantling of Jim Crow in the military. Fellow communist James Ford wrote an introduction to her pamphlet, arguing that the imperialist powers were sounding the drumbeat of war while the Soviet Union remained the only voice for peace. In the US, money could not be found for job training, but it was always available for war production, and the unions became scapegoats as war production trumped worker's rights. Ford also noted that as the war escalated in Europe, suppression of antiwar sentiment was emerging at home. As Donna Haverty-Stacke has confirmed, this was in fact the case. As the US military shifted to preparation for war, the intelligence agencies began to target radical unions and their members out of fear that the mobilization would be sabotaged.[31]

Jones viewed the war as another imperialist venture, like that of WWI, in which Black soldiers would be asked to fight for democracy so that the imperialist states could snatch up more colonies and continue to exploit Black people at home. In a *Weekly Review* article, she invoked the false promises of WWI, highlighting the failure of democracy when Black soldiers returned to a segregated country and racist violence, including the lynching of soldiers. Charles Lindbergh, famous for his transatlantic flight (but whom Jones called the "lawful spouse of the fortune of [banker J. P.] Morgan"), had said the quiet part out loud: that the war would cost white people their supremacy and that if they did not win, the "darker peoples" would take over. Lindbergh, an isolationist, described the war as a race war, one he feared white people would lose.[32]

For Jones, however, war was always to the detriment of Black Americans. She argued along lines she would return to later during the Korean War: that the imperialist powers used people of color as cannon fodder and that capitalists were the only ones to benefit from war. In 1939, after an anti-lynching bill was passed in the House, it was filibustered into oblivion by the Senate. One southern representative shouted during the debate that the bill was only to placate "N\_\_\_r Communists," which Jones took as an "unwilling tribute" to the Black communists who had fought for the bill. Meanwhile, President Franklin Roosevelt, who "never once raised his voice in support" of the bill, was calling for unity.[33]

Jones also noted that, during WWI, Black soldiers in uniform were "stoned, jeered, and mobbed," segregated in public accommodations and in the military, left to do menial labor, and, in one unit, prevented from carrying weapons. This treatment led to an "antiwar sentiment" among Black Americans, who understood the paradox of fighting in a war for democracy when no democracy was to be found at home. Jones reasoned that, when Black soldiers returned from the war to race riots and lynching, they also returned to an economic lynching as they remained discriminated against in work and wages. Even as the federal government called for patriotic devotion to the country, it failed to confront racist violence with law enforcement. Though the Party's opposition to the war sounded confused and hollow to its critics, after it had spent years opposing fascism and calling for action, Jones's pamphlet outlined the very real urgency of the problem of racist violence and the treatment of Black troops.[34]

The YCL launched an anti-draft campaign in response to the Burke-Wadsworth conscription bill introduced in August 1940. The bill called for the first peacetime draft and required all men over twenty-one and those who had not yet reached their thirty-sixth birthday to register. The YCL issued a statement opposing the bill and launched a two-week campaign against it, holding rallies, circulating a petition, and selling Jones's pamphlet to raise funds. The bill was passed in late August. Many of the rallies at which Jones was a featured speaker opposed legislation like the conscription bill because it appeared to move the US toward war. In February 1941, Jones shared a stage with her friend and ally William Foster, national CPUSA chairman, to protest the Lend-Lease bill which provided the UK with military equipment.[35]

As late as May 1941, Jones featured in antiwar actions. A special Mother's Day antiwar rally was planned for May 10 to highlight the uniquely gendered aspect of war. Jones was an advertised speaker along with Elizabeth Gurley Flynn and other Party notables like Mother Ella Reeve Bloor (a longtime Party figure and organizer) and John Gates (a Spanish Civil War veteran). Flynn and Jones were close Party comrades and later served time together in prison. Flynn had been a leader and organizer in the International Workers of the World (IWW) union; she also had impressive radical credentials coming from a family with links to the Irish resistance. Her parents had been friends with James Connolly, one of the leaders of the 1916 Easter Rebellion against the British Empire. She and Jones joined the Party the same year and would work closely together.[36]

Jones's war opposition focused on the abuse of Black soldiers abroad and the abuse of Black Americans at home. But gender was central to her antiwar ideology as well. She would later theorize about war as a particular threat to women, arguing that, as civilians, they were uniquely endangered. Women were caught in the line of fire and exploited as war workers and breeders of soldiers. Attention might be focused on soldiers, but for Jones it was women who were most vulnerable in war and most exploited in war industries. This was rooted in antifascism as well: communists regularly pointed to Nazi Germany's use of women's reproductive labor for its military machinery. Jones invoked what the Party came to call the fascist triple K – *Kinder Küche Kirche* – children, kitchen, and church. The fascist triple K encapsulated what Nazi Germany expected of women – to be breeders for the war machine – something Jones feared might become expected in a militarized United States.[37]

The Party's position changed in June 1941, when the German army marched into the Soviet Union. The invasion meant that the USSR was now in the war, and its allies in the Party pushed for US intervention to secure the socialist homeland. This shift in policy from an antiwar position to full-throttled support for mobilization has been criticized by scholars and anticommunists. Though there was genuine opposition to war in the Party's ranks, the invasion was seen as an attack on socialism by avowed anticommunist fascists. The left then, as now, was a favorite targets of fascists, and the Party feared what the invasion might mean for the USSR and for themselves. Jones and her colleagues shifted their policy priorities and over the next several months urged the US to prepare for war against fascism.[38]

Jones's journalism transitioned to supporting the war effort and rallying young people to register for the draft. She also urged the opening of a second front to support the Soviet Union. Scholars have been divided over how Jones and other Party members handled this new policy. Christina Mislán analyzed Jones's wartime *Weekly Review* articles and argued that she put "superexploited" voices at the center of nationhood, race, and war politics. Mislán highlighted three main aspects of the articles: First, Jones advocated for US intervention in WWII by linking segregation to fascism and promoting military service and transnational solidarity. Second, she centered the "superexploited" and employed a discourse that intersected racial justice with the CPUSA's Popular Front platform. Finally, her journalism was complicated because she "contributed to the growth of US global power, even while she critiqued its policies." This last aspect is particularly notable because after WWII Jones was a vocal critic of US military expansion and intervention.[39]

During the war, the Black press placed itself "within and outside national interests" by arguing for the defeat of fascism both abroad and at home; meaning that Black journalists promoted war service while also advocating the destruction of Jim Crow in the US – partly as repayment for that service, but also in order to secure victory against fascism. Mislán is interested in how Jones's journalism navigated the intersection of her Black newspaper writing with her communism. Studying over a hundred editorials written by Jones, she argues that her writing reflected the Party's policy shift from "radical, anti-imperial(ism)" to "wartime mobilization." These editorials centered the "Black Struggle" within "US national interests" by "equating Jim Crowism to Fascism," something Jones and her colleagues had been doing for at least a decade before the war. The editorials also promoted a link between "national unity," "military participation," and "trans/national liberation."[40]

As Carole Boyce Davies notes, Jones's *Weekly Review* journalism was an extension of her role as YCL's educational director, a position she took up in 1940. Her columns were part of an effort to reach the "multiracial and mixed-gender audiences" in the youth organization. Sarah Dunstan and Patricia Owens argue that Jones's articles reflected a geopolitical discourse that became prominent in the 1940s – a discourse that was generally deployed in "response to threats to global white supremacy." Jones "reoriented" it by centering the "material resources, agency, and power of the colonized." In contrast to Mislán, Dunstan and Owens argue that Jones did not contribute to empire making, but instead reimagined a future for colonized peoples in their own nations.[41]

Jones's articles frequently connected Jim Crow to Hitlerism and linked the defeat of the one to the defeat of the other. Despite the segregated military institutions Black Americans labored under, Jones believed participation would form part of the "dissolution" of the "domestic and global repressive system." Mislán argues that Jones engaged in what she calls a "Du Boisian framework," referring to

W.E.B. Du Bois's analysis in *Black Reconstruction* which positioned Black Resistance as central to resistance to a new "slave system" under Jim Crow. Jones insisted that since defeating Jim Crow meant that Hitlerism also had to be defeated, advocates against Black participation were not helping the struggle against segregation, and in fact were "impeding" progressive causes.[42]

While Jones also insisted that encouraging Black work in wartime industries did not mean workers should endure exploitative conditions or accept wartime profiteering, she was toeing a difficult line in arguing that big business was fascist but also necessary for war participation. Jones was "selectively" critiquing US imperialism, while remaining hopeful that Black military participation would lead to "national inclusion, full citizenship" and an end to "repressive domestic politics." This was not a radical stand, especially since it was one several mainstream Black newspapers were also taking. Jones was simply expressing it in an "alternative medium" in the communist presses.[43]

There were several contradictions in Jones's writing, especially given her later theoretical corpus that rejected militarism as inherently fascistic. In her wartime reporting she linked antifascism to anticolonialism and anti-imperialism, ignoring the colonialism of the Allied powers. She would make "anti-imperialist arguments" about Western nations, but at the same time claim that though capitalists had too much power in the US and UK, basic democratic rights were still respected there. According to Mislán, Jones depicted German imperialism as more insidious than that of the Western powers. She was paradoxically arguing that the US maintained some basic commitment to democratic rights while also arguing that the US failed to practice democracy, particularly regarding Black Americans. This, Mislán points out, was in the years before she and her comrades faced the fascistic tactics of the Cold War era that would eventually lead to her deportation.⁴⁴

For Dunstan and Owens, in contrast, Jones was issuing a warning that Hitler's goals were global conquest, and that the Soviet Union, the world's foremost socialist power, was threatened by his objectives. She deployed an anticolonial argument informed by Marxist Leninism to urge support for the war effort. That did not assuage the *Weekly Review* readers, or the anticommunist public who noticed the abrupt shift in policy and the contradictions in the Party's new prowar stance. In response, Jones began a series of articles titled "Quiz," in which she responded to questions regarding the new policy. Following the Nazi invasion, she answered the question "Why not negotiate with Hitler?" She was very clear that such negotiation would mean "surrender to Hitler and Hitlerism" and surrendering the US's destiny to the "whim and wish" of German fascism. She pointed to the French collaborationist government in Vichy as evidence that negotiation led to complete domination by the Nazis. Striking an optimistic tone about the US, she argued that negotiation would mean the loss of any advances made by Black Americans. She also pointed to Hitler's own words in *Mein Kampf*, arguing that he would never be satisfied as he envisioned total Aryan domination.⁴⁵

The following week Jones answered one of the paradoxical questions that troubled so many communists: How could they support the imperialist US and UK? She once again invoked the fear of fascism, noting that all people would suffer were Hitlerism to triumph, the oppressed would find no route to freedom, and there would be a return to "barbarism." The invasion of the Soviet Union was clear evidence of Hitler's desire for world domination and the destruction of socialism. For Jones there was a larger lesson to be learned from the invasion. It was not in the end an abrupt policy shift: the Party recognized that Germany sought total domination and destruction, as evidenced by its foolhardy invasion of Russia. She reminded readers that there was no such thing as a "just" war and noted that it was important to remain "vigilant" about the US's and UK's "unjust aims," but insisted that in the end the "main enemy" remained Hitlerism. This of course failed to address why the Party had not remain committed to that position after the Nazi-Soviet pact was signed, but Jones and her comrades now framed the invasion as evidence of Hitler's true goals.[46]

The questions Jones answered were submitted by readers and addressed nearly every question they had about the Party's policy: Was the war about socialism? What about worker's rights in the war? Should the Party support conscripting women? Why should the US get involved since the USSR was putting up such a strong resistance? Does labor have to give up its rights in order to defeat Hitler? The questions went on for weeks and, to Jones's credit, she faced up to them – but turned to the threat of Hitlerism as her primary response. When one reader asked whether the struggle for Black rights wasn't more important than defeating Hitler, she responded that a victory for Hitlerism would "exterminate the Negro people," as was proven by the Nazis' extermination of Jews. She insisted that the Nazi drive for conquest threatened to destroy "every vestige of individual rights, of freedom and liberty," and that isolationists like Lindbergh welcomed a Nazi conquest which would lead to "re-enslavement." For Jones, the "struggle for Negro rights" could not continue to advance unless Hitler was defeated. More than that, a Nazi victory would mean the end of independence and would "thwart the possibility of decolonization" and "worldwide socialism."[47]

The war was more than theoretical for many of Jones's colleagues, including Henry Winston and Abner Berry, who both served; it would also affect Jones's husband. Jones's rise in the Party and its shift in policy coincided with her marriage to Abraham Scholnick. Scholnick was the son of Russian Jewish immigrants, Adolph and Pauline Scholnick. His father worked as a presser in a laundry and his mother stayed home with the children. Adolph died when Abraham was young, leaving Pauline to care for him and his older siblings, Sadie and William. At the time of his marriage to Jones, Scholnick was working as a "Baking Factory Worker" for the Tastee Bread Company. The wedding ceremony took place late in the evening of September 15, 1940, with clergyman Theophilus Alcantara presiding. Alcantara, a fellow Trinidadian, was the pastor of the St. Ambrose African Orthodox Church; he was also a radical. He served with the Brooklyn Interdenominational Ministerial Alliance and was active in the NNC. In 1938, 1940, and 1944, he ran unsuccessfully for local office with the American Labor Party, a New York socialist political party. It seems likely that Alcantara was chosen to preside for his politics rather than his religion, as Jones had early on rejected her mother's Catholicism.[48]

One month after the wedding, Scholnick was required to register under the conscription law that his new wife had been protesting. After the Party dropped its opposition to the war, Scholnick organized a ceremony to celebrate the conscription of his fellow Tastee Bread employees, and by 1943 he was himself in training with the 1060th Flying Squadron. Marriage to a US citizen gave Jones another opportunity to apply for citizenship, after a failed attempt made shortly after joining the Party. But her marriage did not make her case any stronger and she was eventually once again denied. As Boyce Davies argues, Jones's struggle to secure citizenship testifies to the lengths the state will go to define "what constitutes an appropriate citizen." As an active and proud Black communist, Jones was not what constituted an "appropriate" citizen for policymakers, even after she married a US citizen.[49]

Jones's sisters had better luck in gaining citizenship. Yvonne was the first to do so, filing an intent in May 1941 and eventually becoming naturalized on December 16, 1943. Sylvia was naturalized on April 15, 1946, but Lindsay, for unknown reasons, did not become a citizen until August 17, 1959. The date of Jones's parents' naturalization is unclear. Her mother filed an intent in 1927, and her father in 1936, but there is no record of either's naturalization. It is unlikely Minnie was ever naturalized given that she died in 1928. In order to gain citizenship, Jones's parents and sisters had to confirm that they were neither anarchists nor polygamists. It was not until the passage of the Internal Security Act in 1950 that being a communist specifically disqualified someone from citizenship; the fact that this remains the case today highlights the continued power of US anticommunism. Jones was prevented from becoming a citizen because of her radicalism – immigration officials likely conflated anarchist and communist, as intelligence and other government bodies frequently did.[50]

What Jones felt about the prospect of having children is unclear. She understood childbearing and childrearing to be inherently political and frequently wrote about the struggles of Black motherhood. But her lifelong struggle with her health may have eliminated any chances of her carrying a child. She suffered from the lingering effects of her teenage bout with tuberculosis, and reported severe headaches, bronchitis, and pneumonia. It did not help that she was a smoker. In 1944, she underwent "major gynecological" surgery which put her into "premature" menopause at the age of twenty-nine. Had she wanted to become a biological parent, it was now impossible.[51]

In 1942, the same year she became associate editor at the *Weekly Review*, Jones produced a pamphlet titled *Lift Every Voice* which argued for Black participation in the war. She opened with the historic 1938 fight between the Black boxer Joe Louis and the "Nazi hope" Max Schmeling. In defiance of "Aryan supremacy," Louis roundly beat Schmeling and proudly announced he was fighting for the US. The fight served as a metaphor for the interracial unity Jones and her comrades pushed for to achieve victory over fascism. The pamphlet was a complete change in tone and objective from her 1940 pamphlet assailing the Jim Crow army. In 1942 she celebrated figures like Joe Louis and Dorie Miller, a US Navy cook killed at Pearl Harbor, as exemplars of Black America fighting against Hitlerism.[52]

The pamphlet followed Jones's articles in arguing that with a fascist victory Black people would be treated as "latent brutes" and there would no longer be "constitutional liberty and democratic rights." It struck a rather optimistic tone in presenting the United States, not as the land of liberty, but as a land of potential liberty. Unions, Jones argued, would be destroyed under fascism along with literature, art, and culture. While the United States was certainly guilty of poll taxes, literacy tests, and lynching, there was an "opportunity to fight" against such injustices. She quoted Paul Robeson telling an audience in Kansas City, Missouri that while there were "weights" against full participation in citizenship, there were also efforts to introduce change, including Roosevelt's 1941 Executive Order 8802 which created the Fair Employment Practices Committee to end discrimination in the defense industries. Jones argued that while some Black leaders were fighting a "Double V" campaign – referring to the campaign started by the Black newspaper *Pittsburgh Courier* to defeat fascism abroad and at home – there was only one Victory to be achieved, victory over fascism everywhere, and it was the

CPUSA that offered a model for the interracial organization needed to achieve that goal.[53]

After Jones was promoted to editor-in-chief of the *Weekly Review* in 1943, her articles focused on continued support of the war effort and on educating readers about historical and contemporary figures. In June that year she interviewed Paul Robeson, who was then enjoying national acclaim as an entertainer but was also a committed radical. In 1937, Robeson had set up the International Committee on African Affairs (ICAA) with Max Yergan, a communist and former NNC leader. Founded in solidarity with African anti-colonial movements, in 1942 the organization changed its name to the Council on African Affairs (CAA). Yergan would eventually leave both the Party and the CAA, accusing the latter of being a communist group. Scholars and activists Alphaeus Hunton and W.E.B. Du Bois became CAA officers and helped drive the organization until its forced dissolution in 1955 as a result of anticommunist harassment.[54]

Jones interviewed Robeson at the CAA offices, asking him about the war and his admiration for the Soviet Union. Robeson noted "proudly" that his son had been educated in the USSR and said he believed all Americans should be better informed about the country. More important, Robeson felt that in order to defeat Hitlerism and demolish fascism there needed to be a deep friendship between the US and USSR. It was in the US's own interest to ally with the Soviets for "our own good" in the war effort. They discussed the investment colonized states in Asia and Africa had in Hitler's defeat, and Robeson insisted that the USSR was a friend to all people and thus important in anti-imperialist efforts. Jones and Robeson were simultaneously encouraging solidarity with the Soviets while remaining critical of the US's segregation policies without explicitly saying so. Robeson would later be accused of being a secret CPUSA member;

whether a member or not, he would remain closely affiliated with people in and around the Party, including Jones. His wife Eslanda Robeson would also become an outspoken radical activist and Jones's friend.[55] In October 1943, over 300 Young Communist League delegates met in Detroit, Michigan to officially dissolve the organization and recreate it as American Youth for Democracy (AYD), removing "Communist" from the name in an effort to appeal to a larger constituency of young people. Its magazine *Weekly Review* became *Spotlight*, with Jones as editor. With a new name on the masthead the magazine retained its mission to drum up support for the war. The AYD had agreed at its founding meeting to make urging a second front in the war one of its priorities, along with improving relations between the Soviet Union and the United States, pushing Roosevelt for an executive order to desegregate the military, and securing the right to vote for eighteen year olds.[56]

Jones's early journalism offers some insight into her later theoretical corpus. She was committed to desegregation – a not particularly radical goal – but also to radical economic transformation. Support for an increasingly militarized United States, as Mislán has argued, seemed contradictory. But at the same time, Jones saw war and fascism as kin and particularly treacherous for Black Americans and women. In a 1944 Mother's Day article in *Spotlight*, Jones focused on women's experience of the devastation and ruins of war. The Party had long been pushing to use Mother's Day not as an occasion for what they called "sickly sentiments" found in cards, but as a call for political action on mother's pensions and insurance, better housing and schools, and peace. Jones's Mother's Day peace speech in 1941 had exemplified this effort. In her 1944 article, she wrote that women in the Soviet Union mourned their dead while also cleaning the "fascist scum" off the streets. But American fascists were also invoking dead sons and husbands in their attempt to persuade mothers to reject US involvement in the war. Jones specifically mentioned Charles Coughlin, a right-wing Catholic radio priest whom the Party targeted as an American fascist. She accused Coughlin of wanting to negotiate with fascists by encouraging women to denounce the war effort. In contrast, she argued that defeating fascism would "herald the dawn of a better world" for all.[57]

The following month's issue included Jones's editorial letter celebrating the D-Day invasion as the most "powerful bulwark" against world fascism and what it stood for, including "outrages against women and children" and "Aryan race ideology." Those who preached pacifism or antiwar were essentially siding with fascists intent on seeing the destruction of socialism and ending any chance of Black or women's liberation. In a July 1944 editorial she argued that while peace was preferable, it was important to mobilize against fascism to ensure that it would be "utterly crushed." She emphasized that racism and sexism in policy and practice were fascistic, thus the US was not immune and had to maintain its own two-front war against fascism.[58] That same month, Jones wrote a report on *Spotlight*'s first six months. The magazine had 16,000 subscribers, which included the AYD membership as well as their "adult friends." She described the magazine's "single-minded" focus on the effort to "crush Nazi-fascism" and provide a sense of unity among readers. *Spotlight*, she claimed, was the only antifascist magazine devoted to educating youth on the war effort and progressive causes. Remarkably, Jones wrote that one of the policies the magazine supported was a "permanent program for universal military service." In a few short years, she would reverse course on military conscription. War against fascism was justified, but fascistic war, like the one against communism the US would later take up, was not.[59]

The magazine was not doing well financially and by May 1945 *Spotlight*'s poor financial situation forced it to stop publication. Jones had resigned as editor in February 1945 to take over as the AYD's educational director, and she was appointed the Negro Affairs editor for the *Daily Worker*. Her work with the youth communist movement was ending, but in 1946 she was elected to the CPUSA's National Board.[60]

## Surveillance

Jones's growing visibility and leadership in the YCL captured the attention of intelligence agencies, who began actively surveilling communists during the war. The YCL and New Age Publishers, one of the Party's outlets which produced *Spotlight*, were listed as her employer, indicating that Jones was not just a Party member but also an employee. In 1942, the Federal Bureau of Investigation opened a file on Jones and began surveillance that would last fifteen years and result in her expulsion from the country. In June 1940, the Smith Act had been passed, making it illegal to advocate or belong to any organization that advocated the violent overthrow of the US government. Haverty-Stacke argues that, in a preview of Cold War redbaiting, the Bureau used the law to monitor and harass radical labor organizations and arrest labor activists, using war production as cover. By 1941, the FBI had extended its authority to focus on civil rights groups, progressives, and communists on the pretext that they were engaged in plots against the government.[61]

Both the Roosevelt and later Truman administrations feared that American communists were passing information to the Soviets. Roosevelt issued "secret executive directives" expanding the FBI's "investigative authority," which included wiretapping. Athan Theoharis has argued that, during this period, the Bureau began to use extralegal methods by misinforming the executive branch and using external filing methods or the destruction of records to avoid documentary audits. FBI chief J. Edgar Hoover took the opportunity to authorize bugging, "break-in operations" and "mail-opening programs" in the course of "non-criminal investigations" into alleged subversives.[62] Jones and her colleagues were followed, reported on by informants, and had every written and spoken word of theirs catalogued. The information gathered would be used after the war to arrest, detain, and deport communists on the pretext of their being a national security threat.

In the early years, however, the Bureau struggled to identify Jones's origins. Its information often came from informants already within organizations or individuals who had been directed to infiltrate an organization. After FBI agents were instructed to compile information about Jones's birthplace and family, an informant told them she was from Lawrenceville, Virginia. Informants were notoriously unreliable, often feeding agents their own conspiracy theories or repeating hearsay information. There is no indication why the informant believed Jones was from Virginia, but this piece of misinformation, along with her use of a pen name, meant that the FBI did not discover Jones was not a US citizen until 1947.[63]

Agents in Lawrenceville not surprisingly found nothing on Jones. They searched the Bureau of Vital Statistics records looking for a birth certificate and questioned registrars at county offices and school officials – all reported they had no records or recollection of a Claudia Jones. In New York, agents scoured the *Weekly Review* for information on her, finding an article giving her birth year as 1915 – the informant had said 1917. They requested information from New York City colleges to see if she had attended. When her building supervisor was interviewed, he told the agents that she was a good tenant who had no kids. The New York agents indicated in their report that she spoke "unlike [a] southern Negro," which led to doubts about her Virginia origins.[64]

Jones remained a mystery to the agents as they searched marriage and criminal records and explored city directories and phone books. She had no passport, and they could find no school records in New York. They did find her social security number on a job application, but since these numbers had only been in use for seven years and were not the ubiquitous identifiers of personal information they are today, the information led to another dead end. The agents early on identified her parents' first names but could not find their surname. Jones's pen name protected her identity for nearly five years. The endless misleading information the FBI collected could be read as a comedy of errors, but it demonstrates the Bureau's relentless pursuit of individuals who were dedicated to the Black Freedom Struggle.[65]

Jones was also placed on Hoover's "Custodial Detention" list. In 1939, Hoover had set up an "emergency detention program" called "Custodial Detention." It was directed at "persons of German, Italian, and Communist sympathies," and those who were listed were deemed "dangerous to the public peace and safety" and thus would be detained during a national emergency. Hoover knew that his program was illegal and a violation of constitutional rights, so urged his special agents to keep it secret. When he eventually briefed Roosevelt and Attorney General Francis Biddle on the program, they questioned its necessity and legality. While the program was not approved by the Roosevelt administration, Hoover and his agents nevertheless continued to maintain the list.[66]

Recent studies on J. Edgar Hoover have shown that his preoccupation with communism and communists bordered on obsession. Even when suspected individuals or organizations had no affiliation or connection to the CPUSA, Hoover assumed it had not been discovered yet. His Bureau also focused undue attention on the Black Freedom Struggle, reserving its more underhanded methods for Black activists.[67] This focus on Black activism and the FBI's surreptitious efforts to discredit the individuals and movements involved has left a troubling legacy in the United States. Lerone Martin argues that Hoover enabled the rise of Christian nationalism and that he built up the Bureau as a "white Christian force." White evangelicals saw Hoover as a partner in their attempts to "bring America back to their God"; they did not merely ignore his unconventional and illegal methods but embraced them, because Hoover's machinations ensured the perpetuity of white supremacist institutions and power. His "worldview," which dominated the FBI for over forty years, "determined legitimate statecraft from subversion" – meaning that Hoover decided what was legal or illegal and chose who should be surveilled and punished. For Martin, while Hoover's own lifestyle and habits, and his Presbyterianism, were hardly evangelical, Evangelicals embraced him as a nationalist hero because he used the Bureau to enforce his own values of anticommunism, white superiority, sexism, heterosexism, and small government (with the notable exception of his own agency). This has enabled the Bureau to exercise power almost without any oversight. Even today, many of its own agents have noted that the FBI has failed to anticipate white supremacist violence and terrorism as it continues to focus disproportionate attention and resources on Black activists, including Black Lives Matter activists, whom it labeled "Black Identity Extremists." After a backlash, the Bureau abandoned that phrase, but instead lumped BLM in with white supremacists by considering both to be instances of "Racially Motivated

Violent Extremism." Though Hoover has been dead for over fifty years, his policies directed at communists created a framework that still influences today's Bureau.[68]

Communists knew they were being surveilled, but it is not likely they knew the full extent of it, until the courtroom dramas that would start to unfold from 1949. On May 19, 1943, Hoover wrote Lawrence Smith of the Special War Policies Unit recommending that a card be made for Jones "in view of the existing emergency." The unit was part of the Department of Justice's War Division created to monitor the threat of espionage. In June, a card was created for Jones. As Theoharis notes, Attorney General Biddle did not formally ban the practice, and allowed a list of aliens to be maintained under the title "Security Index." By August 1943, the War Division had been absorbed into the Department of Justice's Criminal Division, and Hoover was told that he could not have his Custodial Detention program. He nevertheless continued to maintain the list, now using the label "Security Index Cards" rather than the more loaded "Custodial Index Cards." He was also not yet aware that Jones was not a US citizen and so could be included on the alien Security Index. It was in this period that Hoover set up what would later be called COINTELPRO (Counterintelligence Program), which would employ illegal and underhanded methods, sometimes with deadly consequences, against activists, including Jones and her colleagues. It was later used against another generation of activists, including Martin Luther King Jr. and members of the Black Panther Party.[69]

## Browderism

Even as the CPUSA and its members were being described as a subversive threat to the nation, Party policy was shifting to embrace Americanism and tone down the emphasis on class struggle. This new policy came to be known as Browderism, referring to Party chairman Earl Browder's emphasis on "conciliation with the ruling class," which included politicians in Washington, DC and capitalists on Wall Street. As Gerald Horne has described it, the logic behind the policy was that the wartime alliance between the US and the Soviet Union had demonstrated the ability of capitalism and communism to cooperate. The Party began to preach unity and threw its support behind Franklin Roosevelt, the New Deal, and the war effort. Leading Black figures like Ben Davis were eager advocates of the new Browder line and supported Roosevelt's reelection campaign in 1944. That same year the CPUSA changed its name to the Communist Political Association (CPA). Horne argues that this shift was not completely Browder's fault, and that it was more "emulation than dictation" as the Soviet Union had dissolved the Comintern that year. But it occurred at a time when the Party began to "deprioritize" its calls for racial justice. Browder himself cast doubt on the Black Belt Thesis and began to express concern over whether Black Americans "could be integrated into the class struggle."[70]

There were Black members in the Party who "popularized" the new Browder line, including for a brief period Jones. In March 1945, as the war was ending, Jones wrote an article for *Spotlight* on the Yalta conference that was the basis for Browder's belief in the cooperation of socialism and capitalism. She wrote that at the conference the big three leaders – Stalin, Roosevelt, and Churchill – had all agreed to the independence and liberation of the people of Europe, and had adopted a plan to allow for elections and universal suffrage. She was complimentary about Roosevelt and the decisions made at Yalta, and hoped that "a world of peace, security and mutual trust between nations" would emerge. Jones's primary concern was demolishing fascism and preventing its resurgence in a defeated Germany. Yalta, she claimed, had set out a plan to achieve both. The article was optimistic, praising the Yalta plans going forward, and suggesting that a prosperous postwar alliance with the Soviet Union was the goal. Jones also looked toward the April 1945 meeting in San Francisco that would formalize the United Nations proposals for global cooperation made the year before at the Dumbarton Oaks conference. She counseled readers to treat the Yalta decisions as a basis for the future. Only months later, however, Jones would wholly abandon Browderism and become one of its most vocal critics.[71]

Jones's friend and former lover Howard "Stretch" Johnson described her as a one-time hero-worshipper of Browder, but the latter's new policy began to sow seeds of doubt. Some Black Party members, like Doxey Wilkerson, were already questioning the policy. Johnson, who had been wounded in action, returned to the US to find the Party "furiously" debating Browderism. He was recuperating at an upstate New York hospital and had not been released from the military, so his information about the debates came through his friends Jones and Henry Winston. They were worried because the struggle for Black rights in some districts had been "blunted" or even "completely eliminated" under Browderism. Before being deployed, Johnson had experienced "creeping Browderism" when he was disciplined for writing a pamphlet about Jim Crow in the military. He was told by Abner Berry that it could be "demoralizing" to the war effort. He also noted that the Party had rejected the "Double V" campaign, with Browder counseling both labor and Black members to give up their campaigns in the "interests of unity to win the war." Johnson joined a group of Black communists who opposed the policy.[72]

The month after Jones's Yalta article, a French communist leader, Jacques Duclos, published a letter critical of Browderism. It was from a document that came out of Moscow and was not widely circulated. William Foster later complained that he had to search to find a copy of it. The letter was concerned with Browder's intervention in communist parties in South America, where they "emulated" the CPUSA. When the Party was officially dissolved and the CPA was formed, the membership subsequently dissolved as well, with nearly half the members leaving. In May 1945, after the Duclos letter was circulated among communists, Ben Davis shifted his allegiance and confronted Browder about his "intransigence." The following month, the ILD leader William Patterson attacked Browder at a national meeting, singling out his abandonment of the Black Belt Thesis and the Black Freedom Struggle. The Duclos letter sparked debates about Browderism and many began to express their regret at accepting it, including Jones's white comrades Elizabeth Gurley Flynn and Alexander Bittelman. In July 1945, Earl Browder was ousted from the Party, and it was reestablished as the CPUSA.[73]

In August, Jones made her objections to Browderism known in a position paper presented at the Party's convention. She admitted to having accepted it without "study, thought, or true conviction." She rejected Browder's belief that Black Americans had used their self-determination to choose integration, and acknowledged that, though progress had been made, the evidence suggested that self-determination was still central to the struggle. Browder had also given up on the Party's revolutionary goals and argued that liberation could be achieved under capitalism. Jones attacked Browder's assumptions that he understood what it was that Black Americans had chosen and that their struggle was no longer necessary or separate from the class struggle. Since Browderism had also counseled an embrace of Roosevelt's New Deal, Jones argued that it ignored the "liberal-bourgeois policies" of the Roosevelt administration. The CPA had assumed a mythic wartime unity that it expected to continue into the postwar world, but it ignored persistent problems and the nearly immediate shedding of wartime gains. Jones also claimed that efforts to dismantle the Fair Employment Practices Committee were already underway.[74]

She concluded by noting that the need for the struggle for Black rights was more important than ever. She also took herself and her Black comrades to task for accepting "Browder's opportunist thesis" and thereby embracing "the false and bankrupt logic of reformism." Worse still, they had accepted a "less than equal status" for Black Americans in the future. She proposed that a commission be formed to study the Black Belt Thesis and the work needed for Black equality, and argued that the CPA would not be an effective organization when it came to confronting and dismantling racist institutions and practices.[75]

Jones articulated what many Black Party members felt about Browderism. Thelma Dale, the executive secretary of the NNC, added her voice to the debate by insisting on more work for equality, particularly regarding Black women who faced the "major brunt of the lay offs" after the war. In January 1946, Jones published a lengthier article on the Black Belt Thesis that further articulated her stand on self-determination and the Party. She argued for the preservation of the Thesis and further work by the Party to support its Black comrades. She went on the attack against what she called fascist "imperialist forces" within the US, concentrated in "monopoly capital" and "reactionary Republicans." At the war's end, the lynching of Black Americans recommenced and "Hitler-like incitements" by Congressmen intended to divide labor from the Black Freedom Struggle worked to undermine all wartime progress.[76]

The Party, Jones continued, had been the "vanguard" of the Black Freedom Struggle because it recognized the "Negro Question" as a "special" issue. It taught white workers that it was in their own "self-interest" to fight against the "imperialist ideologies and practices" of the ruling classes in the United States. Jones defended the Thesis as one that grounded the Party's understanding of white supremacism as the ideology of the ruling classes – an ideology deployed to divide and conquer working people. As Boyce Davies has argued, Jones was a Leninist rather than a Stalinist, and her written work exemplifies this. Jones argued that the Black Belt Thesis followed the Leninist understanding of a nation as a "historically evolved, stable community of language, territory, economic life and psychological makeup."[77]

She then went on to describe how the Black Belt in the US south resembled the Leninist notion of a nation. She argued that though Black people shared a "common language" with the white majority, Americans shared the same common language with their former British oppressors, and no one would have argued that liberation from the British Empire was a mistake. In 1913, Lenin himself had made the argument that Black Americans were a nation. But most important for Jones's purposes, it was Browder who had abandoned the Marxist Leninist thinking that had guided the Party. She argued that as communists, the belief that socialism would liberate all oppressed people was a guiding principle, and that "as Leninists" the Party must not deny any oppressed people the right to self-determination. This was a policy Browder had abandoned and to which Jones was reaffirming the Party's commitment.[78]

The break with Browderism was significant in terms of the Party resuming its work and leadership in antiracism, but also in creating a new focus on women's rights. As Higashida argues, when William Foster ascended to Party chairman, communist women (including Jones) renewed their efforts on the "Woman Question," as they called it. Kate Weigand has noted that even under intense FBI scrutiny and harassment, the Party became an important voice in articulating women's oppression within a Marxist Leninist framework in the 1940s. This, coupled with the Party's renewed embrace of antiracism, helped lay the foundation for Black Left feminism and a focus on Black women's triple oppression.[79]

Jones had risen in the Party ranks early on, but it was her stand on Browderism and the Black Belt Thesis that earned her more attention and respect from the Party leadership as well as rank-and-file members. Harry Haywood, a long-time communist and leader in the Party, claimed that it was her 1945 position paper that had "stimulated" his interest in the ongoing Party debates over Browderism and self-determination. Both the 1945 position paper and 1946 article made Jones a recognized communist thinker. She was to be instrumental in creating the Party's new policy on the "Negro Question" and was becoming an important leader and ideologue within the Party. In the postwar years she would continue to climb in its ranks. This did not go unnoticed by the FBI, who were still dizzily trying to figure out exactly who she was, while also trying to find ways to punish her and her comrades.[80]

Jones and the Party also articulated a still relevant theory that US fascism was a pertinent and omnipresent force. Though the term was not coined during Jones's lifetime, "racial fascism" was recognized by Black radicals when they described US racism and sexism as fascist, especially as expressed in law in restrictions on birth control, segregation, and other oppressive laws. In practice, racial fascism was apparent in law enforcement violence and in the indifference of state actors toward punishing racist violence. It was and has remained a powerful strain in Western nations, and the fact that it remains a problem is unsurprising. Racial fascism is embedded in the liberal democracies that have defined citizenship based on exclusion. This is because monopoly capitalism has had (and continues to have) a grip on domestic and foreign policy, leading to the recognition that the Western powers have no claim to democracy. The US fascism Jones theorized came to include the growing anticommunist apparatus that would single her and her comrades out as a threat and openly trample on their civil liberties, while liberals abandoned their own commitments to justice and engaged in redbaiting. In the final analysis fascism in the Western states is not anomalous.

# 3

# The Early Cold War (1945–1950)

*To Elizabeth Gurley Flynn*

I think I'll always see you everywhere –
At morn – when sunlight's radiance bathes all things like verse
Proclaiming man, not beast
Is king of all universe.

I'll see you in young shooting sprouts
That sneer at weeds – age-gnarled in doubt
Of users who defile in epithet
A life well-lived in service built from strife.

I'll see you too at noontime
When the sun in orbit
Flings it's rays like thyme through skies on days that hurt
Causing you to weld anew full courage spurt.

I'll see you oft at twilight's dusk
Before the sun will fade
I'll conjure up your twinkling laugh
Your eyes so much like jade.

I'll see you in the dark of night
When nature seeks her rest
Except the reedy crickets
Who muse in watch, I guess.

I'll think of you forever
And how your spirit rings
Because your faith leaps as a flame
Sweet nurture to all things.

Of all the times I'll miss you most
Is when I'm least aware
Because you will intrude I know
Upon my inner ear.
Beloved comrade, when from you I tear
My mind, my heart, my thoughts, you'll hear!
      Claudia Jones[1]

American communists had reason to be optimistic at the end of World War II. The United States had allied with the Soviet Union in the defeat of Nazism. The Atlantic Charter agreement between Franklin Roosevelt and Winston Churchill seemed to suggest that independence for colonized nations would follow. Women and Black Americans had found work opportunities in industries that had previously denied them employment, and there were efforts made to include women in the workforce by adopting funded child-care programs. But there were also signs of problems. The federal government grudgingly enforced non-discrimination laws in war industries, women's wages were still significantly lower than men's, jobs remained coded by gender and race, and wartime gains in wages, hours, and benefits began dissolving with the war's end as did the job opportunities. The Fair Employment Practices Committee (FEPC) created by executive order to enforce non-discrimination in war industries was quickly abandoned.

Perhaps the most troubling sign of the new age ushered in by the war was the atomic bomb. Policymakers, pundits, historians, and military personnel continue to debate the efficacy of the bombing of Hiroshima in ending a war that was already on course to end. The second bombing, this time of Nagasaki, only days later has proven even more difficult to justify or understand. Militaristic conservatives today quickly silence dissent from those who question its use, ignoring the fact that conservatives were some of the most vociferous critics of the bomb in 1945. But more troubling for Black America was how easily and efficiently the bomb (and then a second bomb) was dispatched against Japan, a nation of color.[2]

As wartime alliances between the Allied powers dissolved, and the United States began posturing as the world's only nuclear power, backed by a powerful military, anticommunism emerged as the dominant policy both at home and abroad. Gradually, criticism of US policy was depicted as treasonous and anticommunist witch-hunts zeroed in on American communists and their allies. Claudia Jones would remain optimistic for a time as progressives tried to counter the hostility and focus on making substantive change; fascism, after all, was defeated. But US fascism in the guise of anticommunist politicians and law enforcement agents would violate constitutionally protected citizenship rights and silence influential radicals in the Black Freedom Struggle. Jones would become a target, but even in the face of legal harassment she wrote some of her most influential theoretical work and helped to shape Black socialist feminism.

Scholars have long recognized that anticommunism has been a predominant aspect of US politics. Nick Fischer argues that it was deployed after the Civil War to quell dissent, particularly among labor activists. With a free Black labor force, anticommunism became a tool to silence dissent and delegitimize (and make illegal) claims to equality. Charisse Burden-Stelly argues that a "Black Scare," propelled by anti-Blackness, fed white anxiety about being dominated racially, socially, and economically by "inferior Black populations." This operated in tandem with anticommunism to become part of the "architecture of racial capitalism" in the modern United States. Because anti-Blackness was motivated by fear of Black power over white people, and anticommunism was justified by a fear of radical takeover, claims for progressive change appeared subversive. Fischer contends that it was not simply the federal government that propelled anti-radicalism. The government worked as an agent of monopoly capitalism to criminalize dissent. "Defiance" against capitalist institutions became "sedition." These sentiments remain powerful today as right-wing leaders continue to attack moderate social justice demands as communist conspiracies.[3]

For Burden-Stelly, "war and imperialism" became the primary drivers of profit in the modern era. While the United States was just emerging from war, it was staking its claim as the so-called defender of democracy in the world. This defense led to the build up of the largest and most expensive military in world history. This was justified by the "endless construction of 'threats'" from, as Burden-Stelly argues, "primarily racialized and socialist states" and, in the United States, from radicals and Black Americans. The US government expanded its anti-radical and anti-democratic infrastructure in the name of defending "progress, prosperity, freedom, and security." As Fischer describes it, the reality was that US officials had to construct "semantic contrivances" to mask their attacks on democracy and freedom and to convince Americans of the righteousness of anticommunism. What anticommunists criticized in the Soviet Union was often also happening in the US, including attacks on labor organizations and against populations of color. Anticommunism was taken up by a growing and influential conservative movement that described civil rights as an attack on white America. These conservatives allied with liberals who abandoned radical demands in order to protect themselves from redbaiting and obfuscated the perpetuation of social inequality.[4]

Especially important in this context is police violence, which has been a consistent problem for Black Americans and one that continues to galvanize activists. Christopher Vials and Bill Mullen have argued that continued police violence proves that "racial capitalism" can "turn fascist." Activists today have taken Jones's analysis further by arguing not just for an end to police violence and for police to be held accountable, but that law enforcement agencies, as agents of capitalism rather than the public good, need to be abolished. Abolitionists argue that the police have historically been empowered to police the "color line," as armed state agents tasked with protecting "the state and private property." Increasingly, police forces have been militarized while social welfare has been eviscerated. For Ruth Wilson Gilmore this "organized abandonment" means that the state has replaced the limited welfare programs that existed with more violent policing. She argues that "we actually see the abandonment of one set of public mandates in favor of another – of social welfare for domestic warfare." This form of fascism was something Jones and her allies focused on; and it was not just violent, it was genocidal. Piecemeal civil rights reforms were not enough to eliminate fascism.[5]

Gerald Horne notes that the US government made reformist concessions to the civil rights movement while simultaneously silencing its comrades in the Communist Party. The CPUSA had its own problems with internal racism and sexism, but it was one of the few interracial organizations that made efforts to confront them. It also denounced reformism as piecemeal and not enough to effect radical change, while mainstream civil rights organizations acquiesced to the Cold War state and pushed for integration. Today's abolitionists have coined the phrase "reformist-reforms" to describe policies that fail to address systemic structures and therefore perpetuate the status quo. Horne argues that during the Cold War, while the breakdown of segregation made it appear that real progress was being made, questions about economic justice were silenced and framed as communist plots. As Horne points out, the movement could secure the right of Black Americans to sit at a lunch counter with their fellow white Americans, but it could not help them secure the economic resources to eat there. White supremacy and anticommunism became the "major forces" defining US life after World War II, and this guaranteed there would be limits on any civil rights gains. The limited reforms of the time failed to make the substantive changes that were needed to create an egalitarian society, leaving racist structures in place to this day.[6]

## US Fascism

Jones would confront the Cold War state and rail against anticommunism. She recognized its basis in anti-Blackness and pushed for radical change, even in the face of legal harassment. The US policy of containing communism both at home and abroad emerged just as Jones was becoming an important CPUSA leader. In the immediate postwar years, she was elected to the Party's National Board as secretary of the Negro Commission, and became the editor for Negro Affairs at the *Daily Worker*. Throughout 1946 and into 1947 she wrote a regular column for the paper on news events and political campaigns, many of which she was involved in. Her postwar journalism focused on the Black Freedom Struggle and white supremacist harassment, expressing a growing concern with what she described as bipartisan efforts to criminalize dissent and the rise of domestic fascism.

Jones argued that, rather than the defeat of fascism, the US was witnessing its growth, and she feared what this meant for liberation movements. For Jones, as Burden-Stelly notes, this fascism was "manifested" in "white supremacist terrorism," "Wall Street imperialism," and "economic domination internationally." The US's military domination, and its growth in the postwar years, was a hallmark of fascism, and it deployed anticommunism to "cripple all progressive thought and activism." Antiradicalism – defined by Burden-Stelly as "the disciplining of communists, socialists, and other anticapitalists" whose ideas, activism, and political orientation were "deemed subversive" – was fascist. Jones recognized many similarities between US and European fascism, including the control and censoring of the press, increased nationalism, fraudulent elections (with the disenfranchisement of Black voters), and violations of human rights, among others. However, as Burden-Stelly identifies, for Jones US fascism had four distinctive aspects: anti-Blackness, capitalist imperialism, militarism and warmongering, and anticommunism.[7]

Jones's "Negro Affairs" articles reflected her concerns about these four aspects of US fascism. Anti-Blackness and racist violence remained a constant specter for Black Americans despite their efforts in the military and war industry. The police killing of veteran Charles Ferguson in 1946 would lead to an important CPUSA campaign and highlighted for Jones the continued danger of being Black in America. As Mullen and Vials argue, racial fascism has always been experienced by Black Americans, with violence against "part" of the Black population being used to "discipline the whole" population. Though Jones and the Party had hoped that the defeat of fascism and the alliance with the Soviet Union, coupled with the New Deal state, might usher in a new era, anticommunism instead fortified racial fascism within the body politic. Anticommunist legislation "imperiled the citizenship" of even the native born and demonstrated that repression could exist and thrive under liberal democracy.[8]

On February 5, 1946, Charles Ferguson and his brother Alfonso were murdered by Long Island police officer Joseph Romeika outside a diner. Witnesses could not agree on the events, but they confirmed that Romeika had lined Charles and Alfonso up against a wall along with their brothers Richard and Joseph. A group of women claimed that before the men were lined up, they saw no behavior out of the ordinary, but a bus driver accused Charles of cursing out a diner employee. Joseph Ferguson said in his eyewitness testimony that his brother Charles admitted to the officer he had a gun and when he reached to show him, Romeika shot him and Alfonso. The bullet that killed Alfonso also struck Joseph in the shoulder.[9]

By April, the US Army had cleared Charles of any wrongdoing and agreed to pay his widow his pension. Meanwhile, the CPUSA demanded that New York Governor Thomas Dewey launch an investigation. Several prominent attorneys became involved, including Thurgood Marshall of the NAACP, Arthur Garfield Hays from the American Civil Liberties Union (ACLU), and Osmond K. Fraenkel from the National Lawyers Guild. Jones and the Party called for a new grand jury after an all-white jury had exonerated Romeika of the killings and Joseph's wounding. It was a familiar story of a white officer using homicidal force against Black men and a white jury endorsing his actions.[10]

The Party sent telegrams to Governor Dewey demanding an investigation; they also sent a delegation to speak to him and organized pickets to demand justice. Jones reported on the actions and urged other New Yorkers to contact Dewey and their state representatives to demand action. She described Romeika as the "anti-Negro killer" and the case as one of "lynch justice." This emphasis on lynch law would become central to the Party's opposition to the Cold War: while the United States claimed to be securing democracy with its anticommunist interventions abroad, it was failing to deliver democracy for its Black citizens at home. Lynch mobs were replaced by police, prosecutors, juries, and judges, and Black defendants had no rights in this system. Dewey eventually called for an investigation, but it resulted in Romeika's second exoneration. The case and its disappointing resolution appeared in the 1951 Civil Rights Congress *We Charge Genocide* petition accusing the US government of genocide against Black Americans.[11]

Jones was also concerned about a rampant anti-Blackness in the labor movement, which fortified capitalist imperialism. She focused some of her journalism on the efforts to unify the labor movement, arguing that the only beneficiary of these racial divisions was monopoly capitalism. Jones offered an important critique of monopoly capitalism as it began to operate as an imperialist surrogate during the Cold War. Even if states were no longer explicitly practicing empire, it was fast becoming apparent that corporations would lean on state militaries to ensure capitalist global control. Jones counseled that interracial class solidarity had to counter monopoly capitalist power. She wrote several articles on the National Negro Congress (NNC), which worked to consolidate unionization and social justice issues and included some of the biggest names in the Black Freedom Struggle at the time, such as Paul Robeson, Alphaeus Hunton, and A. Philip Randolph. Throughout the spring of 1946, Jones reported on the NNC's efforts to organize and support interracial unionization ahead of its tenth annual conference. In a column from April that year, she argued that Black workers were some of the most militant in the labor movement and white workers would do well to ally with them. The article is an early reflection of the disillusionment that would come with the Truman administration. While communists hoped that Roosevelt's New Deal laid a foundation for more expansive progressive change, and that as his former Vice-President Truman would pursue that expansion, Jones became troubled by the new President's labor policies. She wrote about a bipartisan effort that was eroding Roosevelt's promises of "unity, peace, security, and progress," as evidenced by Truman's role in breaking a railroad strike. When coal and railroad workers went on strike in 1946, he threatened to use the US Army as strikebreakers, and Congress approved. Truman would go on to interfere in at least two more railroad strikes.[12]

The NNC conference theme was dealing a "death blow to Jim Crow," and it was endorsed by the Congress of Industrial Organizations (CIO) union federation. CIO President Walter Reuther sent his blessings to the meeting. One of the goals was to address the loss of wartime jobs and the growing unemployment among Black workers. Wartime job loss was an important theme in Jones's writing as Black workers were the most impacted by it. She was especially interested in Black women workers, whom she would later describe as the last-hired and first-fired in the war industries. Another concern was the bipartisan effort to dissolve the FEPC, which was "filibustered to death" in Congress in 1946.[13]

Truman's suppression of strikes, coupled with Cold War policies like the Truman Doctrine (which used financial aid to bolster governments in Greece and Turkey against left-wing challenges), worried the Party. Jones described these policies as an "Anglo-American drive" toward an "atomic war." Though the nation was war weary, US troops were still stationed in overseas territories in the hundreds of bases that remained in the war's wake. As colonized people's movements gained momentum, the US took the side of the imperial powers to shore up its own anticommunist alliances and growing military might. In April 1947, along with several Black Party leaders including Ben Davis, Henry Winston, Doxey Wilkerson, and Audley Moore, Jones signed a statement claiming that the Truman Doctrine compromised the safety of Black America. The statement argued that the administration's "imperialist ambitions abroad" were only a "smoke screen" that would destroy democracy in the US and "usher in a Fascist regime." It continued by arguing that the Doctrine worked together with anticommunist hysteria to deny Black America its rights. Only ten days after the Doctrine was announced, Truman signed an executive order mandating loyalty screening for civil employees, requiring them to confirm they were not communists. This, the signers of the statement believed, would target any person, Black or white, who advocated equality, and that Black Americans would be "the first and worst sufferers." The statement concluded that the growing power of anticommunism to silence any criticism of capitalists or the government was fascist.[14]

The demise of the NNC was a harbinger of things to come. As Erik Gellman notes, the NNC coalition of communists, unionists, and liberals became difficult to sustain during the Cold War. By 1947, the conflicts in the coalition became "insurmountable," and though the CIO might have endorsed its conference, it did not list the NNC as an affiliate organization. For Gellman, this was one of the early signs of a liberal retreat. As liberal groups and individuals began to abandon it, the NNC merged with the International Labor Defense organization to create the Civil Rights Congress (CRC). Under the leadership of communist

William Patterson, the CRC acted as a legal organization that defended working-class people in criminal trials. Jones wrote about some of the tensions in the NNC in 1946, accusing A. Philip Randolph, President of the Brotherhood of Sleeping Car Porters union and an NNC official, of facilitating the filibuster against the FEPC. She claimed that he had undermined the goals and tactics of the National Council for the Permanent FEPC by discouraging organizations from traveling to Washington to support it. Randolph appeared to want to keep communists quiet and out of the spotlight. Years earlier, he had denounced redbaiting, but became disillusioned after the 1939 Nazi-Soviet pact. For Jones, Randolph was another liberal who had traded redbaiting for limited concessions, which in her view amounted to collaborating with segregationists.[15]

This liberal retreat reflected the larger trend toward the bipolar world that was emerging as the liberal democracies declared their disagreements with the Soviet Union. In March 1946, Winston Churchill gave his infamous "Iron Curtain" speech in Fulton, Missouri. Jones wrote that this speech did not impress Black America, especially given that Fulton was a segregated town, and the Westminster College campus, where the speech was delivered, did not accept Black students. But it was a "fitting setting" for Churchill to propose his "Anglo-Saxon military alliance," which was no different than Hitler's "Aryan supremacy." Black Americans saw through the speech; it was just a "smoke screen" to preserve the British Empire. Jones noted that Black editors across the US had denounced the speech and its imperialist language, with some acknowledging that the Soviet Union was a friend to Black America and not a threat to world peace, as Churchill was suggesting. The speech was really a cover for the US, the "pied piper" of world imperialism. The postwar tides were turning, and Jones feared that anti-Soviet hostility would lead to further conflict.

She counseled the labor movement to unite with the Black Freedom Struggle to resist war and secure peace against the rise of a renewed fascism.[16]

The FBI made a note of Jones's article in her file, recording her criticisms of Churchill's speech and her claim that Black Americans were not interested in the growing tensions between the US and the Soviet Union. Bureau agents frequently noted that Jones was critical of the way Black Americans were treated, and that she regularly spoke out against racist violence. Her leadership in protesting the Ferguson brothers' killings, as well as her role in the march to Washington on their behalf, were also included in her file. Jones was increasingly critical of US militarism, a position that was fast becoming practically illegal in the US.[17]

In July 1947 Jones participated in a radio debate broadcast on Pittsburgh, Pennsylvania's KQV station about universal military training. She was joined by Nathan Albert, described by the FBI as representing the "communist side." They debated Blair F. Gunther, a county judge, and Colonel J.S. Irwin, the leader of a Pennsylvania organization advocating universal conscription. As Christina Mislán has argued, Jones's Cold War opposition to military preparedness and the draft was radically different to her eager advocacy during World War II. But as Jones explained, while World War II was a struggle against fascism, US Cold War policy was itself fascistic. Rather than promoting "peace and democracy," universal military training served the interests of "warmongers." Her view was thus consistent in its opposition to fascism. Early in the debate, Jones was attacked for her communism and forced to defend universal military training in the Soviet Union. She pressed her point by asking her opponents for what war were they preparing.[18]

Days later, when Jones wrote about the debate in the *Daily Worker*, she outlined the position she and the Party would take as the "cold" part of the Cold War began to heat up in several parts of the world; namely, that "military might" could not contribute to peace without being combined with a "democratic foreign policy." Jones claimed that both Roosevelt and his second Vice-President, Henry Wallace, were committed to democracy, but that commitment had died with Roosevelt. Her opponents argued that military preparedness and universal military training were necessary for peace; Jones pointed out that the influence of outsiders in Greece's civil war and the Indonesian independence movement hardly counted as an effort toward peace. The Soviet Union, she argued, had more reason to maintain a well-prepared military because of the invasions and interference from other nations it had experienced. Her final point in the debate was that the government had a greater responsibility to fund schools, clear slums, build nurseries and address domestic problems in order to keep the peace. The US military was also "anything but fully democratic" given that it was segregated. She asked the same question she put during the war: How could a Jim Crow army secure democracy abroad? The CPUSA, she wrote, had supported the antifascist resistance during the war, but it would not support the US's imperialist ambitions abroad while it exercised fascist control at home.[19]

## The "Woman Question"

Jones had forged her communism at the height of the Popular Front, which had used the idea of antifascism in a broad sense. Fascist states shared many things in common, amongst them the marginalization of women as breeders for the war machine. As mentioned earlier, the Party called this *Kinder Küche Kirche*, a German phrase describing women's expected devotion to the home, children, and church; Jones called it the fascist triple K. Fascists specifically sought to return women to a mythical subservient role in which their devotion was to a masculine figure and their brood of white children. This was the Nazi vision of a white supremacist future. The fascist triple K also existed in the United States, and Cold War anticommunism sought to further delimit women's political power. Though Jones would be one of the Party's most important theoreticians on race, she was also active in the Party bureaucracy on women's affairs, and her body of writing included an emphasis on women and broader understandings of gender (which she called "sex"). She was active in the National Council of Negro Women and the Congress of American Women (CAW), and in 1947 she became the secretary of the CPUSA's National Women's Commission. In 1948 the Party assigned her to reorganize some of the women's commissions in US states that had Party chapters.[20]

The CAW was an attempt to create an interracial women's movement. Kate Weigand argues that for American women the postwar years "bred disappointment, dashed hopes," and led to "forced retreat" in the face of an "intense and widespread" antifeminism. As Jones frequently noted in her writing, women had proved more than capable during the war, but were expected to vacate their jobs when the men returned. This specifically hurt Black women already forced to work in low-wage jobs before the war, and now once again facing racial and gender exclusions. With these disappointments being immediately felt at the war's end, radical and liberal women activists created the CAW to address the issues.[21]

The CAW was founded on International Women's Day in 1946 at a convention attended by 600 delegates. It focused on three major issues: "international peace, child welfare and the status of women." Its leadership was made up of fellow travelers like Mary van Kleeck and Muriel Draper, and communist leaders such as Jones's friend Elizabeth Gurley Flynn. The organization became the US branch of the Women's International Democratic Federation (WIDF), a "pro-Soviet ... antifascist" women's organization based in France. At its inception, on the cusp of the communist purges, the CAW attracted a "broad constituency" of radical women, liberals, and union activists. Weigand notes that while the CAW would draw in politically diverse women, from the beginning communists had a strong presence, starting with Flynn as one of its leaders, joined later by Jones.[22] It organized around several goals shared by communists and progressives, including material support for mothers, funded childcare, and peace. Peace was envisioned not just as an end to war but as a way to secure social equality. Because war threatened the lives of everyone, and represented a failure of the state to protect its people, women and children often became its victims.

The organization became an early casualty of the Cold War purges because of its association with the WIDF. The House Un-American Activities Committee (HUAC) published a report on the CAW in 1949, concluding that the organization was an "arm of Soviet political warfare" in the peace campaign. This was an early attack on the peace movement, and it led to the CAW's dissolution.[23]

The HUAC report featured Jones several times. Association with communism effectively became a political crime during the Cold War, whether on the part of an organization or an individual. If a group or a person had links to the Party, however tenuous, then the association forever linked them to communism and thus sedition. In the case of the CAW, the problem was the organization's association with WIDF and members like Jones. Among the organization's supposed crimes were that Jones had appeared in a photograph with a delegation of CAW women protesting the Smith Act trials in 1949. The report described her as an "alien Communist leader." Jones was also featured at a "Women Fight Back" event protesting anticommunist arrests and trials. The report included an article she had written in support of the CAW in the "official organ of the Communist Party," *The Worker*, and identified her as a featured speaker at a "Communist-inspired" peace gathering that accused US foreign policy of being the greatest present threat to global peace. Jones was recorded as having attended a 1948 CAW meeting where she spoke and received enthusiastic applause. At the meeting she noted that 1948 was the 100th anniversary of both the Seneca Falls Women's Convention (which inaugurated the US women's suffrage movement) and the "great and scientific movement called Marxism." Jones's speeches to, support for, and role in the CAW were enough to link the organization to the imagined communist conspiracy.[24]

Around this time Jones's marriage to Scholnick fell apart. In February 1947 she filed for divorce on the grounds of "incompatibility" in the first civil court of the City of Juárez in Chihuahua, Mexico. Since US divorces at the time were prohibitively expensive and required cause, many Americans traveled south to obtain what was known as a "Mexican divorce," while others simply stayed married to avoid the hassle. Jones was represented by attorney Xavier Rosas Cevallos before Judge Jesus Barba Cornejo. The divorce was granted and affirmed at the US consulate in Juárez. The two had no children, thus simplifying the procedure. The court declared the marriage dissolved and returned Jones's surname to her.[25]

That same year she became the Secretary of the CPUSA National Women's Commission and turned her attention to its work on women's rights. In this role, Jones wrote an article titled "For New Approaches to Our Work among Women" challenging the Party's draft resolution on women's issues, which she felt was inadequate in addressing the "special social, economic, and political needs" of women. In Carole Boyce Davies's view, Jones's main contribution to Marxist literature was her integration of women and Black diasporic people's needs into the canon. Jones moved past the economic determinism of Marx by arguing that social conditions would not simply change under socialism and instead needed special attention. Boyce Davies argues that Jones, therefore, is "Left of Karl Marx" in considering gender and race not as subcategories of class but as material conditions with material consequences.[26]

Jones argued that women were an important population for the CPUSA to organize because of their militancy. Since monopoly capitalism in its own way recognized women's power, this meant that the Party had to compete with capitalism itself in order to organize them. Monopoly capitalists were attempting to appeal to women, not as political agents, but with the "Hitlerite slogan" that women belong at home and by trying to entice them with material goods. These attempts were obscuring the gains made by women during the "antifascist war," particularly the gains they made in industrial work. What the capitalist rhetoric ignored was the need of many women to work outside the home. Jones called on unions to take up the call to protect women's jobs and to continue to support wartime programs like nurseries and price controls.[27] She also urged the Party to appeal to women by articulating its support for programs like medical care and improved public education.

Scholars have often dismissed these familial concerns as the "maternalist" preoccupations of women's politics, but this only perpetuates essentialist beliefs about women's focus on the home and ignores the politicized nature of women's and children's existence. For a communist like Jones, revolution had to begin with personal relationships in the home because women's domestic conditions were determined by politics. As she noted in her "New Approaches" article, capitalist interests sought to encourage women's domesticity for the sake of their own profit margins, while politicians circumscribed the lives of women and children by denying basic medical care, underfunding public schools, and likening social welfare to racialized handouts. In Jones's time, as today, restrictions on access to birth control and abortion also delimited women's rights and led to poor medical outcomes. These restrictions evidence the state's fascist control over women's bodies. Jones noted that Black families were imperiled because capitalists and politicians saw them as laborers first. Since family issues are gendered as well as racialized, the communist focus on the household cannot simply be dismissed as maternalist. The fate of the family, especially the Black family, was influenced by politics, but for Jones and others the family also had revolutionary potential.[28]

Jones saw women not as an auxiliary in the class struggle, but as its "vanguard." In 1947, when the Party reinvigorated its Women's Commission with Jones as its leader, it created local organizations to collect information on local needs, but also helped to convince women comrades that their needs would be addressed. Thanks to Jones's growing influence, the Party's 1947 platform included a demand for "full equality of Negro women from segregation, discrimination, intimidation, poll tax and downgrading in employment." It also encouraged women to run for and serve in political office. Jones warned the Party that it needed to put more effort into integrating this work into its other departments. Women's needs were not separate from the class struggle, but were essential to it. Jones took the Party to task for leaving women's issues to female comrades rather than considering them part of the struggle. This would not be her only such warning to Party leaders.²⁹

## Arrest

Her work reorganizing the states' women's commissions would keep her busy, but Jones's ascendency in the Party ranks meant that US intelligence saw her as a growing threat. In 1946, the FBI had discovered her sister Yvonne Cumberbatch's naturalization papers, but did not yet know that they were related. At the time, Yvonne happened to be living with Jones and her then-husband, and the FBI found the naturalization papers by following Yvonne's voting records. After nearly five years of surveillance, the Bureau was closing in on finding the one piece of information they could use to silence Jones: she was not a US citizen and was therefore deportable. Using her high school records, the FBI finally worked out that Claudia Jones and Yvonne Cumberbatch were sisters. By early 1947 the Bureau had found the manifest for the ship that carried the Cumberbatch children to New York and, by May of that year, had confirmed there was no evidence to show that Jones was a naturalized citizen. Bureau agents were instructed to ascertain whether "action" could be "taken against her."³⁰

The Bureau had determined that Jones was a CPUSA leader and as such required "continuous, active investigative attention." The New York agents assigned to monitor Jones's activity noted several times in her file that her written and spoken work "concerned the negro"; they continued to investigate what involvement she had with the Party's alleged conspiratorial apparatus. In 1947, the Bureau was extending its own surveillance authority, without express permission or constitutional mandate, and focusing a great deal of attention on the CPUSA and its leaders. Its own criminal division determined that Jones had not committed any crimes, so the Bureau decided to pursue deportation using the Alien Friends Act of October 1918, which allowed for the deportation of anyone accused of trying to overthrow the US government.³¹

Barely two weeks into 1948, Jones was arrested. At 8:40 pm on January 10, the FBI raided Jones's home on 143rd street in New York City. Her sisters Yvonne and Sylvia were both present during the arrest. Jones refused to sign an affidavit giving the Bureau permission to search her apartment. She was allowed to dress, and then removed from the apartment at 8:55 pm. The agents took her to Ellis Island where she was left with a security officer and a matron. The arresting agents described her as "militant," writing in their report that she had "ridiculed being arrested." She was bailed out the next day on a $1,000 bail by her attorney Ira Gollobin, who worked for the American Committee for the Protection of Foreign Born (ACPFB).³²

The CPUSA wasted no time in denouncing the arrest. The following day the National Board issued a statement insisting that the arrest was unlawful and warning that the "drive against progressives" was moving into "high gear." The same week Jones was detained, another CPUSA colleague, the Russian-born writer Alexander Bittelman, was arrested. The National Board was right: the attempt to silence the CPUSA and other progressives was underway, as was Jones's legal struggle. The Party immediately moved to organize in her defense, using the courts and a mass action strategy to raise awareness around the legal issues by holding rallies, writing letters, circulating petitions, and spreading the news in the Party's many outlets.³³

Jones and her peers had become increasingly concerned about and critical of anticommunism, and recognized that anticommunists were focusing on suppressing Black voices. Two weeks after her arrest, a *Daily Worker* article noted that the CPUSA forbade its members from advocating the overthrow of the US government, but that it did advocate ending Black oppression. Jones was armed only with a typewriter; unlike the state or federal government, she never lynched anyone, or pulled the switch on an innocent person in the electric chair, or denied anyone the right to vote. She was part of "America's submerged tenth," the "JimCrowed, the lynched," and this was why the FBI and Congress wanted to silence her. As Burden-Stelly notes, "radicalized Blackness" exposed the "rootedness of racial discourse" in the global capitalist economy and menaced the class and racial hierarchies in the United States, therefore silencing Black radicals was essential. The Party recognized this. The *Daily Worker* article said Jones was a "bright and wide-awake girl," and a CPUSA member because the Party worked to improve the lives of Black Americans. Her only crime was trying to help Black America, which the FBI admitted in noting that her political work focused on Black Americans.[34]

Ben Davis, Jones's friend and colleague and a member of the New York City Council, took up the fight against the racist anticommunist persecutions. He wrote in an editorial that the "Negro people" condemned all attacks on communist and labor leaders by the federal government, but that Jones's arrest was particularly galling. He went on to attack an article written by Almena Davis in the *Los Angeles Tribune*, a Black weekly. Almena Davis had once worked for Charlotta Bass's *California Eagle* but left because, as she told the FBI, Bass began following the "communist line." In her article, she argued that Jones had "deserted the cause of her own people" to "espouse" the cause of another. The article was an indication of the liberal retreat from radical politics that was happening while the CPUSA dealt with their legal woes.

Many Black newspapers and liberal civil rights organizations, including the NAACP, sought to distance themselves from the harassed communists. In the process, they advocated the (illegal and immoral) suppression of radical Black politics, and tacitly acknowledged the accusation that a communist conspiracy lay behind calls for radical change. In other words, liberals were playing into the hands of US intelligence and career politicians, ultimately assisting them in limiting civil rights gains. Almena Davis wrote that Black Americans should be indifferent to Jones's arrest. Ben Davis fired back, accusing her of being a "strikebreaker or scab" and the one turning her back on the cause. He noted that "Miss Davis" might gain some popularity by taking such a stand, but it would be akin to being a "Tokyo Rose" or a "house negro."[35]

Almena Davis's article went directly to the heart of the problem the Party would face over the next decade of legal harassment: the abandonment of the cause in the name of liberal accommodationism. Ben Davis compared "Miss Davis" to Jones, describing the former as a "troubadour of filth" and a "political trollop." In contrast, Jones was an inheritor of the militant legacy of Black women with the "courage and honor" to stand up for Black womanhood against their "ruling class oppressors." The liberal Black leadership was instead embracing capitalism and the exploitation that accompanied it.[36]

Even while the CPUSA leadership faced hearings and scrambled to raise legal funds, Jones and the Party continued with business. The Party was planning for its 14th National Convention, in August 1948, at which it would formally endorse Henry Wallace's candidacy for President under the Progressive Party ticket. This became a real opportunity for radical Black Americans to try to counter the escalating Cold War. Wallace, Roosevelt's former Vice-President, had decided to run because he worried about what the bilateral contest between the world powers would mean for peace. The Progressive Party platform embraced "labor rights, peace, racial justice, self-determination" and a "dialogue" with the USSR. Radical Black activists like Eslanda and Paul Robeson, Shirley Graham and W.E.B. Du Bois rallied around Wallace. Jones was also part of the coalition of labor and civil rights activists who endorsed him. Though Wallace himself advocated a managed capitalism, he did not denounce the communists in the Progressive Party ranks. But their presence became a liability for the campaign as the Cold War rhetoric increased, and anyone or anything associated with communism was targeted as treasonous. In a sad reflection of the state of US politics, Wallace's Progressive Party failed to secure a single state, while Strom Thurmond's segregationist Dixiecrats, who had split with Truman's Democratic Party over civil rights, gained four states. This was an early indication of the Democrat's loss of power in the segregationist south and, for some, evidence that fascism remained strong in the US.[37]

The CPUSA convention's platform was critical of the US's containment policy and wary of its increased militarization. The platform had nine points, including eliminating the "huge military budget," withdrawing American troops stationed in other countries, offering "no-strings attached" economic assistance to "war-ravaged countries," and securing a peaceful settlement with its allies over Germany. The convention denounced the "attacks on the Communist Party" and argued that it was "reactionaries" not Marxists who practiced "force and violence." It also called for the abolition of the HUAC, the dismissal of all charges against Party members, and the outlawing of the KKK. Party members re-elected every officer on the National Committee, to which Elizabeth Gurley Flynn was added.[38]

The Party's 1948 platform put it at variance with US Cold War policy and made it and its members some of the lone voices denouncing the militarization of the country. It also coincided with a Soviet initiative the same year called "Struggle for Peace in all the World." This was in many ways a cover for the Soviet Union's lack of military materiel compared to the US. The US was also at that time the only atomic power in the world, which frightened Black American activists, particularly because the bomb had been used against a nation of color. The Soviets, meanwhile, were trying to rebuild after the war and could not keep up with US military proliferation. US intelligence linked all criticism of the containment policy to the Soviet initiative, depicting the peace movement as a Soviet conspiracy. Activists were targeted because their peace politics were about more than just ending war. Jones believed that peace was a prerequisite for achieving an antiracist, antisexist, anti-imperialist socialist world. As Burden-Stelly argues, anticommunism became a "tool of policing, surveilling, and repressing the nexus of anti-systemic struggle" that linked the Black Freedom Struggle to colonial wars abroad. Anticommunism became so powerful that it could "transmute seemingly universal ideas like peace and progress" into a criminal conspiracy. When the Soviet Union became an atomic power in 1949, Jones argued that it was the only force that could counter American militarization and ensure peace.[39]

Jones would become an important voice in the Party's peace initiative, but first she had to deal with the attempts to have her deported as the "full machinery of anticommunism was arrayed against her." After her arrest, Claudia Jones Defense Committees were created and rallied to raise money and challenge the proceedings. The FBI paid attention to these efforts, noting the demonstrations and those organizing on her behalf. The day after her arrest an "emergency committee" was created to raise funds and organize demonstrations. The organizers included leading Black communists Ben Davis, Audley Moore and Richard B. Moore. Richard B. Moore was a leading organizer in the Scottsboro campaign and in the Harlem CP branch; he was eventually expelled from the Party, but nevertheless stepped up to aid Jones. In February, a delegation of communists went to the New York US Naturalization and Immigration offices to deliver a protest letter to the Immigration Commissioner against the deportation order. Police barred the doors and at least one demonstrator, Bill Norman, a CPUSA state committee member, was roughed up by them. In Harlem, Richard Moore became chairman of the Claudia Jones Defense Committee and planned another rally the day after their comrades had been attacked by police. The FBI noted that Jones herself had appeared at a rally on February 2.[40]

Jones's deportation hearing was set for September 13. The FBI included in its files the information that Jones admitted to being a communist and that she had made efforts to become naturalized. After her second attempt to become a citizen, in 1940, she was denied because of her association with the Party and, she suspected, her race. This made her what Carole Boyce Davies describes as a "deportable subject." For Boyce Davies, Jones was a citizen of the Caribbean diaspora and thus a stateless person. Michael Hanchard has argued that states construct their ideal citizens via immigration and deportation laws that act as tools to ensure white populations and exclude people of color. This history, Hanchard argues, is bound up with the history of radicalism. Countries such as the United States craft immigration laws that delimit the rights of Black immigrants and by extension Black citizens as well as radicals. Jones's radicalism and her challenge to the white racial order made her particularly vulnerable to deportation and exclusion from the US.[41]

Elizabeth Gurley Flynn attended Jones's hearing in September and noted the baseless grounds of the deportation charges. She was accused of having multiple aliases when the only names she ever used were her married name and her pen name. The witnesses at the hearing were the arresting officers from Ellis Island and a fingerprint expert. Flynn wondered why the fingerprint expert was needed when Jones had never denied her identity. The witnesses noted Jones's entry into the US at a young age, which led Flynn to wonder if they worried that Jones had been a "precocious infant" carrying a "volume of Karl Marx" into the country. Jones refused to testify but made a statement to the press that the Truman government saw her as a threat because she had called out a "reactionary administration" that refused to "prosecute the lynchers, the KKK or the anti-Semites." She claimed that the hearing was "illegally constituted" and violated her rights as an alien facing deportation proceedings. Her attorney Carol King protested the proceedings because she was not given enough time to prepare. Jones argued that being threatened with deportation because of one's political beliefs contravened the Bill of Rights and the Constitution. The federal government was not prepared to present its case because its key witness was not present, and the hearings were postponed until September 30.[42]

As it turned out, the government's key witness, George Hewitt, would appear the next day for a different deportation proceeding. The CPUSA had a field day with Hewitt as a witness. Professional witnesses were generally former communists who worked with the FBI and appeared at legislative and criminal proceedings to testify against their former comrades. Hewitt was reportedly receiving $25 per day to testify. The Party claimed that he was facing perjury charges in Washington state and argued that his "stool-pigeon" testimony would never stand up to scrutiny. The government also subpoenaed Angelo Herndon to testify at Jones's rescheduled hearing. Herndon appeared for the hearing but read out a statement that he would not allow himself to be used by the courts against Jones, and would not let the Department of Justice "brand" him as a "traitor."[43]

King told the press she believed that the hearings kept being postponed not because of Hewitt's failure to show or other witnesses' refusal to testify, but because the Department of Justice knew that the proceedings were not justified. The deportation threat against Jones would drag on into 1950, until Joseph J. Mack, the hearing officer for the Immigration and Naturalization Service (INS), concluded that the deportation order was legitimate. By that time, however, the FBI and the INS had a new weapon in their arsenal: the McCarran Internal Security Act, passed that year, which eased the standards for deporting radicals. Jones was taken back into custody on October 23, 1950, along with other communists, to be held for deportation. Among the group was Betty Gannett, who Jones would later serve time in prison with. Jones, Gannett, and fifteen others were held at Ellis Island in what they called the "McCarran wing."[44]

On November 8, the *Daily Worker* published a letter from Jones describing Ellis Island. She contrasted watching the birds make their nests with a place where people were detained for their personal beliefs. She described the group on the McCarran wing as a veritable "United Nations," since they represented so many countries, and noted that the Statue of Liberty had its back turned to Ellis Island, suggesting the injustice of the charges against her and her comrades. Jones argued that not one of the people she was imprisoned with were guilty of crimes; they were guilty only of devotion to the labor movement, the "fight for Negro rights," and the crusade against discrimination. But what they were most guilty of was advocacy of "peace and security." In another letter published days later, Jones described the conditions in the prison. One of her fellow detainees, Rose Nelson, had been put in solitary confinement, but following protests led by the Party and the ACPFB she was eventually released. Jones and Gannett had been sick; Gannett with sinus issues and Jones with bronchitis. In the letter, Jones continued her assault on the war state, describing the need to secure release for her and the others from the "atom makers of war and fascism" and the "would-be lynchers." Meanwhile the ACPFB was working to secure their bail.[45]

Elizabeth Gurley Flynn wrote about the detainees and Jones in particular, arguing that they were not criminals because they were charged with "ideas" not "crimes." She described Jones's arrival in the United States as a young child and her "fruitless" attempts to secure citizenship. She shared details from a letter Jones wrote her about the people she was detained with, and their high spirits given the circumstances. Flynn urged people to write Eleanor Roosevelt, who was serving on the UN's Human Relations Commission, asking for her support in the release of the detainees. After nearly three weeks imprisoned on Ellis Island, Jones and the other McCarran detainees were released on bail.[46]

The hearings for each of the communists threatened with deportation took place within the next month. Jones described them as being rushed "mass-production" style. Carol King, who served as lead counsel for the ACPFB, had tried to argue that the hearings were a violation of a previous Supreme Court case that found deportation proceedings violated the Procedure Act, which was meant to guarantee all defendants due process. She also argued that the INS hearing officer was prejudiced against communists and thus should be recused. These legal appeals failed. Jones went before a judge on December 21, 1950, for proceedings the *Daily Worker* described as "Yuletide" deportations. The next day she was ordered deported to Trinidad. Because of appeals, the deportation order was not issued until November 1952, when she was ordered to Ellis Island for departure. During the appeals process Jones remained free on bail, but her bail conditions were extreme, requiring psychiatric evaluation, weekly reporting to Ellis Island, confinement to a fifty-mile area in the Southern District of New York, and an end to her CPUSA membership and association with Party members. The FBI noted Jones's failure to comply with the bail terms as she was often seen in the company of Party members. On November 14, 1952, the Justice Department cancelled the deportation order because Jones had been arrested again, this time accused of violating the Smith Act.[47]

## Theoretical Corpus

While the FBI's threat to deport Jones was no doubt stressful for her, even under state scrutiny she carried on with her work and her influence in the Party continued to rise. Her most important contributions to the Party and the Marxist canon largely came while she faced FBI and state harassment. As Boyce Davis argues, Jones's work on gender and race dealt with what she saw as shortcomings within the Party, and her hope was that "working class women would respond" if the CPUSA were to "address" their issues. Her 1947 position paper on the Party's failures on women's issues laid the foundation for two important articles that would appear in 1949: the piece she is best known for, "An End to the Neglect of the Problems of the Negro Woman!" and "We Seek Full Equality for Women."[48]

Jones's Neglect article was a response to Betty Millard's 1948 pamphlet *Woman against Myth*, which has been considered an important early work in arguing that women's subjection has been a defining feature in both capitalist and socialist formations. But as Kate Weigand argues, white Party women like Millard failed to provide any substantive analysis on Black women's oppression. Weigand claims that while Millard's pamphlet was an important stimulus for the Party to expand its theory on women's conditions, because of its omissions it also became the "catalyst" to understanding Black women's oppression. Jones's response article would bring Black women's "experiences and perspectives" to the "center" of CPUSA writing. It was published in June 1949 in *Political Affairs*, and is Jones's best-known article because of the influence it had on the Party and because it theorized about Black women's social conditions, a topic peripheral in the Marxist canon.[49]

For Weigand, the Neglect article emphasized that although women shared a common gender oppression they remained "different." This difference feminism was a hallmark of radical communist women's organizing, and an important foundation for what we now call intersectionality. Communists like Jones were not exploring the interconnected relationship between social and material categories as intersectionality does, but they did lay the ground for rejecting essentialist beliefs that all women's experiences are the same. For Boyce Davies, the difference between Jones's triple oppression and intersectionality is that Jones focused on the "superexploitation" of Black women in a way that was "layered within" a Marxist framework. Superexploitation recognizes that under capitalism "all workers" are exploited, but it also points out that some workers have the "ability to exploit the labor of other class fractions." Black women are in the "class fraction" that has their labor "superexploited." For Boyce Davies, this means that white women and Black men with the "class power and access to it" can also exploit Black women's labor. Erik McDuffie agrees, arguing that Jones's understanding of the superexploitation of Black women derived from Marxist Leninist thought; superexploitation is one of the "uniquely severe, persistent, and dehumanizing forms of exploitation" that are necessary to maintain capitalism. What Jones did was to extend that analysis to include Black women, whose labor was "assumed."[50]

The idea that Black women faced gender and race oppression, often called double jeopardy or Jane Crow, had circulated for decades among activists like Anna Julia Cooper, an education activist, and Amy Jacques Garvey, Pan-Africanist writer and Marcus Garvey's second wife. But it was communist women who integrated the idea into the Marxist tradition, arguing that class reduced Black women's material circumstances too. Jones took this a step further by arguing that Black women were "the most oppressed stratum of the whole population." This was a direct challenge to the CPUSA's traditional focus on shopfloor politics and the assumption that male industrial workers would foment revolutionary change. One of the important points Jones articulated from the start of the Neglect article was that the Party had failed to recognize Black women's militancy and their historical and present challenge to power. She invoked the historical exploitation of Black women and articulated their resistance – a resistance that arose out of necessity because of the racist exploitation of Black America.[51]

Jones looked to the working class and the Black home to articulate Black women's oppression that was rooted not just in industrial exploitation, but also in the prejudices of her fellow working people. She wrote that a Black woman's working conditions were not like those of white women because of the historic differences in wage earnings between white and Black men and white and Black women, the tendency of Black Americans to be stuck in low-wage menial labor, and the need for Black women to work outside the home at higher rates than white women. She noted that Black women had long been at the forefront of the Black family out of necessity, and that they experienced superexploitation because of their unique economic situation. But even progressives failed to recognize this, and "white chauvinism" perpetuated Black women's precarious economic and social position. Jones called out an idea that continues to plague white Americans – the belief that racism is expressed in interpersonal relationships rather than in larger institutional and state policy and practice. She called this "the worst kind of Social-Democratic, bourgeois liberal thinking" because it ignored the fact that Black oppression cannot be remedied without changing the very institutions that rely on exploiting Black labor and preventing working-class coalitions. This is a problem we conceptualize today as systemic racism.[52]

Boyce Davies argues that scholars who have insisted that Jones's "primary" political identification was with "Marxist Leninism" miss the fact that, while not herself a feminist, she pushed the issue of women's rights beyond its typical framing in 1949. She also expanded the boundaries of the economic determinism that limited so many Marxist thinkers. In her Neglect article she argued that the "Negro question" was "prior to" the "woman question," and that only by addressing and working for Black women's liberation could all people, women and workers included, be free. She called for a "heightened political consciousness" around Black women's oppression and for Black women to take up their "rightful place" in the "national liberation movement." To liberate the most oppressed was to create a foundation for the liberation of all the oppressed. Jones argued for an expansive emancipatory ethos that articulated the need to liberate people beyond just improving their material circumstances. This meant that before the class struggle could succeed, the working classes would have to be liberated from their own racist and sexist tendencies.[53]

John Munro argues that Jones's analysis also "connected race and gender to empire." Jones undermined the US's imperialist ambitions by challenging its alleged commitment to racial and gender equality as it claimed to bring democracy abroad. She wrote that the US's claim to democratic supremacy was false as the government was uninterested in securing citizenship rights and protection for Black Americans, while it simultaneously promised to bring those rights to the formerly colonized. Jones presented a "complex argument" that demonstrated how the "multiple dimensions of social domination" operated together and "constituted one another," and how this was all "entangled" with imperialism.[54]

Cheryl Higashida argues that the Neglect article "irrevocably shifted" the Party's and the left's understanding of "gender and race politics." Boyce Davies agrees, arguing that the article was "pivotal for the history of black feminist theoretics" because it moved beyond other analyses on race and gender. Weigand believes that its value lies not only in what it did for Black women, but also in its explication of the experiences of women from various racial and national backgrounds and its emphasis on "women's differences" that expanded the horizons for communists. Party members began to recognize that class struggle alone could not ameliorate gender or race oppression, especially when so many radicals subscribed to racist and sexist beliefs. More important, the working-class movement could not ignore the fact that the social conditions perpetuated by some of its own adherents and exploited by capitalists were a real barrier to liberation. The article was essential to getting the CPUSA leaders to understand "Black women's special modes of oppression and resistance" and in putting Black women at the center of the Party's work on women's issues.[55]

Jones continued her analysis in September when the *Daily Worker* published her short article "We Seek Full Equality for Women," which reiterated many of the points made in the earlier article. "We Seek Full Equality" celebrated the thirtieth anniversary of the Party's founding, which Jones used as an opportunity to praise the CPUSA for taking the lead in recognizing the "Woman Question" as part of Marxist Leninism. She does, however, note that this required the recognition of women's unique concerns outside of class struggle, emphasizing that the woman question was a "special" issue. But this article was less about criticism of the Party's shortcomings than about praise for what it had already done.[56]

She noted that the Party was the first to introduce Black women's triple oppression to white women and the working class. But instead of taking credit for herself, she claimed that it was William Foster who had "sharpen[ed]" the Party's thinking in emphasizing to working-class men still clinging to bourgeois notions of sex prejudice that women's oppression was unique. Jones also argued that women's social oppression was already partially recognized within Marxist Leninist thought, citing Friedrich Engels' popular *The Origin of the Family, Private Property, and the State*, but that it was Foster who had called on the Party to "correct" its errors and "improve" its work.[57]

Jones rejected biological notions of women's inferiority and discussed the Party's efforts to theorize the woman question, citing the Jefferson School of Social Science conference held in June 1949. The Jeff School, as it was known by its teachers and students, was a Marxist institution providing workers' education. Jones taught courses there, as did several of her colleagues, including W.E.B. Du Bois, Lorraine Hansberry, and Doxey Wilkerson. The school also served as a site for events and conferences hosted by Party members.

Jones opened the conference, titled "Marxism and the Woman Question," with a report on the "theoretical basis of the Marxist approach to the woman question." Betty Millard chaired the opening session, and there were 600 delegates in attendance.[58]

The Jeff School compiled a detailed outline for the event which included an extensive reading list featuring both Jones's Neglect article and Millard's *Woman against Myth*. The outline also included several topics and questions that needed to be addressed. Many of these issues included the problems that Jones had written about, including women's exclusion from labor unions and the marginalization of Black women in labor. The conference was premised on the assumption that "Socialism is the ultimate solution of the woman question."[59]

Though the Party was far ahead of others on women's equality – largely thanks to the work of Jones and other Party women – in her article Jones counseled that it was important to use the thirtieth anniversary to "strengthen" its work on the woman question. This was important because women represented a militant group invested in political action against the forces that threatened them, their homes, and their children. Most importantly, women were invested in peace, an issue Jones would have much more to say about in the years to come.[60]

## Anticommunism and Racism

Jones's most important and influential theoretical work sought to awaken the Party to its own shortcomings as well as its possibilities. But it came just as the federal government was working to eradicate US communism. In 1948, J. Edgar Hoover wanted to take down the fifty-five people on the CPUSA's National Committee. Because advocating communism was not illegal, he intended to bore from within in the hope that eliminating the leadership would make the organization collapse. As Ted Morgan has demonstrated, prosecutors had only twelve of the leaders arrested because proving that all of them were conspiring to violently overthrow the US government was too difficult. The prosecutors decided to focus on the most high-profile leaders, including Ben Davis, Henry Winston, and the Party's General Secretary, Eugene Dennis. The trial of the twelve began in January 1949 and ended ten months later in October.[61]

The arrests and trials prompted Jones to write a three-part series of articles on racism and anticommunism. In the first article, she argued that if it was not enough that Black Americans faced daily racist indignities and violence, anticommunism criminalized Blackness by putting "14 million" Black Americans "under suspicion" in the House Committee hearings. Black Americans were being treated as "wards or field hands" by the "imperialist state." The hearings, Jones claimed, "unwittingly" acknowledged that Black America was "nationally oppressed" in the "Black Belt," and argued that the drive to fascism, exemplified by the HUAC hearings, could "wipe out" progress. The Committee members "shout their pious concerns" about civil rights while they "wink" at poll taxes, lynching, and the harassment of communists. Jones pointedly contrasted the Committee's indifference to racist violence with its active undermining of the rights of citizens and residents who confessed devotion to Marxism. The hearings were a "smoke screen" that allowed people to ignore racist violence and imperialism. She likened the Committee's attacks on communism to Hitler's attacks on leftists; both operated as a distraction from the government's devious ends: war and genocide.[62]

Jones carried this analysis further, demonstrating that anticommunism was racist and focused American attention on a fictitious communist plot, while Black Americans were regularly met with violence and discrimination. She wrote about her comrades Davis and Winston – the only two Black leaders among the twelve arrested – and their attempts to draw attention to the travesty of the trials. Winston was remanded to prison and had his bail revoked because he stated in court that "5000 Negroes had been lynched" and none of their killers brought to justice. Davis did the same, indicting the "Jimcrow lynch system," while the prosecutors claimed it was he and Winston who were the real threats.[63]

In an article about Winston, Jones called him a "hostage of white supremacists" and argued that anticommunists were afraid of the interracial unity that the CPUSA symbolized. Anticommunists could not understand why white communist leaders would risk arrest and prison to speak out against racism and imperialism. These anticommunists, Jones argued, were beholden to capitalists and thus invested in racial division to keep the working masses acquiescent to their demands. White supremacy was a powerful tool to prevent labor's success, and anticommunist political leaders were only too happy to oblige their capitalist benefactors.[64]

Jones had little time for liberal Black figures either. In the second article in the series she focused criticism on Jackie Robinson, the famed athlete who integrated major league baseball. Robinson, Jones argued, became a symbol of "fair play" among Americans, but he was a tool in HUAC's anticommunist trials to denounce radical Black activists. The anticommunist playbook included a "divide-and-rule" tactic that used prominent Black voices to rescue the US's imperialist ambitions. Robinson went before HUAC as a "friendly witness" and denounced on the stand Paul Robeson's remarks at a 1949 peace conference in Paris. Robeson claimed that Black Americans would not fight in the US's imperialist wars; Robinson countered by claiming that Black America was loyal to the United States. Jones argued that Robinson's views were not surprising given that he was part of a more comfortable class of Black Americans. As Gerald Horne has argued, Robinson's career might not have been possible without Robeson's tireless campaigns to integrate baseball; his testimony, therefore, felt like a betrayal. Additionally, Robeson's comments at the conference were taken out of context and led to increased hostility toward the entertainer. Jones's final article in the series noted that while liberal Black leaders were abandoning the movement, the interracial Communist Party and its leaders were being harassed and imprisoned for their devotion to antiracism. She argued that, if not for the CPUSA, there would have been no progress toward equality, and that this was why the state sought to silence them, and why she remained committed to the Party.[65]

But the Party's fortunes continued to decline. On August 27, 1949, Robeson went to Peekskill, New York to hold a concert to raise funds for the CRC, only to be met by a violent mob. The violence forced the postponement of the concert until September 4, when a mob once again attacked the concertgoers. Jones wrote in an article a week later about the "Heroines of Peekskill" – the women who organized in the face of violence to hold the concert. The women who returned to Peekskill, knowing the risks, demonstrated what she had been telling the Party for years: that women were a radical force that needed to be organized. The Peekskill incident confirmed that "lynch law" and "brutal assaults" were sanctioned by both political parties and represented the "disastrous path" anticommunism had put the United States on. She hoped Peekskill would be a "clarion call" for the "masses of women who love democracy and civil rights" to unite against the fascist forces of the anticommunist state.⁶⁶

By October 1949, eleven of the original twelve CPUSA leaders, including Davis and Winston, had been convicted. Davis was ejected from the New York City Council because of his conviction, a position he had held since 1943. As Ellen Schrecker argues, the convictions of CPUSA leaders "removed ... many restraints" the federal government faced in its harassment of communists, giving it the ability to increase its anticommunist arrests and trials. The CPUSA was a legal organization, but the successful prosecutions meant that the state could engage in "whatever politically repressive measures" it sought to pursue. By the 1950s, the Party "had few rights that any official body had to respect." Anticommunism's "apocalyptic vision" of the danger communism posed had been so effectively disseminated that those who remained "openly associated" with the Party could barely lead "a normal life." The convictions affirmed the state's undemocratic attacks on the Party. The Cold War demonstrated not just the limits on citizenship rights, but also the ability of the state to oppress its own citizens under the guise of democracy.⁶⁷

The anticommunist arrests and trials of the period have often been viewed as an historical aberration, a troubling time in US history. Just as often the period has been referred to as McCarthyism, a term historians reject as a misnomer since Senator Joseph McCarthy only operated for a handful of years, while the machinations of individuals like J. Edgar Hoover continued for decades. The reality is that these arrests, trials, and convictions are part of the long history of the US carceral state and of its violent agents of social control including the police, the courts, and juries. As Vials and Mullen argue, in the past and today, there has been an "overlap" between fascist movements and policing, and the anticommunist arrests and trials in the US are another chapter in that history. While law enforcement has focused on left-wing movements, right-wing organizing has been under-policed. As Beverly Gage's biography on J. Edgar Hoover has shown, the FBI chief obsessively focused on progressives and the left, assuming that, even if they were not outwardly communist, there was likely a communist plot yet to be discovered. Gage has suggested renaming this period Hooverism. Today, studies have shown that white supremacists actively recruit in the US military and in law enforcement agencies.[68] Policing – whether during the Cold War targeting communists, or today targeting Black Lives Matter activists – is crucial to "race-making." Criminals and criminality are a construction of the fascist state, which in the United States has been an expression of racial fascism. Just as anticommunism was and remains anti-Black, law enforcement continues to target communities of color through over-policing and violence. This was something Jones understood, though she used a different language to articulate it.[69]

# 4

# Anti-Cold War and Deportation (1950–1955)

*Farewell to Claudia*

Nearer and nearer drew this day, dear comrade,
When I from you must sadly part,
Day after day, a dark foreboding sorrow,
Crept through my anxious heart.

No more to see you striding down the pathway,
No more to see your smiling eyes and radiant face.
No more to hear your gay and pealing laughter,
No more encircled by your love, in this sad place.

How I will miss you, words will fail to utter,
I am alone, my thoughts unshared, these weary days,
I feel bereft and empty, on this gray and dreary morning,
Facing my lonely future, hemmed in by prison ways.

Sometimes I feel you've never been in Alderson,
So full of life, so detached from here you seem.
So proud of walk, of talk, of work, of being,
Your presence here is like a fading fevered dream.

Yet as the sun shines now, through fog and darkness,
I feel a sudden joy that you are gone,
That once again you walk the streets of Harlem,
That today for you at least, is Freedom's dawn.

I will be strong in our common faith, dear comrade,
I will be self-sufficient, to our ideals firm and true,
I will be strong to keep my mind and soul outside a prison,
Encouraged and inspired by ever loving memories of you.
                    Elizabeth Gurley Flynn, October 24, 1955[1]

The CPUSA was an early and relentless critic of anticommunist policy, and Jones was a leader in theorizing it as an opportunity for the US to expand its empire. Even while she faced the threat of deportation and her fellow communists were being imprisoned, Jones would continue her leadership role in the Communist Party and write some of her most important work on gender, race, peace, and Marxism. As she continued to theorize about Black and women's liberation, her written work would articulate a Marxist feminism and discuss how oppression operated differently for women – in the process laying a foundation for intersectionality. US intelligence agencies used the escalating Cold War to expand their surveillance powers and criminalize radical dissent. The war in Korea and the Party's opposition to it further inflamed law enforcement. The Korean War, beginning in the summer of 1950 and lasting until the uneasy (and unresolved) truce in 1953, represented everything the Party feared. Anticommunism provided the US with cover to interfere in nations of color and impose its will.

American communists pushed against anticommunist policy that positioned the United States as a global police force while criminalizing peace advocacy and civil rights at home. The CPUSA argued that anticommunism strengthened global capitalism's power through relentless military incursion, particularly in Asia and Africa. American Cold War policy required the subjugation of people of color abroad and the silencing of critics in the United States. Jones warned Americans that the containment policy would commit the US to endless war, a bloated military at the expense of social welfare, and a weakened commitment to racial justice. She identified the trajectory that would put the US and the UK on a path to upholding white supremacist capitalism while convincing American and British citizens they were spreading democracy. In the final analysis, the only thing the US managed to contain was the spread of democracy. Jones and her peers predicted the future we live in today.

The most relevant aspect of Jones's critique for activists today is that she recognized that the national security state was white supremacist and that it relied on inventing enemies in order to sustain monopoly capitalism. The state neither needs nor requires the consent of those it governs, nor of the people to whom it purports to bring democracy. Jones reasoned that peace was a prerequisite for freedom because the state can use war and the threat of war as an excuse to trample the civil liberties of its own citizens and transmute the demand for equal citizenship rights into treason. Today, the reach of the US military has been extended even further, the US now has the largest prison population in the world, its police forces are armed with military weaponry, and its authoritarian laws continue to limit constitutional rights to dissent. The fascist state that expelled Jones has continued its expansion.

## Half the World

In 1950 Jones began a bi-weekly column in the *Daily Worker* titled "Half the World." As Carol Boyce Davies argues, the "logic" of the column was rooted in the "materialist-feminist assertion" that women as "half the world" deserved more attention and resources. In her analysis of these articles, Cristina Mislán argues that Jones "constructed complex narratives" about the "relationship between gender, nation, and war," and anticipated later feminist arguments by positioning the personal as political. For Jones, women were the most vulnerable during wartime and thus the political decision to go to war had personal consequences. As Mislán highlights, the column also focused on the Korean War – a war largely forgotten among Americans – as being central to the "McCarthyite era of surveillance and persecution." As both Mislán and Boyce Davies have shown, Jones's journalism in the "Half the World" series reflected her own political commitments, her personal involvement in Party campaigns, and Party policy on the devastation caused by Cold War militarism.[2]

Jones's column addressed issues of concern for women and communists, including the education of children, free speech on college campuses, FBI harassment, and food costs. Jones's (and other communist women's) focus on women and household concerns has been misinterpreted as an appeal to maternalism, perpetuating the assumption that women's issues are specific to the domestic realm and thus are not political. But Jones understood the household as a political institution and as a site in which to make radical political change. Borrowing from their Soviet comrades, during the Depression decade communist women regularly invoked the household as a political unit and rejected essentialist notions of women's domesticity. In 1935 Lenin's widow, Nadezhda Krupskaya, articulated this for American communists when she argued that "we do not want women to devote their lives to rearing children only," and that "married life" should not prevent women's "public work." This was the point Jones emphasized in much of her written work on gender, insisting that women were an unseen political bloc. She also emphasized that the household, especially that of the Black family, was political because capitalist interests supported by the imperialist state chose war and profit over social welfare and the well-being of Americans. Depoliticizing the home and failing to see its relevance to political and capitalist interests was (and remains) another factor that prevented progressive men from confronting male chauvinism. This was an especially grievous exclusion given that women's physical bodies and reproductive abilities have been and continue to be policed by those same political and capitalist interests. Jones and her generation were calling out these elisions.[3]

In one of her first columns, appearing in April 1950, Jones weighed in on a controversy over "male chauvinism" that had split the Party ranks. Poet and communist Walter Lowenfels published a story in the *Worker* on Christmas Day 1949, titled "Santa Claus or Comrade X," about living in a house full of women (his wife and four daughters). As Kate Weigand notes, the article garnered both praise and condemnation. The story focused on the women's care and concern over clothes, and some readers argued that this perpetuated the notion that women are only concerned with appearance. Jones's issue with Lowenfels's article was that all it did was parrot "ruling class ideology" grounded in women's "inferiority," thereby doing the work of the "capitalist ruling class" in sowing division among the working classes. The danger above all was that the story would discourage women's activism. These were the exact issues Jones had reprimanded the Party for in her Neglect article. She warned that publishing material that reduced women to stereotypes would demoralize the very women she hoped to rally to the cause.[4]

Many of Jones's columns focused on war, and the Cold War in particular, as a specific peril for women. In the months leading up to US intervention in Korea, she raised the alarm about the conflict and atomic weaponry. Vincent Intondi argues that Black Americans were some of the most outspoken opponents of the atomic bomb, and they often noted that it had only ever (and has still only ever) been used against a nation of color. In March 1950, concerned about President Truman's approval of hydrogen bomb construction, the Permanent Committee of the Partisans of Peace, a group with links to the Soviet-backed World Peace Congress, wrote a petition denouncing atomic weapons. Known as the Stockholm Peace Appeal, or pejoratively as the "Ban the Bomb" pledge, the petition demanded a "ban on all atomic weapons" and a call to indict for "crimes against humanity" any nation that used them. Jones and other communists took up the call to collect signatures. In a "Half the World" article a few weeks after the petition was written, Jones called for American women to organize to ban atomic weapons. She criticized the values of a war state that devoted "$40 billion" to its military budget, but only "5 percent" of its annual budget to social welfare. "Warmongers" she argued, used anticommunism to "paralyze" the will of the people to "fight for peace."[5]

This point is one that scholars have come to agree with: the US has since that time been involved in a "forever war" that most Americans have little knowledge of as the national security state does not require their consent. As David Vine has argued, "Cold War" is an egregious misnomer since the death toll from this period was upwards of 10 million people. Mary Dudziak has shown that "wartime" is a constant state for the United States; furthermore, as Marilyn Young has argued, the Cold War and its first hot conflict in Korea taught US policymakers that they could wage war using tax revenues without taxpayers' consent. This was a fear Jones articulated from the start: that the government was misrepresenting monopoly capitalism's imperialist ambition as a contest to spread democracy when in fact it was all about securing resources, labor, and ultimately profits.[6] For Jones, peace and justice required capitalism's destruction; she believed that you could not reform your way to liberation. On International Women's Day in 1950, Jones gave a speech on women's role in the peace struggle that was later published as an article titled "International Women's Day and the Struggle for Peace." She recounted the work of several local and national women's organizing efforts, both religious and secular, to counter what she called the "Truman-Acheson Doctrine," accusing Secretary of State Dean Acheson, along with President Harry Truman, of seeking to "inaugurate [a] suicidal atomic and hydrogen weapon race." Jones was clear that these efforts were bipartisan, as both the main political parties were pursuing war in the name of anticommunism. She once again counseled the Party that it had to make organizing women a priority, because the "monopolist rulers" were hard at work trying to prevent unity for peace. She hoped to arouse women's "internationalism" to get them to identify with their "sisters the world over" in their struggles against imperialism and fascism.[7]

Jones and the Party opposed Cold War policies like the North Atlantic Treaty Organization (NATO) and the Marshall Plan as assaults on the Soviet Union and a foundation for the next war. The Marshall Plan was especially targeted as a capitalist tool to spread US favor and wealth and disguise imperialism as a benevolent effort to rebuild countries devastated by war. Jones saw both NATO and the Marshall Plan as tools for "war and fascism" and as efforts by "monopoly capital" to enforce the fascist triple K, *Kinder Küche Kirche*. This was because, even as the Party failed to see women's potential, capitalists feared that the mobilization of women for peace would spell the end of their power. Behind the attacks on women's "femininity or womanliness" was a concern that women's power and their demands for social and political change would challenge capitalism's strength and spell the end of the war state.[8]

Jones's work on women's rights was specifically grounded in the class struggle, even as she challenged her fellow Marxists to include social issues, which she insisted were already addressed in the canon. Her International Women's Day speech articulated the Party's objection to the Equal Rights Amendment (ERA) as a bourgeois feminist attempt to impose "equalitarian" politics and endanger labor. She argued that women's "complete emancipation" was only possible under socialism and described the Party's goal as being to create a socialist United States. Emancipation, she argued, would only ever be complete under socialism because "class division and human exploitation" would be "abolished." Most importantly, she articulated a criticism of "Bourgeois democracy" that highlighted both the Party's rejection of the ERA and its skepticism about reform. In the bourgeois state, equality could never be achieved because it required "constant struggle." In the capitalist democracies, a reformist law required more laws to uphold it and those laws required constant enforcement; reform would often beget more reform that needed more laws and more enforcement, and so on. A socialist state required the dissolution of oppressive institutions that depended on war and profit. Her critique of the growing war state insisted that freedom could never succeed in a country that put on the appearance of equality while its power was sustained by capitalism and militarism. War was the lifeblood of monopoly capitalism; peace and freedom required the destruction of both.[9]

She closed her speech and article by warning that the left could never secure liberation while its own ranks resisted women's and Black emancipation. She emphasized that "Progressive and communist men" had to become the "vanguard" in fighting "male supremacist ideas." She did not care for "glib" talk from progressive men about "women as 'allies,'" pointing to the lack of "effort" on their part to see women as integral to their struggles. She argued that Marxist Leninist teachings recognized women's oppression and that this had to be communicated to the masses, both women and men, to counter the encroachment of bourgeois feminism. Socialism was the "final guarantee" of peace, women's rights, and "freedom."[10]

Bill Mullen argues that Jones's speech carefully toed the line regarding Stalinism. That the CPUSA and its members were Stalinists who took direction from Moscow is an often-repeated claim made by anticommunists. The show trials, purges, and the 1939 Nazi–Soviet pact became a litmus test for many; those who left the Party made a clean break but those who remained, like Jones, were seen as devout Stalinists. As Mullen argues, Jones's speech centered women and "not the Soviet State" by pointing to Marxist Leninism as the promoter of women's independence and not the Soviet Union. The 1930s had witnessed the USSR's aggressive rollback of women's rights legislation and its adoption of pronatalist policies similar to those of other nations. Communist women thus had to strike a delicate balance in praising the promises of socialism while avoiding discussion of the dictatorship under Stalin.[11]

Jones believed that it was this speech that led to her eventual deportation, but it was only one part of her body of work attacking US militarism and Cold War policy. Weeks before the Korean War began, she wrote a front-page article in the *Daily Worker* about organizing women against the war. The Ban the Bomb petition offered an opportunity to organize, and she noted that women across the US were "spearheading" the effort to get 5 million American signatures on the petition. These women, she wrote, were aware of the dangers of war and of the "reactionaries in their own land" who were downplaying the need for peace. They did not accept the "monstrous doctrine spread by imperialists" that war was "inevitable."[12]

Jones's written and spoken work inspired many activists, including W.E.B. Du Bois, who would articulate a theoretical framework for the argument that peace was necessary to secure emancipation from imperialism and US racism. But to US intelligence officials, peace activism was synonymous with treason, and support for the Ban the Bomb petition signaled subversion.[13] In 1949, Du Bois attended the Paris Peace Congress, the same meeting at which Robeson's antiwar remarks had sparked controversy. Upon returning to the United States, Du Bois and others set up the Peace Information Center (PIC), an organization devoted to circulating information about the global peace movement. The PIC had to be very careful politically, since it could not openly advocate any campaign associated with the peace movement without inviting FBI scrutiny. The group conferred with attorneys in an effort to stay within the limits of the highly restrictive anticommunist legislation. In May 1950, the PIC published its first "Peace-Gram," a monthly newsletter about the peace movement. It included the text of the Ban the Bomb petition. In July, Secretary of State Acheson called the petition Soviet propaganda. The following month, the PIC was ordered to register as a foreign agent under the Foreign Agents Registration Act. The organization chose to dissolve rather than register, but the State Department considered the now non-existent group still liable and had Du Bois and other PIC leaders arrested. Du Bois would eventually be acquitted, but the peace movement was now alert to the danger it was in.[14]

For Charisse Burden-Stelly, this episode indicates the threat that "Radical Black Peace Activists" like Du Bois and Jones presented. Their activism was "antagonistic to US interests" because in its politicization of Blackness it exposed how racial discourse was rooted in US policy. The Cold War state was also wary of the activists' connections to overseas struggles, interpreting their "internationalism" as an "egregious form of anti-Americanism." The defense industries, or what we today call the military-industrial complex, were becoming "so essential" to the economy that criticism of them became "akin to subversion." Indeed, recent studies have shown that defense spending became part of a bipartisan strategy to secure economic security and political alliances. As Michael Brenes argues, even in the absence of war, defense spending was foundational to political and economic politicking in the US, at the expense of social welfare. This continues to be a bipartisan issue today, as the US under a Democratic President (Biden) has approved the largest military budget in world history. More concerning, the privatization of military units, which concretizises capitalism's investment in war, has made oversight nearly impossible and brutality a regular practice.[15]

For Jones, peace was the "antidote to anti-Blackness, labor exploitation, and perpetual war." War and violence were "played out" on the bodies of Black men, both those fighting wars abroad and those facing racism at home. This is the important connection Jones and others made between the war state and the "lynch law" state, as the US deployed Black people to wage war abroad while ignoring the danger racist violence posed at home. For Jones, war victimized women the most, partly because it diverted funds away from social welfare but also because women bore the brunt of the economic burdens of wartime. Furthermore, as she pointed out, the effects of capitalist "warmongering" and "profit-driven imperialism" fell "disproportionately" on Black women.[16]

Jones argued this point about women's heightened consciousness of the dangers of war in a February 1951 article titled "For the Unity of Women in the Cause of Peace." As the Korean War heated up and the death notices increased, women were increasingly becoming aware of the actual cost of war. Black women especially understood the injustice of a war that was waged in the name of preserving democracy while Black men continued to be lynched at home. Though Black men's bodies were on the line, it was women who bore the brunt of war, Jones argued, because they faced the loss of their kin and reduced circumstances at home. War entailed the exploitation of women in industry and the exploitation of their reproductive labor for cannon fodder. The evisceration of already limited social welfare programs combined with the massive expansion of the military was the worst-case scenario Jones had warned against.[17]

Jones again called for her comrades to prioritize recruiting women into the peace movement, a dangerous gamble since such involvement was branded as treason. Her article included three demands: to "develop and strengthen" a women's peace movement, to root that movement in the working class, and to bring the "fight for peace" to Black women specifically. In her discussion of organizing Black women, Jones connected peace to the fight against lynch law. She cited the Willie McGee case, an episode that had haunted American communists and revealed the motivations of the lynch state and the role of Cold War policy in securing white supremacy. McGee was a World War II veteran arrested in November 1945 in Laurel, Mississippi, allegedly for the rape of a white woman named Wiletta Hawkins. All indications were that Hawkins manipulated McGee into a sexual relationship and harassed him to the point that he left the state for a time. After he returned and rebuffed Hawkins again, she accused him of sneaking into her home and raping her. McGee was arrested, forced to confess, convicted, and sentenced to death in the matter of a month. Once alerted to the case, the CPUSA and the Civil Rights Congress led a movement to free McGee, which Jones participated in. When she wrote the article, McGee was still alive waiting to hear if his execution order would be stayed. Jones wrote about McGee's wife being an essential part of the campaign to free her husband, which evidenced the importance of Black women's organizing. Unfortunately, on May 8, 1951 McGee was executed. His death haunted the CPUSA and revealed the indifference of the state toward Black America. Jones led memorials across the country, and even a year later she was still invoking McGee's execution as evidence of the US's moral bankruptcy. The McGee execution was just one example of the injustice Black America faced while the US claimed to be ushering in democracy in Korea.[18]

Jones's outspoken advocacy on behalf of McGee and her devotion to the CPUSA meant that she often faced attempts at censorship. In 1951, at a memorial meeting at Roosevelt College in Chicago, a group of faculty objected to her talk. She wrote about the attempt to silence her in her "Half the World" column. Communists had spoken on the campus in the past, but the "appearance of a Negro woman communist" speaking out against the "legal lynching" of a Black man provoked anger. She believed that what upset the faculty was her linking of the "fight for peace" with the "fight for freedom." White supremacy was a weapon wielded against both, a tool to "divide and split" the unity of working people. The *Chicago Tribune* reported that several students "booed and heckled" as they tried to disrupt her talk. The college dean claimed that most of the students were opposed to her speech – which was sponsored by the Labor Youth League

(LYL) – but he wanted to respect the students' freedom of speech and allowed Jones on campus. The LYL was a communist adjacent organization that was involved in the peace movement and advocated racial equality. The dean later stated he would prohibit any future talks by communists.[19]

Jones took issue with the *Chicago Tribune's* reporting: it claimed that twenty students had interrupted her, while she insisted it was only six. The students used racial epithets against her, chanting "speak monkey speak," but this was not reported on. The "Red Squad" (referring to police) was in attendance for surveillance, but, contrary to the *Tribune's* report, they did not escort the hecklers out; it was left to others in the audience to silence them. Contrary to the dean's claim that most of the students opposed her speech, Jones believed that the opposition came from a small fraction of fascist-minded youth who faced an "unsettled outlook" as the US was at war. She wrote that the audience were open to conversation, even the anticommunists among them, and that she had challenged them to think more critically about things they took for granted. For example, when asked whether Marxists believed in free speech, she countered by asking why Marxists are accused of violating free speech when it was the state that was attacking the free speech of communists. She urged the students, especially since they were of draft age, to recognize the link between war abroad and white supremacist violence at home.[20]

The campaign against legal lynching was part of the peace movement because it revealed the US's priorities: war was paramount, Americans were not. The Korean War and the legal lynching cases led to the founding of the short-lived Sojourners for Truth and Justice (STJ), a Black women's organization. According to Erik McDuffie, the founding of the Sojourners was inspired by Jones's Neglect article and Beulah Richardson's poem, "A Black Woman Speaks of ...

White Womanhood, White Supremacy, of Peace." The poem described the contradictions radical Black activists saw in the state's concerted efforts to wage war and uphold white supremacy. Richardson and Louise Thompson Patterson issued a call to Black women in September 1951 to travel to Washington, DC, to pressure politicians to act on racist violence and end the Korean War. The group converged on Washington in October.[21]

Jones was not a founding member of the STJ and was unable to attend its first meeting in DC because her bail terms confined her to New York, but she would become a member and an advocate. McDuffie recounted an incident that Louise Thompson Patterson shared about Jones and the STJ. Allegedly the Party did not like the organization or Jones's enthusiasm for it because it feared "losing . . . its most visible Black female leaders." When Jones told Thompson Patterson and Beulah Richardson about the Party's concerns, this led to a physical confrontation between Jones and Richardson. Thompson Patterson reported that she "had to pull Beulah off Claudia." McDuffie argues that if the story is true then it "contradicts" reports of Jones's enthusiasm for the group, and shows that there were divisions within Black Left feminism. Whether the fall out occurred or not, publicly Jones was an enthusiastic endorser and promoter of the STJ.[22]

In her November 25, 1951 "Half the World" column, she celebrated the founding of the Sojourners as the most "heartening development" in the "Negro liberation movement." She praised the group's meeting in Washington, DC, as being important for the movement against "lynch terror" and "national oppression," and especially for the movement for "peace and freedom." She believed that the Sojourners demonstrated that Black women's leadership in the movement was both essential and on the horizon. She claimed that the organization was already spreading across the country, as indicated by the "report backs" from groups forming across the US. Jones attended the "report back" meeting in New York with sixty other women, including domestic workers and professionals, housewives, and "lynch widows" of Black men killed by the state. They were there to fight back against every "insult" and "indignity" that had been faced by Black people for centuries. She insisted that they had power as "Negro women" and that the STJ organization was a first step toward Black women's leadership.[23]

Jones also publicly challenged white progressives who questioned the founding of the organization. "Since when is it the prerogative" of white progressives, she asked, to "determine the direction of the liberation movement" of oppressed people? The critics claimed that the organization was "nationalistic," but Jones countered that no organization was less so because it dedicated itself to "full freedom." Since Black women were "triply oppressed," the organization represented something new and necessary in the struggle. She counseled white progressives not to "worry too much" about any potential nationalistic trends in the group because it was Black progressive women who would lead the way in overcoming such tendencies. The best thing white progressives could do was lend their support and see the group as a "heartening sign" of radical Black women's leadership.[24]

The Sojourners had rallied in support of Willie McGee, but the Rosa Lee Ingram case was especially important to the group because it involved sexual violence against a Black woman. Ingram was a widowed Georgia sharecropper with twelve children. John Stratford, a white sharecropper and neighbor, had repeatedly made passes at Ingram which she rebuffed. In November 1947 he tried to force himself on her but she fought back. Four of Ingram's sons joined the fray and by the time it was over Stratford was dead. Ingram and two of her children were arrested, tried, and found guilty in hasty proceedings based on forced (and inconsistent) confessions. The CRC and the CPUSA saw in the Ingram case another instance of lynch law and of the sexual violence, intimidation, and, in Jones's words, "daily insults" that Black women faced. Jones wrote that the case exemplified the "oppressed status of Negro womanhood" and indicated the "degradation" of Black women as "bourgeois democracy" became more fascist. It also highlighted for Jones the Black woman's "historic role" as protector of the Black family. The treatment of Black women was the greatest "indictment of the capitalist system" because their lot in the US was one of "continuing indignity" as a result of "American monopoly imperialist oppression." When Jones wrote about the Ingrams they were still in jail (where they would remain until paroled in 1959). The Sojourners organized visits to them in prison – including with Rosa's other children – raised money for their care, and signed a letter written by W.E.B. Du Bois that was sent to the UN to request intervention in the case.[25]

For Jones, the STJ presented the opportunity she had longed for: the organization of Black women, against war, lynch law, and the exploitative capitalist state. This was a movement founded by Black women, "conceived by them, organized by them, and led by them." Party comrades who failed to understand the importance of the Sojourners were guilty of the worst kind of "phrase mongering." Jones was not interested in rhetorical support for the movement; instead, she wanted to see vigorous action on the part of white comrades.[26]

The link between the peace movement and the campaigns against lynch law coalesced in the 1951 *We Charge Genocide* petition. Lawyer and CRC chairperson William Patterson compiled data on murders, rapes, and assaults against Black Americans between 1945 and 1951 and presented it to the United Nations as evidence that the United

States was engaged in genocide against Black Americans. He argued that the Korean War and the growth of the US military also counted as violence against Black America. US warmongering was taking place not just overseas, since the federal government was willfully ignoring the rights of Black Americans as guaranteed in the 14th and 15th amendments. Cold War policy, the petition insisted, was a white supremacist policy that degraded the lives of people of color at home and abroad.[27]

The Sojourners rallied behind the petition and Jones gave speeches urging support for it. Unfortunately, neither the Sojourners nor the petition would survive anticommunist harassment. The STJ leaders were all under FBI investigation, the organization was "riddled" with informants, and the Bureau was joined in its surveillance of the group by the Secret Service, the Counter Intelligence Corps of the Army, and Naval Intelligence. One informant told the FBI that the STJ was trying to start a revolution and planned to march to Georgia to free the Ingrams (FBI agents did not believe the claim). The Bureau expressed concern that the Sojourners would ally with the UN against the US government. The *We Charge Genocide* petition was dismissed as a Soviet plot and Patterson was arrested. The "noose" was beginning to tighten over the CPUSA, its members, affiliates, and fellow travelers. As McDuffie argues, the anticommunist climate made it impossible to build the kind of movement Jones and the STJ envisioned, and the organization folded in 1952. The CRC would itself collapse in 1956.[28]

## Arrest and Trial

Anticommunism further alienated Jones and her colleagues from the alleged promises of democracy, a democracy that was increasingly proving to be illusory. Joseph Keith argues that in her writing Jones "located" her life story as a story of "unbelonging" within the United States. This sense of "unbelonging" due to racism and sexism drove her to communism and helped her to formulate an emancipatory ethos "within a larger framework of racial capitalism and empire." Jones knew that her written and spoken work was increasingly putting her under threat, and indeed by 1950 she had been arrested twice and was detained for a month following her second arrest. More than just her activism, it was her lack of citizenship that made her existence more precarious.[29]

While dealing with the legal harassment, Jones also had to contend with poor health. Her bout with tuberculosis as a teenager may have imperiled her long-term health, as her adult life was plagued by illness. While detained in 1950, she complained of a "flare up" of bronchitis, and in June 1951 the FBI reported she was being treated for bronchitis again. Jones's health would increasingly become a topic of concern as it continued to deteriorate. Taking the issue more seriously, she began to reflect on her long-term smoking habit. When Joseph North wrote a column for the *Daily Worker* arguing that tobacco use was dangerous, his article created a furor among readers. Jones contributed to the debate in the *Worker* noting that her comrades Gus Hall and Ben Davis had long warned about the dangers of smoking, and revealing that she herself had managed to break a pack-a-day habit. She admitted that it was a little "trying" on her friends' nerves when she dramatically asked for windows to be opened as the "cloud of cigarette smoke" became too intense. Ever the communist, she noted that quitting was difficult because "bad habits" can be as hard to get rid of as "bad ideology." Though the article was in good humor, with a teasing but encouraging tone, she did note that the "tobacco monopoly" was eager to maintain smoking habits

– but, she claimed, once you experience the "pleasure" of non-smoking, you come to long for it, just like the movement longed for peace. Unfortunately, Jones returned to her habit and remained a heavy smoker into her later years.[30]

FBI harassment and another arrest would further jeopardize her health. On June 4, 1951, the *Dennis v. United States* decision upheld the convictions of the CPUSA leadership. Jones likened the Supreme Court's decision to a "fascist danger" not unlike what had occurred in Nazi Germany. The anticommunist state was now further empowered to make communist advocacy illegal, essentially denying constitutional protection for certain Americans. As Jones herself noted, she and many of her persecuted friends were hostages of "white supremacists" who targeted them for their devotion to equality.[31] Government officials saw the Court's decision as an opportunity to extend their focus, and less than two weeks later Jones and several of her comrades were arrested for violating the Smith Act – her third arrest. On June 20, she was taken into custody along with sixteen other CPUSA leaders. Across the country dozens of other communist leaders were also arrested. Among them were her friends Pettis Perry, Elizabeth Gurley Flynn, and, once again, Alexander Bittelman and Betty Gannett.[32]

Jones described her arrest in a "Half the World" article. She was awoken at 7:00 am by "FBI characters," who never seemed to be around "when lynchers, Ku Kluxers and anti-Semites are around." They arrested her and other "working-class leaders," including the "seriously ailing" and elderly Israel Amter, who was seventy years old. Meanwhile, neighbors went about their business oblivious to the fact that the federal government was engaging in "the denial of free speech and thought." Jones was searched for weapons and the agents watched her dress before taking her into custody. She, Flynn and Gannett were taken to the Women's

Detention Center in Greenwich Village. She encouraged her readers to rise up against the harassment as a constitutional violation. The detainees were given exorbitant bails: Jones's was "literally" her "weight in gold" at $20,000 with an additional $5,000 tacked on for deportation charges. Bail for all the defendants totaled nearly $200,000. She was freed on bail on June 23.[33]

The FBI had been staying close to Jones in these years, following her every movement and noting each of her publications. She remained on the Security Index and agents were instructed to focus on any "revolutionary statements" she made. They noted that Jones never denied being a CPUSA member, proudly admitted to her leadership appointments, and was regularly featured in the Party press and on the radio as a CPUSA representative engaging in debates. The Bureau also included in its file statements she had made denouncing the military draft and war preparedness before the Korean War, and even logged the slogans chanted at rallies she had attended. The FBI had long planned to arrest and deport Jones and worked for years between her first and last arrests to build its case. The problem was that, as the Bureau admitted, she focused on the plight of Black America and women and, though she advocated socialism, nowhere did she advocate the overthrow of the US government.[34]

In its attempts to criminalize communism, the federal government employed tactics that often shifted the focus of trials away from the specific charges of sedition. As Ellen Schrecker argues, the government "fashioned" its arguments, evidence, and witnesses around the "contention" that the CPUSA was a "criminal conspiracy." The trials were not just about the defendants; they were public exhibitions intended to get the American people behind anticommunism. The courts deployed what were often "highly distorted" stereotypes about communists, which were then linked to individual communists. Schrecker argues that in the early Cold War there were few nuanced criticisms of the government's tactics, and the "stereotypical communist" image was played out "everywhere" – in news and media, politics, congressional hearings, and in Hollywood.[35]

The case against Jones would be made using her own words – words that the Bureau admitted focused on extending civil rights. The FBI also had a habit of massaging the evidence to make it appear more insidious. Under the category "False statements made by Subject. . ." it included the claim that Jones had listed her birth date wrong on her INS records, contradicting the date given in her high school records (which were likely completed by her father); the Bureau planned to subpoena the superintendent of schools as a witness. The issue of her "aliases" came up again, with the Bureau listing her birth name, married name, and pen name as aliases, all no doubt to make her appear dishonest. It also listed several of Jones's articles in its case against her, including "For New Approaches to our Work among Women," "An End to the Neglect of the Problems of the Negro Woman!" "International Women's Day," "Foster's Political and Theoretical Guidance to Our Work among Women," and "For the Unity of Women in the Cause of Peace!" The most common (and problematic) government tactic was to use professional witnesses – as they had with Jones's earlier deportation proceedings. The witnesses could vary from an official confirming high school records, to an FBI special agent, to a Library of Congress archivist. But the Bureau's favorite type of witness was the former communist who could claim knowledge of an alleged communist plot, even if they could not link individual defendants to the purported conspiracy.[36]

With dozens of Party leaders either in jail, on trial, or forced to go underground, the families that were left behind found themselves targets of government harassment and often experienced financial difficulties. In September 1951, Peggy Dennis, whose husband Eugene Dennis was among the original twelve leaders tried, helped found and run the Family Committee of the Smith Act Victims (FCSAV). The organization helped the impacted families by raising funds for childcare or supplemental income, and for social events including summer camps for the children. They also raised awareness of the targeting of the families of those convicted or accused. In one notorious case, Jones's friend Esther Cooper Jackson was left to care for her two children when her husband James Jackson became "unavailable" – a euphemism for someone advised to go underground (a tactic some communists and historians have argued made the Party appear guilty). FBI agents staked out the family house, followed the family around, interrogated teachers and neighbors, monitored and questioned James's parents, and even approached the two young daughters. After their youngest, Kathy, was kicked out of her preschool because of the harassment, the FCSAV raised awareness of the incident and public pressure led to her readmittance.[37]

Jones wrote about the organization's important mission in her column. Shortly after its founding, she participated in a massive event to help raise funds and wrote about the need to care for the family members and shield them from state repression. Some children lost contact with their fathers, for others it was both their parents. Deborah Gerson, whose own parents were caught up in the red scare, would later note that even as the federal government claimed the white heterosexual family was a bulwark against communism, "progressive and Communist families" were afforded no such respect. The FCSAV was founded nearly simultaneously with the Sojourners, and Jones saw it as another example of "unity in action in sisterhood." She hoped that the group could "bring closer the day" when "peace, life, friendship, love, tenderness and happiness" could be enjoyed by the Smith Act families and "the world as a whole."[38]

In February 1952, Jones's thirty-seventh birthday celebration was used as an occasion to raise money for her defense and that of her co-defendants. Abner Berry, a Party organizer and writer, described the event in an article, noting that Jones was someone the government feared "instead of honored." She was feared because she dared to think that "peace was possible, and freedom could be won." The Trade Union Committee for Claudia Jones, which had organized the event, was "bowled over" by the support given to Jones by her neighbors and friends. The group collected financial gifts as well as "jewelry, perfume, blouses, bags" and other presents for her. Jones's co-defendants attended the celebration, as did Esther Cooper Jackson; a chair was left empty in honor of her friend and imprisoned comrade Ben Davis. Her father Charles Cumberbatch was also there, and gave a speech in which he said that he had raised her to respect "others' opinions and ideas." In her own speech, Jones noted that the CPUSA had helped her to understand how to "fight better for the liberation" of her people. On a separate occasion, the Sojourners hosted a cocktail party in honor of Jones's birthday. Her trial began only weeks after the celebration.[39]

Between the arrests and the trial in March 1952, four of Jones's co-defendants were either acquitted or deemed too ill to be put on trial. The remaining thirteen included Flynn and the only other Black defendant, Pettis Perry. The trial would last thirteen months and involved all the now typical aspects of the anticommunist trials – admission of Marxist Leninist literature as evidence of a violent plot, records of the defendants' written and spoken work (though Jones accused the court of refusing to read her work into the record because it feared creating communist sympathies), and professional witnesses. One of these witnesses would later provide material that enabled the CPUSA to attack the injustice of the trials. In July, Harvey Matusow, a former communist expelled from the Party, took the stand. He had worked briefly at the Jefferson School of Social Science where Jones and others taught, held conferences, and studied Marxist literature. The school itself would come under pressure from the federal authorities and be forced to close. Matusow testified that he had seen Jones, Gannett, and Perry at the school – something none of them would have denied, but since it was a maligned Marxist institution, association with it supposedly confirmed their guilt. In 1955, Matusow published a book titled *False Witness* in which he admitted he had lied on the stand and accused other professional witnesses of doing the same. The authorities dismissed his confession as another tool of the communist conspiracy in an attempt to delegitimize his claims. His confession would do nothing for the defendants already serving their prison sentences by the time of the book's publication.[40]

In January 1953 the defendants were found guilty. On February 3 they were sentenced to between one and three years in jail and taken back into custody. Jones was sentenced to one year and one day and fined $2,000 – a lighter prison sentence because of her poor health. In the middle of the trial she had contracted bronchitis and was hospitalized because of heart failure. A steep bail was set, which the Party and friends and family managed to raise so the defendants could remain free during the appeals process. Jones was placed on supervised parole with the INS under the provisions of the McCarran-Walter Act, passed in 1952, which allowed for communists to be deported. She told agents that she would not "desist" in the fight for peace, and she did not. She was appointed editor of the *Negro Affairs Quarterly* and worked on the CPUSA's National Peace Commission during the appeals.⁴¹

At the sentencing each of the defendants made a statement. Jones began by asking the Judge, Edward Dimock, whether she deserved one year of incarceration for advocating equality, for believing that Black liberation could only be achieved through alliances with the working class, or for her adherence to Marxism. She argued that she was being sentenced to prison for advocating peace and an end to the Korean War, for exercising free speech, and for believing that socialism was the only means to achieve equality. She called out the "despicable forced admission" of the witnesses, particularly the Black witnesses used against her who had been paid to memorize a "script" and who could not answer questions other than those they had been primed to respond to. The almost total lack of Black and Puerto Rican jurors (there was a Black alternate) revealed the "white supremacist ruling class prejudice" against them serving on juries. Jones told the judge that she held the trial in "utter contempt" because it was a "trial of ideas"; she and the others were "morally free" while the court stood "naked" before the constitution. Jones proudly declared her belief in Marxist Leninism and her opposition to the war state. She reminded the judge that she did not arrive as a child revolutionary – she was radicalized by US racism, and it was US racism that convicted her. Jones's statement summarized not just her belief in her innocence, but also the injustice and racism of the anticommunist trials.⁴²

During the appeals process, the Party also tried to secure parole for the original Smith Act defendants who were already serving time. In December 1954, Jones published a pamphlet titled *Ben Davis: Fighter for Freedom*. Featuring an introduction by Eslanda Robeson, it was a call for "amnesty" for Davis. A *Daily Worker* reviewer described it as a portrait of one of the US's "greatest working-class heroes" and a "testimony of courage and spirit" that would "stir patriots." Jones praised Davis's long career as an advocate for Black America, his attacks on Jim Crow, and his devotion to working-class struggles. She described the segregated prison where he was serving his sentence and linked his devotion to the cause to the long history of Black resistance to oppression and his own work against lynch law. She ended by demanding "Amnesty for Ben Davis and his colleagues now!"[43]

Jones and Davis's convictions and sentences were not just an attack on communists, but further evidence of the racist court system. In a February 1954 article, Jones continued her analysis of the racism inherent in anticommunism by arguing that the "aims of fascist McCarthyism" were to "stamp out the imperishable achievements" of abolitionists, anti-imperialists, and those devoted to Black equality and working-class unity. She argued that McCarthy and those who backed him were "patently anti-Negro" because they opposed democracy and peace, because they were determined to reverse the gains made for equality, and because they were committed to authoritarian governance and the suppression of political expression. The Party, she argued, had long been opposed to the racist court system in the south; now anticommunist legislation like the McCarran-Walter Act targeted progressives and radicals and limited the immigration of West Indians (a provision set a quota for immigrants from the Caribbean to 100 a year) – a piece of legislation that effectively linked immigration and the fear of radicalism. She noted that even those who advocated for equality and denounced communism were targeted, mentioning specifically the federal government's censorship of Walter White, who led the NAACP, and Gunnar Myrdal, a Swedish sociologist who investigated US racism, whose written works had been removed from embassy libraries.

Both men were anticommunist, but both also advocated racial equality. Their anticommunism did not protect them. Anticommunism pivoted on the belief that Black equality was part of a grand conspiracy. The reality was that anticommunism was an expression of US racial fascism.[44]

## Prison

Jones and the other twelve defendants lost their appeal on January 11, 1955. Jones, Gannett, and Flynn were immediately taken back into custody and held at the Women's House of Detention. Jones's attorney Mary Kaufmann filed an appeal to convert Jones's sentence to "time already served" based on her precarious health. The appeal cited the fact that the court-appointed doctor had recommended her hospitalization for "hypertension" and "reactivation of her pulmonary tuberculosis." The doctor's notes from her examinations in 1952 reveal the extent of Jones's poor health. Dr. Louis Miller, a hospital physician, wrote that Jones had been suffering from "acute pulmonary tuberculosis" since the age of seventeen. During the trial she had run a fever for several days straight. Her condition required hospitalization because her heart was functioning "under severe strain," her pulse was high, and her blood pressure was dangerously elevated. Miller warned that there were several complications that could result, including cardiac failure, cerebral hemorrhage, and Bright's Disease (today called nephritis – inflammation of the kidneys).[45]

Dr. John Wood, the court-appointed doctor, diagnosed her with "hypertensive cardiovascular disease." Miller wrote a more detailed evaluation of Jones using Wood's notes and the results of x-rays and an echocardiogram. Jones had "severe cardiac damage," high blood pressure, and evidence of permanent damage done to her heart and lungs. Her life expectancy was "not too great in terms of years" because she was suffering from "lung impairment" and hypertension, each of which alone could be devastating, but together seriously compromised her health. Miller concluded that Jones needed to dedicate her life to "looking after her health" as there was no known treatment. These conclusions were made in December 1952, during the trial. Kaufmann was still working two years later to try to secure Jones's release from prison. But the judge was unmoved.[46]

Jones, Gannett, and Flynn were taken to the segregated Alderson, West Virginia women's prison to serve their sentences. Flynn was sentenced to three years, and Gannett to two. In 1963 Flynn published her book *The Alderson Story* about her imprisonment. Upon arrival, the women endured the routine strip and cavity search. They were allowed some belongings, which they only knew about from two other Smith Act defendants already serving time at Alderson. They were given army surplus clothes, and a regular cigarette allowance (though Jones had earlier quit, her doctor gave her permission to smoke eight cigarettes a day). Everyone had their hair deloused with DDT, which they were instructed to keep on for forty-eight hours (a troubling procedure given today's understanding of DDT as a carcinogen). The facility had a three-week "orientation" after which the inmates received their cell assignments. Jones, however, was immediately hospitalized and her orientation period delayed. Flynn was sent to maximum security, Gannett to a separate area. The three women did not see much of each other at the beginning, and Jones would not see Gannett at all during her incarceration.[47]

Kaufmann worked to secure Jones an appropriate diet for her medical condition. She wrote a letter on January 26 urging the Alderson authorities to follow the doctor's orders and provide Jones with her prescribed medicine and a no-salt diet. The prison doctor did not agree with Jones's other doctors and resisted providing the recommended food. Meanwhile, Kaufmann was also pushing for a new trial in light of Matusow's false testimony. Jones spent her fortieth birthday imprisoned while her attorney worked on getting her appropriate health care and securing her early release.[48]

Jones wrote her father that she was almost certain that her diet was as "salt-free" as could be had in prison. She told him that she had begun to feel better and had finally been able to leave the hospital after a month. She then had to attend her orientation, which, she explained, was when they instructed the prisoners on how to "keep your things in order," like clothing and living areas. Unfortunately, she was sent back to the hospital because it had not yet received the results of her tests and she was experiencing headaches. She was able to read newspapers and magazines, as well as novels such as *The Razor's Edge* by Somerset Maugham, a book about a World War II veteran traumatized by his war experience.[49]

Jones's letter to her attorney only days later had more urgency, mentioning that she was not only experiencing headaches but heart pain as well, which she had not felt in a long time. The pain had returned when she was forced to eat the regular prison diet. The hospital was giving her different medication than she had been prescribed and her blood pressure was higher. She told Kaufmann that at orientation she felt short of breath doing even simple tasks, so she asked the doctor to recommend less strenuous activity for her work detail. In another letter she noted that even the limited schedule she was put on made her quite tired. She was given digitalis, a drug used to support the heart, and dehydration tablets, as well as medicine for her headaches. She urged Kaufmann to continue working on securing a salt-free diet.[50]

Flynn considered herself, Jones, Gannett, and their comrades across the prison system as political prisoners, a designation the United States refused to recognize, even as the "most tyrannical countries" did. There were other "politicals" in Alderson at the same time. Jones befriended Blanca Consuela Torresola, a Puerto Rican nationalist who had been involved in taking over a Puerto Rican town during an uprising. She was serving a life sentence. Jones wrote a poem about her titled "For Consuela – Anti-Fascista." It read:

> It seems I knew you long before our common ties – of conscious choice
> Threw under single skies, those like us
> Who, fused by our mold
> Became their targets as of old
>
> I knew you in Jarama's hills
> Through men and women drilled
> In majesty, whose dignity
> Rejected shirts and skirts of dimity
>
> I heard you in Guernica's songs
> Proud melodies that burst from tongues
> As yet unknown to me – full thronged
> With Liberty.
>
> Anti-anti-fascistas!
> That was your name
> I sang your fame
> Long 'fore my witness of your bane of pain
>
> I saw you in the passion-flower
> In roses full of flame
> Pure valley lily, whose bower
> Marks resemblance to your name

> Oh wondrous Spanish sister
> Long-locked from all you care
> Listen – while I tell you what you strain to hear
> And beckon all from far and near
>
> We swear that we will never rest
> Until they hear not plea
> But sainted sacrifice to set
> A small proud nation free
>
> O anti-fascist sister – you whose eyes turn to stars still
> I've learned your wondrous secret – source of spirit and of will
> I've learned that what sustains you heart, mind and peace of soul
> Is knowledge that their justice – can never reach its goal![51]

Jones imagined Consuela as a comrade in the larger struggles against US fascism. In Consuela's case, it was the fascist imperialist state that kept Puerto Rico as a colony while the Puerto Rican nationalist movement pushed for its liberation.

The federal prison system was just then beginning to desegregate following the *Brown v. Board of Education* decision the year before. Prison officials enlisted Flynn, Jones, and Gannett's help, but they faced resistance from both the white prisoners and prison guards. Many Black prison guards began to leave after desegregation because they faced harassment from their fellow guards and white prisoners. Jones tried to intercede on behalf of one of the harassed guards, but the woman chose to leave instead. Other Black inmates looked to Jones for advice, and she schooled them on how whiteness was weaponized against Black people, in particular how white women would cry "rape" to protect themselves or their reputations, at the expense of Black men's lives, like in Willie McGee's case. Flynn and Jones brought to the prison a critique of imprisonment itself as a capitalist tool to restrain the peace and anti-imperialist movements.[52]

The women were well taken care of thanks to the FCSAV, which raised money for commissary, books, and newspaper subscriptions and paid bus or train fares for family members to visit. Jones's father Charles Cumberbatch, now seventy years old, was "not too well" but visited her often and the FCSAV funded his travels; but he had to stay at a segregated boarding house. Kaufmann, who also visited, shared information with Cumberbatch about Jones's health. Jones was eventually taken off the digitalis and was being treated for hypertension, but, weeks after arriving, she still struggled to get a salt-free diet. In February 1955, Kaufmann presented the court with a motion to secure Jones her doctor-recommended diet.[53]

Jones described her "pretty hectic" daily routine to Kaufmann. At 6:30 am the inmates were awoken by an officer and were expected to arise "immediately." They were then required to get dressed, clean their cells, eat breakfast and be ready to start work at 8:00 am. Jones was assigned to the "weaving room" in the school, which was a "brisk" six-minute walk (though it took her eight minutes) from the cafeteria. At lunchtime, she was barely able to "get her coat off" as she was expected to get food, sit, and eat, and be back at work by 1:00 pm. Work continued until 5:00 pm when it all happened again – walk to get dinner, then return to the "cottage" where they had duties to attend to. Jones was assigned to clean the laundry room. The inmates all did their own laundry and were then locked in at 7:00 pm, lights out at 9:00 pm. She worked five days a week with two days "off," which she described as equally as hectic since they took classes (Jones was taking Spanish) and had to use the rest of their time to clean. Because there was so little down time,

Jones was unable to fully recover and felt ill and tired much of the time.[54]

Charlotta Bass, editor of the Black newspaper *California Eagle* and former President of the STJ, organized a letter-writing campaign to urge Attorney General Herbert Brownell to release Jones. She also assembled a delegation to travel to Washington, DC, in April to pressure politicians to support Jones's release. Ben Davis wrote from his prison cell in Terra Haute, Indiana, to petition for Jones's freedom based on her poor health. Cumberbatch traveled to DC with the delegation to plead his daughter's case. William Patterson joined him, along with James Ford of the National Committee to Defend Negro Leadership (NCDNL), which had been formed to advocate for Black radical leaders under anticommunist attack. The motions filed to release Jones were denied in April, though she did finally manage to get a salt-free diet.[55]

By May 1955, Jones was eligible for parole. Friends, neighbors, and Party comrades spoke before a New York parole board on her behalf. Cumberbatch testified that during his visits to her she was "very ill indeed," though he noted some improvement since she had been receiving the appropriate diet. She continued to experience "cardiac pain" and remained very sick. Paul Robeson also spoke, saying he was moved by Cumberbatch's appeals for his daughter. As a political prisoner, Jones refused to accept guilt and instead noted that her conviction was a violation of her constitutional rights and was politically motivated. Since she would not beg the parole board for forgiveness with promises of reform, her parole was denied on May 4. The board cited the "gravity of offense" and the "lightness of sentence." In July, the Jamaica Federation of Trade Unions sent an appeal to the Attorney General worried about Jones's health and encouraging her early release. She was in the prison hospital again by August with high blood pressure and "low pulsation"; the CRC contacted the parole board asking them once again to consider early release. In September, the NCDNL shared a letter from the Trinidad Independence Party which registered a protest with Brownell against her continued detention. Unfortunately, the appeals went unheeded.[56]

That summer, the murder of Emmitt Till thrust the issue of lynching into the national consciousness and further exposed the US's contradictions in claiming to be a leading democracy. Jones wrote a poem about the murder:

*Lament for Emmitt Till*

Cry lynch murder!
Sear the land
Raise fists – in more than anger bands!

Mother, mother – you who bore
Son from womb of sorrow know
White washed justice sure will reap
More than it can ever sow . . .

Uncle, uncle who stood
Firm-hand in jim crow dock of wood
Facing lynchers eye for eye
Meeting sadism for parading child.

People, people, you who swore
Vengeance for this brutal hour
Make your unity soar above strife
To swiftly avenge young Emmett Till's life![57]

For Jones and the CPUSA, Till's murder evidenced the hypocrisy in the incarceration of communists whose crimes included denouncing lynching. Though it made headlines across the nation, Jones and the Party had long been pointing out the tragedy of unpunished racist violence and how it compromised the US's promises of freedom.

In April, Jones was moved from the "colored cottage" to join Flynn in maximum security, where there was no segregation. She would remain there until her release in October. Flynn described these months as the happiest she had in Alderson. Both women made themselves busy learning new crafts and taking up work mending and sewing. Jones was given a weaving job in the craft shop, where she completed thirty tablecloths used by the staff. She also learned ceramics, pottery, metal jewelry making, woodwork and leather work; the officer in the craft shop told Flynn that Jones was the most talented prisoner she ever saw. She did clay modeling and taught it to the younger women, and taught another to play piano. A table centerpiece and place mats that Jones created won first prize at a local county fair. As Flynn saw it, she and Jones became mentors to many of the younger women inmates, who were poor, uneducated, and had often been abused.[58]

In August, when Jones was back in the hospital, she had three fainting spells and her pulse was dangerously low. She was diagnosed with digitalis poisoning. Her blood pressure was quite high so she was confined to bed. Three weeks prior she had told her father about her low pulse and the dizzy spells; she had also had regular "sick calls" with the prison physician. She chose a "lock in" – being locked in her cell – so that she could take a day of rest, but when she returned to work the next day she felt ill and was immediately hospitalized again.[59]

While imprisoned, Jones and Flynn reflected on the nature of incarceration and criminality in the US. Jones's letters to her attorney were dominated by health updates, but she also occasionally discussed legal issues and wondered about the use of "freedom of association" in their appeals. She argued that with Cold War tensions high, the prosecution of herself and her comrades was making "dangerous inroads" on freedom. Flynn's Alderson memoir focused in part on the failures of the US prison system itself, raising issues that pre-date the current mass incarceration crisis. She dissected the racialization of criminalization, the inadequate efforts at reform, and the roots of recidivism within the very system itself. The Alderson prison, like many institutions in the criminal legal system, was created as part of an effort at reform, and major progressive women's organizations had input into its planning. Women reformers worked with state officials to plan its construction in hopes that the prison would help to reform those detained there, but so many of the women had ended up in the facility because no efforts had been made to help them secure work, education, and economic opportunity on the outside. Flynn described the broken parole system that failed at every level to lessen the cruelties of prison sentences or prepare the women for life outside. In the end, prison could never address the systemic problems that fostered criminality and punitive measures against the most exploited in US culture.[60]

Flynn desperately wanted to see Jones released, but she also had a feeling of "desolation" knowing she would lose her companionship. They had frequent debates and conversations that the other women mistook for arguments. But it was these conversations that eased Flynn's time. For Jones's part, she worried about leaving Flynn behind in maximum security and urged her to request a transfer. Jones was "indignant" that Flynn was being kept there, and worried that she was being taken advantage of by other prisoners. But Jones's poor health made her release urgent. In September she developed a "painful ailment" in her feet which led to a month-long hospital stay. Adding to the women's anxiety was the looming deportation threat. A British government representative visited her in prison to discuss her pending deportation.[61]

Jones's release date had originally been set as January 13, 1956, but she secured an early release in October 1955 for good behavior. The night before her departure, a fellow inmate did Jones's hair. Flynn also assisted Jones in memorizing her prison poetry because she was not allowed to take any of the poems with her. She left one behind for Flynn, and gave each of their cottage mates a gift – one of the craft items she had made. The next morning, October 23, the guard came for her and she went to Flynn's cell to say a hurried goodbye. Flynn described that day as the "hardest" she ever had in prison, and wrote a poem in farewell to Jones (reproduced at the start of this chapter) describing how she would miss her friend and comrade. The two women would never again see each other in person.[62]

## Deportation

The FBI was eager to get Jones out of the country and continued its machinations even while she was imprisoned. Upon her conviction, the Bureau immediately notified the INS. Agents noted the efforts made for her release, the letters supporting parole, and Jones's behavior and health while in prison. They wanted her released directly into INS custody, and assured themselves that, despite her poor health, Jones's ability to withstand the rigors of prison meant she could be detained and expelled from the country. She was denied an administrative stay that would have given her six months in the US after her release, which allowed the FBI to secure a deportation warrant for her immediate removal. The Bureau confirmed a flight to Trinidad on Pan Am.[63]

Days before her release, NCDNL delegates went to the British consulate in New York to ask what Jones's status would be in Trinidad. They were assured that she would not be persecuted for being a communist and that they would not object to a stay of deportation until her health improved. During the conversation, the British officials let slip that her travel papers were ready and that she was scheduled to leave on October 25, only two days after her release and one day after her return to New York. The delegates managed to get the consulate to contact the INS and request a reprieve until Jones recovered. James Ford urged *Daily Worker* readers to "send a flood of letters" to the INS against the "unscrupulous and vindictive" deportation order. Jones's lawyers worked quickly, securing her release into Kaufmann's custody and an injunction against the deportation warrant so there would be time to evaluate her health. The INS removed the immediate warrant, but this did not give her much time.[64]

On the day before her release, prison officials brought in an outside physician to assess Jones's health. Ford believed that the exam was done to confirm she was healthy enough to be forced out of the country, and the doctor did tell Jones she was safe to travel by air to Trinidad. Kaufmann and Jones's father picked her up at Alderson on Sunday, October 23. On the train she wrote down all the poems she had memorized. The three traveled first to Washington, DC, where they met with friends William Patterson and Ford. They stayed there overnight and then traveled to New York's Penn Station, arriving at 10:55 am. In its announcement about Jones's arrival, the *Daily Worker* noted that in the time that federal officials had eagerly pursued the arrest, incarceration, and now deportation of Jones, the killers of Emmitt Till had been exonerated and the Black preacher

Reverend Joseph A. Delaine was run out of South Carolina for advocating civil rights. While Jones faced the full force of government harassment, the anti-Black violence continued unabated. Jones knew that to stay in the United States meant a constant struggle for the freedom of all Black Americans in the face of discrimination; she nevertheless remained committed to working toward Black Freedom. Two days after returning to New York she experienced a "sudden attack" and was taken to Mount Sinai hospital; yet the government still wanted proof that she was too ill to be sent away.[65]

Ford was deeply worried about Jones's deportation, and was particularly worried that "her friends" were not doing enough to prevent it. He wrote a letter of appeal to W.E.B. Du Bois expressing these concerns. He thought that the efforts made on Jones's behalf were "inadequate," but did not entirely blame her friends. He believed that the federal government was harassing her allies. Ford asked Du Bois for a meeting to discuss what could be done. Whether the meeting occurred is not known, but Du Bois would later send his regards to Jones upon her departure, and Bill Mullen argues that the 1961 Supreme Court decision affirming the McCarran Internal Security Act, under which Jones was detained in October 1950, prompted Du Bois to officially join the CPUSA.[66]

Jones's friend and Party chairman William Foster lent his voice to the others hoping to get Jones's stay extended or the deportation order cancelled altogether. In a *Daily Worker* article, Foster wrote about the farce of the Statue of Liberty, with its false promise as a symbol of freedom and refuge. "Reactionary capitalists" were "animated" by the undemocratic policies that dominated US politics. Jones was a freedom fighter whose radicalization came out of American injustice. Foster attacked the theatrics of the Smith Act trials with their "professional informers" and "stupid" charges of sedition. The "cynicism and brutality" of US policy was evident in the fact that the government was pursuing a sick woman.⁶⁷

On November 2, while she was still in the hospital, Jones was granted a one-week stay. A strategy was devised to buy more time. Since Kaufmann was representing Charles Charney and Alex Trachtenberg in their own Smith Act trials, she subpoenaed Jones to testify on their behalf to hold off the INS. This bought her a few more days. However, by the end of November, having spent most of her days of freedom in the hospital, Jones conceded to the deportation. A deal was apparently made between Jones and the British authorities for her to go to England. Accounts of why she was sent to London are mixed and inconsistent. Jones would later say that the British were accommodating and helpful during the ordeal. In a district court memorandum to oppose the original stay, it was claimed that Jones was going to be sent to Jamaica. The FBI, however, noted that a prison informant overheard Jones say that the British wanted to keep an eye on her and did not want her organizing in the colonies. The struggles she had securing a passport once she arrived in England suggest that the British did want to confine her in the country to keep a close watch on her.⁶⁸

Foster asked Jones to send him biographical information so he could write a letter on her behalf to Harry Pollitt, the General Secretary of the Communist Party of Great Britain. The letter Jones wrote is the most important biographical document that researchers have. In it she recounts her youth facing US racism and her eventual radicalization into the CPUSA. She describes her trials and her health, and, briefly and only as an addendum, her marriage. Foster used the letter to introduce Jones to the CPGB. In his own letter, he recounted the legal harassment that led to her deportation, and explained the health issues that concerned and preoccupied so many of her friends and family. He assured Pollitt that Jones was a true freedom fighter and that she had dedicated her whole life to the movement. Foster asked Pollitt to "assist" Jones upon her arrival given that she had never lived in England and was torn from her family and friends. Foster was losing one of his most faithful friends and comrades and the letter was an attempt to ease her exile.[69]

In early December, Foster authored a CPUSA statement condemning the deportation and arguing that Jones had never been charged with an overt crime and that her trial was based on "hysteria and the testimony of informers." The statement highlighted Jones's poor health and the "fantastic ... hysteria" that led to the deportation. The legal action taken against her was a "vindictive" reaction to a "freedom fighter" whose radicalization had been forged in the United States.[70]

On the eve of her departure, hundreds of Jones's allies, friends, and comrades gathered at the Hotel Theresa to say their goodbyes. Telegrams and letters were read out, including one from W.E.B. Du Bois saying "Hail and Farewell." William Patterson said that he was not going to say goodbye because it would reveal a "lack of confidence" in themselves as Jones's friends and comrades. Patterson insisted that they would "pave the way" for her eventual return to the US, as they continued the fight for the dignity of all humans. In that future he hoped there would be no more Herbert Brownells (US Attorney General) or John Foster Dulleses (US Secretary of State), no "White Citizens' Councils," and no racist governors and senators upholding white supremacy. He cited the Geneva Accords that had ended French hostilities in Vietnam the year before as evidence of the change he saw on the horizon. He told the audience that Jones would remain committed to peace and would spread the message that the "racist rulers" in the US are a threat to "all mankind." Claudia, Patterson said, embodied "all that is best in our vast heritage of struggle."[71]

Essie and Paul Robeson visited Jones earlier that day and sent a message to the crowd. In it they noted that "Claudia belongs to us, belongs to America," and that she gave "new life" to US traditions, and especially for the movement toward "human dignity and fulfillment." The Robesons were assured that Jones would continue the fight for "colonial liberation struggles," and said in their message that Jones would be missed and that "our hearts go with you." Jones's father, whose health had taken a toll from his daughter's legal travails, told the crowd that "wherever she goes, Claudia will do her best." Jones made a few closing remarks reminding her comrades about those still imprisoned like Flynn and Davis, and she read a poem to Flynn and dedicated it to the entire audience.[72]

On December 9, 1955, after thirty-two years in the US, Jones's life there ended when she boarded the *SS Queen Elizabeth* in New York Harbor. She was joined by 200 people on the pier in front of the ship, where she made a statement denouncing the McCarran-Walter and Smith Acts as racist and fascist. She believed that Americans were uniting behind peace and equality, despite the laws she described as the "shame of America." She pledged to continue her fight in England. FBI agents were present and watched on as Jones entered her cabin at 1:20 pm with her friend Mildred Edelman, who was traveling with her. The agents noted that she was not observed leaving the cabin; the ship left port at 2:00 pm. The Department of Justice issued a statement the same day saying that her deportation was an example of the "concerted efforts" of the INS to rid the country of those who "accepted our hospitality" but then became part of the "Communist conspiracy against the free world." Jones was removed from J. Edgar Hoover's Security Index, though the

Bureau kept regular tabs on her until 1957, and recorded her death in 1964 in her file. The Cold War state had succeeded in its goal of expelling an important Black radical, though it would never manage to get rid of her influence.[73]

Jones would never step foot in the United States again, but her communist comrades would keep her in remembrance and continue to write and sometimes visit her. Her prolonged imprisonment and eventual deportation are a testament to her conviction that a socialist US was possible and that usurping the capitalist state could usher in liberation. Her body of work in the US provides today's activists with an early critique of women's intersectional experiences, an account of her confrontation with the national security state, criticism of monopoly capitalism, and a vision of an equitable socialist future. Given how eager the government was to use former communists in its legal cases against the Party, Jones could have taken a different route by abandoning her commitments. Perhaps her most enduring legacy is her optimistic faith in the people; she was able to face the unthinkable because of her unshaken belief that they could achieve liberation. This was her commitment until her last days.

# 5

# London (1955–1964)

*Storm at Sea*

Today I saw a storm at sea,
A choppy, fearful sight,
T'was if it were besides itself,
And running from some fright.

Today I saw a storm at sea,
And oh – it gave delight,
It churned and foamed, it rolled and curled
As if from sheer delight.

Today I saw a storm at sea,
Its bilious white and black
It spent its force as if it knew
The power of its back.

Foaming and churning, happy and sad
Bubbling and bleating, all silvery and glad.
       Claudia Jones[1]

Jones would reflect later that her deportation to England was motivated by her efforts to end racism. While her colleagues in the CPUSA saw it as politically motivated, Jones knew that as a Black immigrant committed to a vision of a socialist United States, she represented a threat to the Cold War consensus. Jones spent most of her adult life devoted to a multiracial working-class movement that set out to demolish capitalism and usher in a more just and humane world. As Erik McDuffie describes it, Jones "proffered a politics of possibility" in order to build a "more democratic world." This commitment never wavered, but Jones's life in England and her experience with the Communist Party of Great Britain led her to shift her focus more keenly to England's West Indian community. She became a leader of "young African, Caribbean, and Asian radicals." When she died nine years after her arrival in London, she left behind a legacy deeply rooted in the Caribbean diaspora.[2]

It is these years that Jones has been most remembered for. In London, she is canonized as the founder of Carnival and the editor of the city's most significant Black newspaper of the time. But this legacy has also obfuscated the reality that Jones remained a committed Marxist Leninist who worked to usher in a socialist US and later UK, who believed that monopoly capitalism was untenable for Black and women's liberation, and who warned about the military power of the US and its grip on its allies and their former empires. Jones's deepest conviction was that socialism represented the key to liberation; that legacy has been obscured and the figure of Jones the revolutionary radical has been lost.

## Adjustment in England

Jones arrived in Southampton, England on December 14, 1955. She was greeted by a delegation of local women and fellow deportees John and Mae Williamson, who had been sent back to England earlier that year. The CPGB ran an article in its *Daily Worker* newspaper that day, assuring Jones that she was welcome in the UK and that the McCarran-Walter Act had once again "robbed" the United States. A month later the CPGB introduced Jones to her new comrades in an article that again extended its welcome to her. The article drew on Jones's autobiographical letter to Foster and recounted her immigration to the US, her life in Harlem, the loss of her mother, US racism, and her eventual radicalization to communism.[3]

Jones was now in her new home, but her American comrades would always remain important to her. She would continue to correspond with many of her friends in the CPUSA, and it would occasionally keep tabs on her. In February 1956 she wrote an article for the CPUSA *Daily Worker* about her friends still imprisoned under the Smith Act. She also described the London flat she was living in after her "forcible ejection" from the US by "political deportation." She wrote the article while listening to a radio broadcast about Abraham Lincoln and the US President's power to grant amnesty – something not extended to her. But "uppermost" in her thoughts were her friends still serving their sentences for the "crime of holding independent political ideas." She described the "indignities" of her own prison experience in an attempt to "arouse anger" and a "more urgent amnesty campaign" to free her friends; she specifically mentioned Elizabeth Gurley Flynn and Betty Gannett in Alderson, and Ben Davis, still serving his sentence at a segregated men's facility. What the article did not talk about was Jones's own struggles to settle in a new country while still trying to recover her health.[4]

Jones reserved her complaints for private conversations. In an April 1956 letter to her friend Stretch Johnson she described the difficulties of illness and deportation. Johnson was a fellow Party member and Young Communist League alumnus with whom Jones had once been romantically involved. At the time of the letter, he was married with children. Jones asked after his family, and mentioned that she had spent two months in hospital shortly after her arrival in London. Though Flynn had hoped that Jones might benefit from the "socialized medicine" available in England, her poor health made adjustment to life in the country more difficult. She told Johnson that it was "impossible" to be both "uprooted and ill."[5]

Compounding these issues were housing and other personal problems. She told Johnson that her housing situation was "quite critical." To begin with she had stayed with John and Mae Williamson, then with two other deportees, Charlie and Mikki Doyle. By the time she was writing Johnson, she was eager to find her own place to live. She told him that England was very different than the US – to secure an appropriate rental unit one had to purchase not only furniture but "heating apparatus" and appliances such as "stoves [and] refrigerators," all of which were "costly." Having been imprisoned for almost the entire year before her deportation, and then experienced worsening health, Jones was in financial straits. She depended on the goodwill of the CPUSA and her friends, who occasionally sent money. She was clearly ready to begin making her own way again; her hosts were looking for new accommodation and she was tired of being a guest. A doctor had assured her that with rest she would be able to return to "normal" life after several months, but Jones felt she was ready immediately.[6]

Not only was housing an issue, but being violently uprooted from her old life and her loved ones caused her pain. In her December 1955 autobiographical letter to Foster, she had added a handwritten addendum noting her first marriage and divorce, and her intent to "remarry in England within the next few months." Speculation is that she was dating someone named Pasquale. There is little indication in her letters whether her deportation or the continued political tumult in the US might have caused friction in the relationship, but by 1957 it was over. Her friend Heloise Robinson assured Jones that she had "so much to offer" a man.[7]

Perhaps the biggest blow in the months after her arrival in England was the death of her beloved father. During her imprisonment, Charles Cumberbatch had been in increasingly worrisome health. Nonetheless, he had been by Jones's side from her first arrest onwards, making appeals all the way to the United Nations on her behalf. In June 1955, the CPUSA held an event in his honor to hear him speak about his visits to Jones in prison. He became well acquainted with many of the leaders of the Black left, including Paul Robeson and William Patterson, having traveled with them on Jones's behalf. She wrote him while aboard the ship, describing the kind letters her friends sent to say goodbye and how all the comrades she left behind, as well as her family, were on her mind as she traveled. Whether due to the stress of the state's harassment of his daughter, or his advanced age, Cumberbatch's health declined dramatically after Jones's departure. Heloise Robinson stayed in touch with Cumberbatch and had him over for dinner. In one letter to Jones, she mentioned that he "misses you terribly," but was holding up well despite his "kidney condition." Only months later he died, on June 8, 1956.[8]

Heartbroken and thousands of miles away, Jones wrote a letter of thanks to her American comrades for their condolence letters and their devotion to her father to the very end. She recalled when her father spoke at a meeting of the Smith Act Victims, saying that though he did not agree with her in "every respect," he "respected" her right to her beliefs. For Jones, her father was everything she hoped all "progressive and peace fighters" would be – people who had a mutual respect for differences but shared a hope for a better world. This was the basis of their relationship. She cherished the pride in their "African heritage" he instilled in her, which she learned from his editorship of the *West Indian American News*. He taught his daughters to "think and fight" for what they "believed to be right." It was from him that she learned to resist racist oppression. She concluded her letter by telling her comrades that knowing so many others valued her father was a "balm" in trying to master the pain of her loss.[9] Jones's family remained important to her, and even after her father's death she was close to her sisters. Yvonne traveled to London to see her the month after Charles's death. Lindsay also traveled to England to visit, and one of Jones's cousins lived in London.[10]

Jones spent time reflecting on her deportation. Carole Boyce Davies uses the concept of "migratory subjectivity" to understand Jones's deportation and her remaking in England. Jones saw her expulsion as "exile," which for Boyce Davies meant that she identified as a Black American. Her trip on the *SS Queen Elizabeth* represented a transition in which Jones found a way to redefine herself in a new place. Jones re-oriented and became "more directly pan-Africanist and ... internationalist" in her understanding of Marxist Leninist "world revolution." Part of this would have to do with conflicts she faced within the CPGB, but some of it had to do with her identification with London's

West Indian immigrant community, a population that had been growing and was facing xenophobic laws and racist violence.[11]

In the summer of 1956, Jones did an interview in the *Caribbean News* with George Bowrin, a Trinidadian labor activist. Bowrin asked her why she thought she was deported and if being West Indian had played any role in it. She responded that she was a "victim" of the "McCarthyite hysteria" that silenced independent political voices opposed to the "official pro-war, pro-reactionary, pro-fascist" policies of the white supremacist "ruling class." She explained that anticommunism was racist and that it interpreted antiracist activity as a threat to the state and agitation against Cold War policy as seditious. It was seditious not because it challenged the state, but because it confronted white supremacist capitalism. In this way Jones linked anticommunist legislation like the Smith Act and the McCarran-Walter Act to a capitalist agenda; in effect she was arguing that the state was merely an appendage of capitalist interests.[12]

She continued by emphasizing that she was deported because she was a "Negro woman Communist of West Indian descent." She became a "thorn" in the side of the US government because she opposed racism, demanded "redress of . . . grievances," and sought multiracial unity. She also noted that her demands for women's rights were a threat. But she believed that it was not simply this that made her dangerous – it was because she understood that antiracism, anti-sexism, and working-class unity were a threat to the Cold War state. She argued for "improving" people's lives rather than a "huge arms budget." For Jones, the McCarran-Walter Act highlighted the racism of the anticommunist state; she told Bowrin that the Act limited West Indian immigration, thus her own West Indian heritage, along with her communism, were central to her expulsion.[13]

She described US racism as a "scourge" that touched all Black America and noted that it was only the CPUSA that stood up to it. It was her experience of racism in the United States that drew her to communism, and her belief was that only the CPUSA could confront it. This was in part why the US government tried to dissolve the Party and criminalized its leadership. Jones's communism would remain strong, but as Boyce Davies has argued, she would remake herself once in London. Not even a year out of prison, and only months after her deportation, Jones was already showing signs that her politics were moving toward Pan-Africanism. In response to a question from Bowrin about West Indian women, she noted that they were triply oppressed, much like their Black American sisters, but their oppression was as women, mothers, and "colonials." These women were "subjected to indignities" because of the "status of their countries." Jones was engaging an internationalist, anti-imperialist feminism outside of a Western framework. She argued that colonial women like her experienced national oppression. But, as Boyce Davies argues, Jones would continue to view anti-imperialism through a Marxist Leninist lens.[14]

Jones's housing issue was temporarily resolved by May 1956. She moved to South London, where she rented a flat on Meadow Road from Reverend Hewlett Johnson, the "'Red' Dean of Canterbury." She asked the CPUSA for assistance and Johnson helped her with the "fixtures and fittings." She lived in the flat until 1960, but would face regular financial problems and had to make a deal with Johnson to cover unpaid rent in 1959. She also took on a sub-letter, but this did not appear to ease her ability to cover the rent. Jones's financial straits would never quite be resolved. Heloise Robinson wrote Lorraine Hansberry a letter in 1960 expressing concern about their "mutual friend" who had just had to move into another flat. Robinson had just returned from a visit with Jones and had discovered that the costs of living in the new place were "atrocious." Jones was only able to afford to eat meat "twice a week," securing a flat was difficult partly because of the "color tax" imposed on people of color in the city, and the situation was worse for Jones because she was in exile with little control over her own circumstances. Robinson also expressed her chagrin at the fact that there had been a lack of "organizational responsibility," even though Jones had been expelled because she was a communist. It's not clear whether she was referring to the CPUSA or the CPGB, but the purpose of her letter was to ask Hansberry for any financial help she could provide.[15]

Marika Sherwood has argued that Jones's dire financial situation was largely down to the CPGB being unable or unwilling to find her suitable employment, even after her years of service to the Party in the United States. She had served as a leading figure in the CPUSA, wrote frequent theoretical articles, served on the National Committee, led the Women's Bureau, and was editor of several Party papers. Since 1936, Jones had not only been a CPUSA member, she was also an employee. Despite William Foster's appeals, the CPGB would never employ Jones in the same way. She was given a job at the *New China News* as a "typist," and maybe as an editor, but was later removed after being accused of inefficiency and of having personal problems with someone named "Comrade Sam." Jones protested her dismissal in a memo, claiming that the staff felt she was just an "invalid" who had been dumped on them. Sherwood notes that between losing her job at the *New China News* and the founding of the *West Indian Gazette* in 1958, it is unclear what Jones's employment status was, but her "financial worries were constant."[16]

She also faced travel restrictions when her passport applications were denied, reminiscent of the harassment she and her colleagues faced in the US. Shortly after her arrival in the UK she wanted to secure a passport and a travel visa for Prague, which was denied on January 12, 1956. In her letter to Stretch Johnson she mentioned her attempts to secure a passport to go to a "warmer clime," and that she had found a hospital in "the land of my birth" that could provide treatment for her heart condition. She had made at least two applications by this point, and provided medical records, but was again denied. In the summer of 1957, she wrote a letter to Dr. Eric Williams – who would later become the first Prime Minister of Trinidad and Tobago – asking him to intervene in her passport applications. She wanted to travel to Nice, France, on a trip likely paid for by friends. Her application was approved but only for France. She tried again the next year, this time in order to attend a peace conference in Bulgaria, but was denied yet again. Ben Davis suspected that the US State Department had been discouraging the British from approving her passport. This was likely, since the State Department intervened to prevent W.E.B. Du Bois and his wife Shirley from travelling to Canada, a country with open borders with the US. Jones had always suspected that the British wanted to keep her close, given her long history of organization. Her passport was not approved for travel to the "British commonwealth and all Foreign countries" until 1962.[17]

## CPGB

The Communist Party of Great Britain publicly embraced Jones, but her relationship with the organization was strained and would remain so for the duration of her life in England. According to Sherwood, to understand Jones's problems with the CPGB it is important to recognize that, while the CPUSA had its problems with racism, it at least acknowledged racism and had Black leadership. The CPGB did not discuss race, and even though it had taken part in anticolonial campaigns since its founding, its antiracist work was limited. One example is the Party's awkward relationship with the Scottsboro campaign, which has been explored by Susan Pennybacker. In 1932, Ada Wright, the mother of Roy and Andy Wright, two of the Scottsboro boys, toured England to raise money and international awareness. She was received well and the CPGB did actively engage with the tour, but its involvement might have been due to a 1930 Comintern memo that derided the Party for its "inexcusable passivity and neglect" on race and anticolonialism and its failure to address increased discrimination in its own country. Pennybacker argues that its interest might also have stemmed from the Labour Party's involvement with the tour at a time when the CPGB was seeking an alliance with Labour. But the Party might also have used it to shift attention from racism within its own ranks and in the UK by focusing on the US's problems instead.[18]

In 1955 when Jones arrived, the CPGB had no Black members in leadership positions. That year it adopted the "Charter of Rights for Coloured Workers in Britain," allegedly in response to outside pressure. The charter had four points: racial discrimination should be a "penal offense"; Britain's discriminatory legislation against "coloured workers" should be opposed; there should be equality in wages and employment; and "coloured workers" should be encouraged to join trade unions. Despite the forceful stand, the Party "avoided analysing" why "colonial workers" were treated as a problem. Evan Smith argues that the Party's policy on the maintenance of trade between the former colonies and the metropole became another issue for its African and Caribbean membership, including Jones. On the surface, the CPGB was anti-imperialist, but it assumed that trade would continue unchanged between Britain and its colonies in the postcolonial world.[19]

The CPGB did have a branch of the Caribbean Labor Congress (CLC) which issued the *Caribbean News*, but the paper did not receive financial support from the Party. The communist Billy Strachan was its editor, and under his leadership it became the first paper to raise awareness of the situation of West Indians in London. It also went beyond the CPGB analysis on race. But by 1956, the CLC was gone. That same year, Khrushchev's revelations about Stalin's purges caused ripples across international communism; the CPGB lost almost a quarter of its members. Jones's arrival in England caused her personal turmoil, but she also faced a Party struggling internally.[20]

In March 1957, a report titled "West Indians in Britain" circulated in the Party. Sherwood believes that the report's tone and forceful language indicates that Jones was the likely author. Jones brought with her two decades of antiracist activism, and she put it to good use in an organization that was dominated by white activists and leaders. In a similar vein to her 1949 Neglect article, the report argues that the CPGB had "seriously neglected" its work among immigrants and "coloured workers." It also suggested that the Party extend its focus to include the equal rights struggles in the colonies. The CPGB's 25th Congress, held the same year, would give the African and Caribbean members an opportunity to confront their white comrades. Jones attended as the "Vauxhall and Tulse Hill" delegate.[21]

At the Congress, the African and Caribbean membership called for the CPGB's programme, *The British Road to Socialism*, to recognize the independence of former colonies from the Commonwealth. This challenged the Party's assumption that the colonies would remain (unequal) trade partners with Britain – a view that dominated because leaders wanted to maintain the "standard of living" in the metropole. It was an "imperialist assumption" and those who had lived in the colonies challenged it. Smith argues that this did, in the short term, change the Party's position on anti-imperialism and led it toward participation in "anti-colonial and anti-racist movements," including the anti-Apartheid campaign.[22]

Jones stood with her African and Caribbean comrades in challenging the policy. She presented a statement opening with a conciliatory remark thanking her British comrades for embracing her after the "American imperialist reaction" to her struggles in the US. She encouraged "greater solidarity" with the "colonial peoples ... and coloured workers," arguing that this was in the "self-interest" of the British working class. All these groups shared similar oppression from "monopoly capitalists" who exploit working-class labor but "super-exploit the colonies." She wanted an acknowledgement of this to help further a "joint struggle against the common evil of imperialism." Jones moved toward anticolonialism and anti-imperialism out of necessity as she struggled with her British comrades for a basic reckoning of their own commitment to the empire.[23]

She argued that the "science" of Marxist Leninism was the "antithesis of exploitation" and represented a total rejection of racist and "chauvinist" ideology. She often warned her American comrades that chauvinism lurked within the CPUSA, and she was now standing before her white British comrades declaring that they were not "automatically" absolved by their colonial comrades, who suspected many of them were infected with "imperialist ideology." This was a safe assumption given the CPGB's imperialist policy and (as Sherwood notes) the common saying that if you "scrape the skin off a British communist you'll find an imperialist."[24]

Jones warned that even after achieving socialism, it was not safe to assume that chauvinism would be gone. She was speaking here of "big-nation chauvinism," in this case the British communists' attitude toward colonials. Jones never accepted the argument parroted by white communists in Britain and elsewhere that socialism would cure the evils of racism and sexism; in England, Party members could not assume that anti-colonialism translated to an embrace of colonized peoples. She counseled that people remember the lessons of Lenin: comrades had to go out of their way to "allay these suspicions and fears" through action and not just talk. This was an important emphasis in the year after Khrushchev's revelations about Stalin. Jones became a communist at the height of Stalin's purges and Party members were all too aware of them; she pitched her stakes with Leninism and not Stalinism. Jones continued her talk by challenging the idea that colonized people were "backward," and listed the struggles against imperialism in Korea, China, and India as proof that this assumption was racist. Jones's group succeeded in getting the CPGB to change its stance and include a change in policy toward the colonies in the Party's programme.[25]

This did not dissolve the tension between Jones and the Party, but it does demonstrate her attempt to engage with the CPGB. In the summer of 1957, she wrote an article titled "West Indians in Britain" for a special issue of *World News* on imperialism. Sherwood argues that the article is "mild" in comparison to Jones's usual writing, but it reads very much like some of her articles written during her CPUSA years. She often wrote about the shortcomings within the Party, but at the same time encouraged her comrades in their work and was committed to the belief that it was communists who should lead the march toward equality. In the 1957 article Jones addressed the question of West Indian immigration and the concerns of the political parties. She began by saying that the West Indians, who had endured hundreds of years of labor exploitation, were emigrating because there were few jobs and poor wages in the colonies. The colonies continued to be exploited for raw materials, and British imperialist interests remained strong. In effect, the increase in West Indian immigration was a direct result of British policy.[26]

She accused the Tories of "making scapegoats of social minorities" by blaming them for taking jobs. This capitalist obfuscation was a tactic used then (as now) to distract from policies that guaranteed capital accumulation among the wealthy, while workers were left fighting over the scraps. Jones's analysis included an account of what today we would call systemic racism – the unseen and not "openly expressed" means of keeping West Indian workers struggling for the lowest paid jobs in the economy, living in poor housing, and facing paternalism from white workers. She warned against fascist tendencies within the ranks of the working class, explicit in the Ku Klux Klan but also present in the resistance of white workers to organizing immigrants into their unions. She urged the Party to focus on the true enemies of the worker: the "Tory ruling class and the imperialist system."[27]

Jones encouraged support for a bill, introduced by Labour MP Fenner Brockway, that would make racial discrimination a penal offense and would guarantee equal access to employment and promotion. She also wanted the trade unions to welcome West Indian immigrants into their ranks. There were several that had already committed in principle to anti-discrimination policies, particularly in industries where West Indian workers could be found in large numbers, like railways and post offices, but the unions failed to uphold their own policies. Jones credited the CPGB with pushing this issue within the unions and drawing in the support of West Indian workers.[28]

The tension between Jones and the CPGB did not affect her commitment to communism; she remained a Party member until her death and participated in campaigns and other programs with fellow communists. But the distance between her and the Party did open up opportunities for her to collaborate with others, including C.L.R. James, a fellow Trinidadian, and a Trotskyite. James was a vocal critic of both the Party and Stalin, and, as Boyce Davies suggests, there is no indication that they worked closely together. But they reportedly appeared on a panel discussion with one another and were both featured in a 1964 issue of *Freedomways*, a radical magazine founded by Jones's American colleagues W.E.B. and Shirley Du Bois, Louis Burnham, and Edward Strong. Whatever their relationship might have been, this collaboration indicates that Jones operated without seeking Party permission.[29]

She did participate in CPGB efforts to rally around harassed American comrades, including Paul Robeson, who was a popular entertainer in Europe. The National Paul Robeson Committee was formed to urge the US government to return his passport. Jones wrote an article for her US friends about the CPGB efforts to secure Robeson's right to travel. She described a meeting of Yorkshire miners who read greetings from Robeson at a gala, and the condemnation by radio personalities like Gilbert Harding who called Robeson's travel restrictions a contradiction of US liberty. She also cited Richard Coppock, a leading unionist, who argued that a nation that sought freedom for others should first secure it for its own people. Jones wrote that the British people recognized the harassment as a reaction to Robeson's vocal antiracism, and encouraged global protests against his persecution. The British *Daily Worker* might not have featured Jones, but her American friends continued to do so in their publications.[30]

The Robesons would have their passports returned to them in 1958. They left the US immediately and moved to London, where they would live for the next five years. Jones greeted her friends when they arrived, and she would frequently socialize with them during their time there. She also worked with the Robesons, particularly Essie, on political programs and in organizations. One such organization was the African Women's Freedom Movement, founded by Essie in 1961. Jones would become an active member. They organized "Africa Women's Day" on December 7, 1961, to inaugurate the group, and the two women shared a stage to discuss the organization and Black women's political issues. The same year that the Robesons arrived, Jones took up her biggest project in England yet.[31]

## West Indian Gazette and Afro-Asian Caribbean News

Donald Hines, one of Jones's friends and comrades in London, wrote about the setting up of the *West Indian Gazette* (*WIG*), later called *West Indian Gazette and Afro-Asian Caribbean News*, for which he was a reporter. He noted that from the beginning it faced conflicts, but at the same time was fulfilling an important need. As the *Caribbean News* had failed to become a popular news outlet for Black and West Indian readers, the West Indian Workers and Students Association, a new organization formed in 1957, discussed founding its own paper. Jones, having had a lengthy journalistic career in the US, wrote a report about creating a paper, and by March 1958 a sample *West Indian Gazette* was being circulated. Its first run reached 25,000 readers.

For its first five years, the *WIG* ran its operations out of a two-room office in South London above a record shop. The paper was not the first Black newspaper in England, but it was the first commercial Black newspaper, and the "sole voice" for the Black community between 1958 and 1965. Jones, who was elected editor, would spend a great deal of time seeking advertisers as a source of income. Meanwhile, there were issues on the editorial board, chaired by George Bowrin, with people leaving after disagreements over competing visions. Boyce Davies argues that the *WIG*, despite its early troubles, would become one of the "defining forces" in England's Caribbean community.[32]

Jones described the *WIG* as a "catalyst" that "quickened the awareness" of England's West Indians and their "Afro-Asian friends." The paper advocated independent, self-governing West Indian nations with "full economic, social, and political equality." It also demanded "human dignity" for West Indians living in Britain. The *WIG* was a political organ that participated in campaigns against "police frame-ups" and sought white and Black unity among workers. It expressed solidarity between West Indians and the "liberation struggles in Africa and Asia," and was modeled on the Black press that "uncompromisingly and fearlessly" fought against "imperialist outrages and indignities."[33]

After some disagreement with the West Indian Workers and Students Association over who owned the paper, Jones eventually secured the *WIG* and began circulating it across the country. Financial problems would plague the paper for its entire existence, making it impossible to take on "paid staff." Jones's good friend Amy Ashwood Garvey was listed as an editor, and Abhimanyu Manchanda (known as Manu) became the "Managing Director and Editor." Ken Kelly from Trinidad, Jan Carew from Guyana, and Donald Hines from Jamaica would all write for the paper without being paid.

This forced them to find income elsewhere while remaining contributors. It also meant that Jones's income would be inconsistent as she struggled to make the paper solvent. The *WIG* offices became a site of political activity and organizing, and some of Jones's political comrades would sometimes provide uncompensated help at the paper.[34]

During her time in London, Jones's friendship with Manu was one of her longest and closest. Born in India, Manu was a fellow CPGB member and it was he who had helped secure her a position at the *New China News*. Jones sublet a room in her flat to him. Manu was a difficult person, and Sherwood notes that there was an almost "universal dislike" of him. Some of Jones's friends feared that he used her financially, but their shared rent was frequently late and Jones was perpetually short of cash. Jones assisted Manu in creating the Indian Workers' Association (IWA) within the CPGB, and he split his time between this organization and the *WIG*.[35]

Amy Ashwood Garvey was in Ghana at the time of the *WIG*'s founding, but she was asked to be the paper's "honorary president" and happily agreed. Jones asked Garvey to write an article on the West Indian Federation – a short-lived attempt by the British colonies to create an independent coalition government – and "possible independence for the Caribbean." Jones wanted Garvey to report on how Ghanaians viewed this development, considering the proposal from Kwame Nkrumah (the first President of independent Ghana) for a similar "Pan-African Federation." The article would be featured in the *WIG*'s inaugural issue. But as Garvey's biographer Tony Martin explains, her association with the communist Jones caused some problems. Garvey opened an "Afro-Woman's Center" in London which served as a "community center, restaurant, boarding house, welfare agency," and the headquarters of several businesses. The building was purchased by Sir Hamilton Kerr of the Conservative Party, and he provided a £500 monthly allowance. Kerr complained that Garvey's association with a communist had led to his phone being tapped and he insisted that she cut all ties. Garvey reportedly told Kerr to "Go to hell," and that he could stick his £500 "where the monkey put the ripe banana." Garvey was not about to abandon her friend Jones; she also served as a "major source of subsidies" for the *WIG*.[36]

Despite the hopes of those involved, the paper never gained the wide circulation needed to sustain it. Its circulation peaked in 1958 at 30,000; the following spring it was down to 10,000. Jones would struggle to keep the *WIG* afloat. She also pushed to make it not just a newspaper but a philanthropic and political organization. In 1963, when Hurricane Flora struck Trinidad and Tobago, Jones organized a fundraiser featuring Nadia Cattouse, an actress and friend. Hines claims that Jones's reputation meant that few people ever said no to her, and she generally managed to organize important West Indian names for her events. The committee for hurricane relief included C.L.R. James, Pearl Connor, and Edric Connor, founders of the first Black theater company, and author George Lamming, among others. This also shows that Jones's distance from the CPGB allowed her to collaborate outside Party ranks.[37]

Jones's US friends celebrated her paper as well. Elizabeth Gurley Flynn wrote about her correspondence with Jones in the CPUSA's *Sunday Worker*. She told American readers about Jones's important work in London and described the *WIG*'s purpose: to challenge British racism and imperialism. Flynn described articles on South African apartheid and Jim Crow in Arkansas, and Jones's success in getting local dance halls to desegregate. She likened the West Indian's experience in England to that of the Puerto Rican in the United States: both were technically citizens but were treated as inferior colonial subjects and denied basic citizenship rights like voting. Flynn was confident that Jones, with her decades of experience in the US, was fully equipped to take on the work of organizing London's West Indian community. She closed by encouraging her readers to subscribe and donate to the *WIG* to help it in its work.[38]

Paul Robeson would often stop at the *WIG* offices to offer his support. In July 1959, the paper hosted a "Meet Paul Robeson" event at Lambeth town hall. Jones billed the event as an opportunity for Robeson to meet with his African, Caribbean, and British friends for the first time since his return to England. In her opening remarks, she praised the Robesons' work toward "equality, security, human dignity, and the brotherhood of all peoples." Jones needed capital to run the newspaper and she enlisted her famous friend to help. As she told Essie in a letter, she did not want to become a "mercenary" about it, but she did want to ensure the work of the *WIG* continued. She mentioned how exhausting it was trying to keep the paper running while also doing all her political organization. In the same letter, she asked if Paul could do another benefit for them later in the year.[39]

The Robesons were among Jones's greatest champions. In September 1959, both were featured speakers at events for the paper. Paul Robeson's speech was reprinted in the *WIG*. He opened by saying that the *WIG* was his favorite newspaper because it was "courageous . . . deeply human" and committed to a "decent life for us all." He discussed his travels and contact with African and Asian people who were devoted to a peaceful, humane future. He specifically mentioned his support of South Africans. Robeson also invoked Black American history, calling up the ancestors Harriet Tubman and Sojourner Truth who had labored for freedom. He then encouraged those present at the talk and those reading the speech later to support "our Claudia Jones" and the

*WIG*. The following year Robeson was again featured in a benefit concert for the paper.[40]

## Riots

Events in London would drive Jones further toward her work in Pan-Africanism and away from the CPGB. Postwar England was in transition as millions of immigrants from Commonwealth countries came seeking work in the metropole just as urban centers were engaging in slum clearance to remake cities. The urban renewal plans uprooted 5 million Britons while over 2 million immigrants arrived. In this atmosphere tensions increased between white communities and immigrant communities and boiled over in August 1958 in the Notting Hill and Nottingham riots. Hundreds of "Negro-baiting" white residents chanting "Keep Britain White!" targeted "West Indian, Pakistani, and African" immigrants for a week, some calling for murder and lynching. The white rioters were encouraged by a Jeffrey Hamm speech. Hamm was a leader in "Oswald Mosley's Union movement." As Kennetta Hammond Perry notes, Mosley's movement was a "fascist organization" that protested the "coloured invasion." Hamm's speech, given days into the riots, was "obviously hoping to cultivate and exploit" the anxieties of the rioters.[41]

News of the riots spread globally at the same time as racist violence was getting press in the US. This led many observers to question England's "moral leadership on a world stage." The riots challenged what Hammond Perry calls the "mystique of British anti-racism" with its "collective myths" about the antiracism of "British liberalism" that existed in the England of Jones's time and still today. This mystique was rooted in British abolitionism and a belief in the nation's supposed tolerance and "benevolence" toward its colonial subjects. For Hammond Perry, this was a "potent element" in the representation of the nation and its people in the postwar world. The riots challenged this image and "tempered" the reaction of the British people. But the "extant racial realities" were "embodied" by England's West Indian community. These contradictions were at the forefront for the Western democracies in the Cold War world as they tried to pose as moral paragons internationally while the reality of life for people of color in those nations was in stark contrast. The riots led to questions about British tolerance and comparisons with the Jim Crow South in the US. Policymakers doubled down on the "mystique of British anti-racism" by "reconciling the violence" and deploying myths that ignored Britain's imperialist history, all of which worked in support of "keeping Britain white."[42]

In the days after the riots, Jones stepped up to try to quell community anxieties and find common ground with neighbors, while political leaders claimed that only troublesome whites were the perpetrators, or that it was caused by massive immigration and West Indian men dating white women. Hines wrote that Jones's exceptional history of political organization meant that she was fully prepared to confront the situation and challenge the scapegoating. The *WIG* offices became a safe place for people who were affected by the riots. Because the building was in the Black community, neighbors came in and Jones would counsel those ready to go back to the Caribbean to remain in the UK and fight. She was also visited by Caribbean leaders like Eric Williams, Norman Manley (who would later become Jamaican Prime Minister), and Phyllis Alfrey of the West Indian Federation.[43]

The same month as the riots, the *WIG* received a threatening letter from the Ku Klux Klan. It demanded that two copies of the paper be sent to its office each month, and claimed that the "Aryan Knights" miss nothing because they had been paying attention to the *WIG*. The letter stated that the paper had information that was of "great value" to the Klan and said, by way of veiled threat, that it wished the paper success while they were "able to run it." It was signed "A. Whiteman." Days later the *WIG* offices were broken into and trashed. Another letter was received that attacked the paper for mongrelizing "our proud heritage" and the Klan's goal to "Keep Britain pure and white!" The CPUSA *Worker* reported on the second letter in September, noting that the US and Britain both insisted they were the "bastions of democracy" while the Klan and its members harassed fellow Americans and Britons. Flynn wrote that the KKK's response to the *WIG* was clear evidence of the paper's success, and its continued determination to publish demonstrated Jones's resolve to fight British racism.[44]

Many have testified that the *WIG* was wildly influential on Black Britons and that it carved out a place in Black British journalism. Bill Schwarz argues that it was certainly influential in the Black community but that it also influenced the white population by "providing the means" for them to understand and accept a post-imperial England. It was the West Indian immigrants who, though legally British, faced daily racist insults and were left to imagine life after colonialism. West Indians had the "means to think through these issues" and brought with them a culture that was integrated into British "metropolitan culture." In the aftermath of the riots, those who decided to stay realized that the only "cultural resources" they could depend on were those they made themselves. For Schwarz, the *WIG*, still only months old during the riots, became a "public voice" to articulate the community's "hopes and fears."[45]

Schwarz sees evidence of the "creolization" of London in the wider circulation of the *WIG* across the city and in its sponsorship of events that brought Caribbean culture (specifically music) into public consciousness. Hinds has argued similarly that in the Britain Jones left behind there was regular prejudice and hostility toward Afro Asians, making the popularity today of things like curries significant given the previous hostilities. For Schwarz and Hines, while Jones's work with the *WIG* made significant inroads, it was the launch of Carnival in the aftermath of the riots that is perhaps her most remembered contribution. The combination of the *WIG* and Carnival were the "means" by which a "West Indian communist conscious of . . . history" made her impact known on "British soil."[46]

## Carnival

The first Carnival, sponsored by the *WIG*, was organized in less than two months. The idea of the event was to unite London's communities and introduce Britons to West Indian culture. The publicity for it indicated that the "proceeds" of the Carnival brochure would be donated to pay the "fines of coloured and white youths" who had been involved in the riots. Jones titled the brochure "A people's art is the genesis of their freedom," making an explicit connection between politics and art. As later observers noted, many expected the communist Jones to be staid and serious, but she liked to party, and she appreciated the political value of art. Carnival was the truest reflection of Jones. The brochure included a statement from her acknowledging that West Indian people wanted to bring their culture to London, but also reminding them of the need for community in the wake of the riots. She wrote in support of the West Indian Federation and her pride in being West Indian and embracing national identity, as well as the contribution of West Indians to the world.

Jones closed by stating that the committee hoped to make Carnival an annual event. Some early participants believed that her goal was not only to bring the community together but also to convince people to stay. It was also a gesture toward interracial solidarity.[47]

The event was held indoors at St. Pancras Hall in February 1959, a seasonally inappropriate time but chosen because it coincided with Carnival in the Caribbean. It was broadcast live on the BBC, bringing West Indian food, music, and dance to a wider audience. Colin Prescod – the son of Pearl Prescod, an actress and Jones's friend – has written that Jones's importance to the larger West Indian community is evident in the number of celebrities she was able to secure for the annual celebration. Jones was in "active contact" with notable Caribbean and African artists, many of whom she brought to London. In 1962, she was able to secure one of the most famous West Indian artists to perform at Carnival, the Grenadian Slinger Francisco, better known as "The Mighty Sparrow, king of calypsonians."[48]

One of the main features of Carnival was the Carnival Queen. As Prescod points out, beauty pageants might offend the sensibility of feminists today, but for the Carnival to assert the beauty of Blackness at that time was bold and revolutionary. Rochelle Rowe argues that Jones modeled Carnival after the Trinidad celebration which annually crowned its queen. She combined her desire to bring attention to Black women's experiences with the goal of challenging the "racist beauty politics" that often "marginalized them." Jones sought to bring Black women "from the periphery to the centre." The pageant was not meant to involve a reductive focus on women's physicality, but was a celebration of Black women and a direct challenge to racist typologies.[49]

For Rowe, the *WIG* and Carnival were expressions of Jones's specifically Marxist view of nationalism as a "community of nations" of oppressed people. Jones understood that West Indian immigrants in the metropole faced British racism daily and she wanted to encourage them to embrace their "common history and culture." The beauty pageant and the *WIG* became a part of this movement and were a form of "cultural and racial resistance." Unlike the beauty pageants in the Caribbean, Jones's version refused to affirm the value of "light-skinned" Black women and thereby confronted the "racial system of British colonialism" perpetuated by many of the middle-class West Indian organizers. Jones's youth had coincided with the rise of a beauty industry whose emphasis for Black women was on hair straightening and skin lightening as an avenue into middle-class "respectability." But in Harlem, Jones was also exposed to resistance to these expectations and a growing embrace of and pride in Blackness.[50]

Rowe argues that Jones was interested in "beauty culture" in order to help Black women acquire the "markers of femininity and beauty." At the Afro People's Centre, a community center, she created the "Black Sash movement," which presented Black women with awards for "special achievements"; she also reportedly used her own hair salon appointments as opportunities for political recruitment, and attended the graduation ceremonies of Madame Rose's Academy of Beauty Culture, where Black women trained as "hairdressers and beauticians." At one graduation Jones gave the graduates prizes and attempted to recruit people into political activism. The *WIG* also featured a beauty column.[51]

The Carnival pageant judges included many of the same people Jones had recruited for the *WIG*, among them "artists, intellectuals, and notable persons" such as Jan Carew, George Lamming, politicians Nigel Fisher and Marcus Lipton, and others. In their selection process, the pageant organizers purposefully included women of various skin tones. Actress Corinne Skinner-Carter remembers that the first Carnival Queen, Fay Sparks, was very dark, which she believed was notable because of the common association between light skin and beauty. Rowe argues that Jones attempted to appeal to women who could show "confidence" and that she rejected the emphasis on lighter skin tone. Even so, her need to generate revenue for the *WIG* was so pressing that the paper frequently featured skin-bleaching advertisements. The pageant contestants were given prizes and the winners were often gifted with international trips. The *WIG* would report on the winners in years after as evidence that women could "pursue viable careers." For Rowe, the pageant "affirmed Black womanhood" as the "cornerstone" of Jones's "anti-racist and community building work."[52]

Part of the work Carnival and the *WIG* did in London was also commercial, which, as Schwarz argues, was another paradox given Jones's communism. The *WIG* advertised Carnival to create interracial friendships. Advertising in the paper included products popular among West Indians, such as Mount Gay Rum and Red Stripe beer. The paper also featured Caribbean recipes and listed places in the city where specific products or produce could be bought. The popularity of these products and others in Britain today is not in itself evidence of impact on white communities, but Schwarz reasons that the colonized peoples who brought their Britishness to the metropole, along with their products and anti-colonial critiques, are evidence of influence.[53]

The 1958 riots prompted much of Jones's political and social organizing within London's West Indian community. Amy Garvey had returned to London after the riots, and served as a judge for many of the Carnival Queen contests. She also helped found the Association for the Advancement of Colored People (AACP), an organization modeled after its US counterpart the NAACP. Tony Martin argues that for Amy this was an important departure from the position of her ex-husband Marcus Garvey, given his frequent clashes with the NAACP. Labour MP Fenner Brockway became a Vice-President, Jones was the organizations secretary, and Manu was an assistant secretary. The AACP was set up in response to the riots, and Garvey and Jones actively lobbied to reduce the punishment for the West Indians involved in the violence. Both women represented the AACP on the United Defense Committee Against Discrimination, which had brought several organizations together in the wake of the riots. It issued "An Appeal to Good Will" articulating the complaint that while white rioters were set free, Black rioters who responded in self-defense were being punished. Manu also served on the committee, representing the *WIG*.[54]

Hammond Perry argues that while the AACP included several leading London activists, it was the collaboration between Jones and Garvey that would prove most significant in pushing the organization forward. The women's ties "ran deep" and they shared an "internationalist and diasporic" perspective on Black liberation. Most important, they were devoted to the idea of Black women as being central to the "quest for radical social transformation." Jones centered Black women and their "(re)productive labor" in the "liberatory possibilities" that would reimagine and remake ideas of citizenship for people of color. This thought was exemplified in her most famous piece of writing, the 1949 Neglect article, but she had been articulating a gendered emancipatory ethos for decades, and she would bring this to her London organizing. It would also tie her to Garvey and Essie Robeson, who shared the same commitment.[55]

The good will that Jones and her friends were working hard to build was nearly shattered in the spring of 1959 when Kelso Cochrane, an Antiguan immigrant, was murdered by six white men. Cochrane had moved to the United States in the late 1940s but struggled financially. When his work visa expired he returned to Antigua but hoped to return to the US. He was prevented because of the McCarran-Walter Act in 1952 which restricted West Indian immigration – the same act that enabled Jones's deportation. In 1954, Cochrane moved to London instead, hoping to pursue a career in law. On the evening of May 17, 1959, Cochrane, a trained carpenter, told his fiancée Olivia Ellington that he was going to hospital to get treatment for his injured thumb after a work accident. Witnesses saw six white men surround Cochrane and call him "Jim Crow"; they then attacked him and stabbed him in the chest. Bystanders took Cochrane to a nearby hospital, where he died. Scotland Yard officials avoided any speculation about it being a racial incident, and emphasized that Cochrane's dying words were that the men were trying to rob him.[56]

The next day the *WIG* sent a delegation to a meeting of the Council of African Organizations (CAO) and signed on to a letter to Prime Minister Harold Macmillan stating that the attack was racially motivated and asking public officials to condemn it. In a press statement the CAO likened the attack to the racist violence seen in the US. A meeting and a vigil were held in the days after the murder. Essie Robeson spoke at both, emphasizing that Cochrane was murdered because of "racial prejudice and hatred" and insisting that the racist attacks had to be addressed.[57]

Jones wrote an editorial reminding the *WIG* readers that racist violence remained a threat. She pointed to the short memories of so many people who seemed to have forgotten the violence of the riots the year before. West Indians faced daily insults, "colour bar" practices, and harassment in public places, while the police and local white community remained indifferent. She wrote about the case of Joseph Dill Simon, who had been shot in the wrist while walking with a friend.

Simon described the white man who shot him, but the police did not believe him, instead assuming that the attacker was a local Black immigrant. Jones lamented that while "fascists" were on the attack, little was being done by officials.[58]

The Inter-Racial Friendship Coordinating Council (IRFCC) organized a delegation to speak to Home Office officials about their concern at the growing racist violence and the fact that blame was being shifted onto the West Indian community. The IRFCC was created as a "burial committee" to raise money for Cochrane's funeral, which was held three weeks after his murder. Jones, Garvey, Frances and Donald Ezzrecco, and actress Pearl Connor and her husband Edric were part of the delegation. They insisted that the West Indian community should not be punished for local white racism and urged that studies be undertaken in the affected communities to help find solutions. They advocated for a bill to make "racial discrimination and propaganda" illegal. The delegation also sent a memo to officials making it clear that inaction and continued racist violence would do serious damage to England's international standing. Unfortunately, British officials seemed to be leaning toward the US tactic of dismissing such demands as communist propaganda and keeping tabs on activists. Scotland Yard claimed that Garvey was close to the communists and that Jones was a "self-confessed communist."[59]

A week later, on June 1, 1959, the Coloured People's Progressive Association (CPPA) sponsored a twelve-hour vigil outside 10 Downing Street. The CPPA was founded by Frances and Donald Ezzrecco after the riots to promote "democracy, interracial unity," and the "social incorporation" of West Indians. Jones was a leading figure in both the IRFCC and the CPPA along with Garvey. Jones attended the vigil, which went ahead despite the rainy weather. While Jones was actively trying to get the government to address the violence, she remained devoted to her hopes for an interracial coalition of people to make substantive change. But even as she and others were preaching unity, government officials were beginning to lean toward introducing restrictions on immigration.[60]

## The Commonwealth Immigration Act

Hammond Perry notes that in the immediate wake of the riots, commentators were already questioning Britain's liberal policies on immigration from Commonwealth countries. Some argued that the policies provided little control over the Black migrants coming to the UK, and whites pointed to this as the problem. This inextricably linked "race and migration" and shifted blame on to the migrants rather than racist whites and colonial policy. British lawmakers were left with a choice of whether to continue to welcome Commonwealth citizens or restrict immigration, thus confirming for the world that "race did indeed matter." Both Garvey and Jones had tried to stem that debate, but it reemerged in the wake of Cochrane's murder. They went to speak to Labour MP George Rogers as part of an IRFCC delegation after he made comments in support of immigration restriction. Rogers back-pedaled on his comments and told the delegation that the Labour Party planned to sponsor antiracism legislation.[61]

Jones was all too familiar with immigration restrictions. The passage of the McCarran-Walter Act in 1952 upheld the United States' restrictive 1924 National Origins Act that had set quotas for immigrants from certain countries; the new bill limited immigration from the Caribbean to 100 people per year. For some the bill seemed to pave the way for immigration reforms since it removed all barriers to Asian immigration as well as "racial, gender, and nationality barriers" to naturalization. But it retained the US commitment to a white citizenry by upholding quotas and placing restrictions elsewhere. Restrictive immigration laws, especially those that appeared racially neutral, were used to police already present immigrants and naturalized citizens because they defined citizenship through exclusion. As Hammond Perry argues, in Britain the framing of the violence against West Indians as the immigrants' fault was used to justify immigration restriction. Ten years after facing the same kind of legislation in the United States, Jones organized in protest of similar British proposals.[62]

The Commonwealth Immigration Act, on its surface, appeared "racially neutral" because it set employment requirements. But, as Hammond Perry argues, it was a form of "institutionalized racism" that specifically disenfranchised "Afro Caribbean migrants." In 1948 Commonwealth residents had been granted citizenship, but the immigration bill would change their status in the metropole to immigrant and thus open up the possibility of their exclusion and expulsion. Like the McCarran-Walter Act across the Atlantic, it created avenues for the state to surveil and deport the UK's Commonwealth subjects. Jones attacked the bill in a November 1961 article in the *WIG*, arguing that despite attempts to portray it as just another immigration act, it specifically targeted "coloured citizens."[63]

The bill having been introduced by Conservative Home Secretary Rab Butler, Jones referred to it as "Mr. Butler's Colour-bar bill." The legislation was crafted during a Conservative Party conference in October 1961 with the explicit aim of limiting "coloured" immigration from the Commonwealth. Jones argued in an article that the bill would "scuttle the commonwealth," preventing the migration of "coloured citizens" and allowing for the easier "ejection" of those already in the UK. The bill gave the Home Secretary absolute control over who was allowed in the country, effectively guaranteeing preference to "white commonwealth citizens." It "tipped its hat" to Canadian, Irish, and Australian immigrants while finding means to restrict "West Indians, Indians, and Pakistanis." Upon entrance into Britain, immigrants were issued vouchers based on their skill level or lack thereof. By 1964, two years after the bill's passage, people with vouchers indicating they had no skills were prohibited from staying in the UK.[64]

The bill also excluded the poor from entering the "gates of the prosperous." The CPGB claimed that it was crafted to act as a "tap" that could be "turned on and off to suit the needs of Big Business." Jones insisted that there were jobs that needed to be filled, despite claims to the contrary. The housing shortage was not a result of too much immigration but of a Tory government policy that was diverting funding away from social programs and toward building the "H-bomb." The Tories' aim was to uphold the British imperialist system through "huge and unnecessary campaigns" against nations seeking "freedom from the foulness of imperialist-colonialism." It was a bill targeting people of color that the empire had impoverished.[65]

Jones called for organization against the bill and support for the "29 Labour MPs" who opposed it. Other organizations, including the Indian Workers' Association and the Movement for Colonial Freedom (MCF), were organizing to oppose its passage. Jones likened the bill to US discrimination and anticommunism, calling it a "McCarthyite threat to the democratic way of life." It was a familiar campaign and piece of legislation, and Jones more than anyone knew the consequences. The bill revealed a "fear of race" and a "perpetuation, stimulus, and encouragement of racialism" among "fascists and the 'lunatic fringe'" who advocated "apartheid everywhere." Jones urged the passage of a bill to make racism illegal; quoting Martin Luther King Jr. she acknowledged that "Legislation may not solve everything," but if it stops someone from "lynching me, I'll take the legislation." Most important, the bill was an attempt to split working people and draw them away from campaigns for their mutual benefit. She closed by arguing that the "cry should be: No Colour Bar for Britain! No Colour Bar on Immigration!" That same month, a meeting called by Brockway to organize against the bill was interrupted by white supremacists throwing fireworks at the attendees, including Jones.[66]

Around the same time Jones published her article, she hosted Martin Luther King Jr. Hammond Perry argues that this was a signal that Jones and the *WIG* were the "local Black political voice," and part of a "broad coalition of anti-racist supporters" globally. Jones was also "in conversation" with representatives from other freedom movements, including the African National Congress, and with "ambassadors from Haiti, Ethiopia, and Nigeria." Jones's internationalism focused on diasporic politics, but she was also committed to anti-imperialism, as evidenced by her alliances with Indian organizations. She was concerned that the UK legislation was not just about immigration control, but would confer on "coloured" immigrants a "second-class citizenship" – something she focused on in the *WIG*. In 1959, Jones had changed the paper's name to the *West Indian Gazette and Afro-Asian-Caribbean News* to demonstrate her "solidarity" with other people of color in the Commonwealth and to identify the paper as a voice for global liberation.[67]

Jones joined a march on January 14, 1962, to protest the bill; 2,000 people attended. Days later she co-founded the Afro Asian Caribbean Conference (AACC) along with many of the same people she had been organizing with after the riots. The AACC's "Public Relations Officer" was Pearl Connor, and Frances Ezzrecco worked alongside the group. Its inaugural meeting on January 18 was attended by the Jamaican Prime Minister, Norman Manley. At the meeting, a statement was written calling for the working classes to unite against the proposed immigration legislation and participate in a "mass protest" outside the House of Commons. Significantly, the AACC used the term "apartheid" to describe the new bill. South Africa had recently left the Commonwealth rather than reform its "policies of White minority rule." The word apartheid became a "synecdoche articulating some of the most virulent forms of white supremacy." The AACC planned a protest for February 13, the same day as the final debate of the bill. Despite the protests, the legislation was passed and took effect that summer.[68]

In July 1962, the *WIG* featured an article on the "New Immigration Rules," noting that they would impact "West Indians, Africans, Indians, and Pakistani" Commonwealth citizens the most. The article indicates *WIG*'s role as an important source of information and a center for political mobilization. Jones had a great deal to say on the issue, specifically about how British policies led to immigration from impoverished colonies and how this was perpetuated by monopoly capitalism's grip on public policy. In 1964, she wrote an article for *Freedomways* about Caribbean immigrants in England. She cited poet Louise Bennett's verse calling this "colonization in reverse," meaning that the formerly colonized were now colonizing the metropole. In the article she argued that the fault lay with British colonialism, which had left its former Caribbean colonies in economic straits. Under "colonial-capitalist-imperialist" relations, wealth in the islands was "dominated by the few" while others lived in "unbearable conditions." Immigration to England had occurred as some of the islands were on the cusp of independence, because "prospects have not qualitatively improved" for them, and "Anglo-American imperialist dominance" was proving to be tenuous. She argued that this was what led to the demise of the West Indian Federation in 1962. Many reasons have been cited for its formal dissolution, but Jones was correct in noting that the continued colonial status of some of its member states made self-government difficult.[69]

With the passage of the restrictive McCarran-Walter Act in the US in 1952, Caribbean residents looked to England, which was encouraging immigration because of labor needs. Jones wrote that though the sum of the immigrant population from the West Indies was 1 percent of England's population, a new racist language had emerged to describe the "Dark Strangers" living there. This growing "racialism" was evidenced in the 1958 riots and the Cochrane murder. Jones revealed the lie behind England's democratic traditions, because the Commonwealth Immigration Act effectively operated to keep Britain a white nation. She also spent time in the article deconstructing racist arguments that blamed immigrants for housing shortages and job losses. These issues, she argued, were all manufactured by a Tory government that had failed to address the problems and pursued policies that often exacerbated them. She cited as one example the Tory defeat of an Anti-Discrimination bill on nine occasions.[70]

Jones argued that this "racialism" was not a new phenomenon, but a deeply rooted part of British history. In the eighteenth and nineteenth centuries, Britain had justified expanding its empire by denigrating people of color and claiming that they were unable to govern themselves. This opened the way for "wholesale exploitation, extermination, and looting" in the Caribbean islands. Once again, Jones was effectively analyzing what would today be called racial capitalism. As Jones describes it: "The great wealth of present-day British monopoly capital was built on the robbery of colored peoples." Even as late as 1964, months before her death, she noted that it was only the communists who were standing against the racist language and demanding antiracist discrimination legislation. She also noted the communist efforts to address racism in the trade unions and union resistance to organizing West Indians. Despite her marginalization within the CPGB, Jones retained some hope that a multiracial anti-capitalist organization was the answer.[71]

In concluding her article, Jones noted that West Indians in Britain shared similar experiences with African and Asian immigrants, and she expressed solidarity with those fighting for independence at home and for respect and equality in the UK. She argued that racialism expressed in legislation like the immigration act affected those in England, who were treated like second-class citizens. While the government introduced restrictions on migration, local communities pushed for segregation in schools, employment, and unionization. Jones wrote that while the West Indian Federation dissolved, and people in the Caribbean began to draw national lines, in England their identity was bound up with one another as West Indians. She expressed her hope for another federation, one that would be founded on socialist principles, as in Cuba, and that would play a role in the "community of nations."[72]

## World Communism

While much of Jones's work in London focused on West Indians, she continued to be invested in international communism. In 1962, she was invited by the *Soviet Woman* magazine to visit the USSR. It is not clear how she was able to afford the trip, or if the magazine funded it. Sherwood suspects that Jones's friend Henry Winston might have helped her.

She left the *WIG* in Manu's care – a controversial decision since he was more dogmatic and less interested in the kind of social news that Jones regularly included and that drew in readers. Manu's generally abrasive style turned some people off, though some suspected that anti-Asian prejudice could have been at play in the complaints about him. Jones was not entirely happy with how Manu was running the paper while she was away. In letters and phone calls she would take issue with some of his editorials and articles. She counseled him to write shorter sentences using shorter words, and described one editorial he wrote as "odd." She took issue with the changes he made to the masthead, describing it as "scrawly"; though she knew this was an "old pet fancy" of his, for her it changed the "character" of the paper. A masthead, she wrote, was not something to be "tampered with lightly."[73]

Traveling took a toll on Jones's health, and almost immediately upon arrival in Moscow she had to go to see a doctor. Her blood pressure was high, and though a cardiogram showed nothing out of the ordinary, her second day in Moscow was spent in bed. She had to return to a salt-free diet and regularly visit with doctors who counseled rest. She also spent some time at a sanitorium in the Crimea. She had been eager to travel to the Soviet Union and work with the women who invited her, but she had to take things slowly. Even as she traveled the country, she continually managed the *WIG* from afar, offering Manu suggestions and sending articles.[74]

In one article she described Moscow as one of the most "splendid cities" she had ever been to. She praised its architecture, the class consciousness of the Soviet people, and its continued growth. She also appreciated it as an international city where she could meet people from around the world. She claimed that Russian families were "at peace" knowing the government would provide things like free education, job training, and maternity leave, and she expressed appreciation for the gender parity she observed in Russia and how it produced satisfied women and children. This, of course, contrasted sharply with her experiences in the US and England, which she attributed to the exploitative conditions under capitalism. Jones's trip, much like the travels of others throughout the Soviet Union, was organized by her hosts to focus on the positives rather than the problems in the nation; thus, just as her hosts intended, she was elated with her trip and the country.[75]

Jones returned to the Soviet Union the following year to attend the World Congress of Women. That same year she moved to North London, into a home with two other CPGB members. During her first visit to Moscow, she and Manu had lost the flat they were living in, which required Manu to try to locate another option. The *WIG* also had to move offices because of conflicts with the landlord. Money was a constant concern, but once her passport was returned, Jones took every opportunity to travel. The World Congress of Women was hosted by the Women's International Democratic Federation (WIDF), an organization she had worked with as a member of its US affiliate the Congress of American Women. There were some conflicts at the meeting between Chinese delegates and others, perhaps reflecting the larger Sino-Soviet debates over who would be the leader of international communism. Differences emerged around who to blame for imperialism, which some delegates wanted to pin on the United States. The Chinese delegation wanted stronger language pushing for disarmament and peaceful coexistence and a statement condemning US imperialism.[76]

The Chinese might have been referring directly to US aggression on China's border with Vietnam (and previously Korea). The Vietnamese delegate to the Congress pointed to the US's "armed aggression in the southern part" of their country, stating that while the Vietnamese loved "peace and abhor war," they had every intention of "crushing" those who "trample upon peace and justice." Some delegates, however, praised US President John F. Kennedy, and the Italian delegation would not support any statement condemning imperialism. Despite the differences, the Congress passed a unanimous report on the struggle for national liberation.[77]

Jones was once again faced with US military aggression, this time in Indochina. She had been paying attention to the US activity there since 1954, when she wrote an article in the *Negro Affairs Quarterly* about it. In the article she described the efforts of the Vietnamese for independence and quoted her friend Paul Robeson calling Ho Chi Minh the "T'Oussaint L'Ouverture of Indochina." She was writing at the opening of the Geneva Conference negotiations when the hope for Vietnamese independence was still palpable. People across the globe, she claimed, hoped for a free Vietnam and to avoid another war like that in Korea. But the United States continued to beat its war drums and, under the leadership of Secretary of State John Foster Dulles, left the negotiations to avoid agreeing to peace. She noted the US support of the French war and the "old tragic pattern" of US imperialism's "Asian against Asian policy." The US, she feared, was on the cusp of intervention again. She also noted that American Black men had no interest in fighting another "dirty war." Jones was aware that the Cold War containment policy committed the US to endless war, and she was all too prescient about Vietnam. Ten years later, the *WIG* was paying attention to increased hostilities in the country. Dr. Rinjana Sidhant wrote about the US suppression of the nationalist efforts in Laos and Vietnam and the potential for the conflict to spread.[78]

Jones remained interested in US foreign policy and also kept a keen eye on the growing civil rights movement. In her letter to Stretch Johnson months after her deportation, she noted the Montgomery bus boycott which had propelled Martin Luther King Jr. into the national spotlight. In June 1963, she was part of a delegation that urged action after the assassination of NAACP leader Medgar Evers in Jackson, Mississippi. That same month she gave a speech on civil liberties in the US. She also helped organize and participated in a march in London in support of the August 1963 March on Washington which urged the Kennedy administration to pass a civil rights bill. Days later she sent a telegram to her comrade Shirley Graham Du Bois expressing her "profound sympathy" after the death of W.E.B. Du Bois, who she described as the "greatest contributor" to the "Negro and African people's freedom movement." She wrote that he would "live imperishably in the souls of Black folk" because of the power of his work. She also knew the activist actor Ossie Davis and the *WIG* featured stories on US civil rights actions and events and reviewed American authors like James Baldwin.[79]

Jones's last editorial in the *WIG*, published posthumously, was on Martin Luther King Jr. She met him twice in London, the second time when he was on his way to Oslo to accept the Nobel Peace prize in 1964. Jones wrote that while he was largely considered a "moderate," he had some "very radical things" to say while he was there. That year the Commonwealth Immigration Act was up for renewal; King said that such restrictive laws were "out of keeping" with the "laws of God" and contrary to twentieth-century trends. In her editorial, Jones argued that while racism might be different in Britain than in the United States, people of color in both countries faced discrimination. Discrimination was "man-made" and rooted in the "exploitation for profit" of "newly independent people." This "racialism" was used to disrupt "working-class unity" and to secure the capitalist hold on power. King spoke about the emerging ghettoes that resulted from discrimination in housing, education, and employment; Jones argued that resistance to this required legislation that prohibited discrimination. She wrote about the language employed by British politicians and clergy that parroted the "Dixie-crat" (referring to the segregationist political party) language used in the US. This included arguing against mixed-race marriages, calling for restrictive covenants, and blaming poor housing on residents rather than landlords. These ideas Jones labeled an "apartheid mentality." She echoed King and Paul Robeson, both of whom argued for unity in the struggle to end racism and encouraged all Commonwealth citizens as well as all white citizens to speak out against racism.[80]

Jones's devotion to interracial unity remained unassailable. She found many white comrades who were willing to step up during the riots, and she appreciated the CPGB's opposition to the Commonwealth Immigration Act. This did not, however, improve her relationship with the Party. As late as 1963, she took issue with a *Daily Worker* editorial written by editor George Matthews in which he echoed a claim made by MP Sir Learie Constantine that the refusal of the Bristol Omnibus Company to hire a young West Indian had nothing to do with racism. She argued that the editorial made it appear that the "colour-bar" did not exist and was not at all an issue. The *Daily Worker* article selectively quoted Sir Learie who, after saying that the case had nothing to do with the colour-bar, had continued by claiming it was because of the "economic fears" of the workers who did not like the company's poor wages and overtime. To focus only on the economic issue was to ignore how the colour-bar was essential to capitalist control and accelerated "disunity" among workers. This was something Jones felt the CPGB should try to avoid – she was essentially schooling the Party on racial capitalism when presumably it should have already had a theoretical basis for understanding it. Her letter was not published, and a year later, after Jones unexpectedly died, the CPGB did not eulogize her in its newspapers.[81]

Another shift was happening in world communism at the time that would change how Jones and other Black comrades and fellow travelers understood the socialist future. A conflict emerged between the Soviet Union – which in trying to ease tensions with the US had abandoned its emphasis on revolution – and China, which had no formal recognition from the US and openly supported revolutionary leaders. In 1963 Mao issued a "Statement supporting Black Americans in their struggle against Racial Discrimination" which endeared him and China to the Black Freedom Struggle. As Zifeng Liu argues, Jones began to look to China as the world's socialist leader. At the advent of the Cold War, she had argued that the Soviet Union's successful nuclear weapons program was the only existing check on US militarism. But now that the USSR was seeking accommodation with the US, she instead turned to China. Liu argues that she celebrated the Chinese nuclear project as an "advancement against US empire," thus linking it to the "global anti-imperialist nationalist movements."[82]

The *WIG* included a statement by Jones praising China's successful test of an atomic bomb in 1964. She was quoted as saying that the test was a "contribution to the world people's struggles against imperialism and for world peace." It was "imperialists" who were worried about the test, while "anti-imperialists" instead "felt joy, satisfaction, and confidence." She saw the test as ending the US's "nuclear monopoly" and its use of atomic weapons as "blackmail" to try to prevent liberation movements from succeeding. She called the Soviet test-ban treaty with the US a "fraud" because it failed to stop the US from producing more weapons, and she believed that possession of the weapon meant China was no longer subject to US threats and could emerge as a leader of global liberation.[83]

For Liu, Jones's praise of China, when she had previously been critical, was part of her general political realignment toward the colonized and "decolonizing world." She came to see Mao and China as leaders in anti-imperialism and as mounting the biggest challenge to global white supremacy. This was part of her "reorientation" away from the Soviet Union and toward "Pan-African and Third World emancipatory designs." Once China had successfully tested its own nuclear bomb, it became the leader of the "anti-imperialist struggle" against the United States, which she saw as the "greatest imperialist threat."[84]

In the summer of 1964, Jones was invited to the 10th World Conference Against the Hydrogen and Atomic bombs in Japan. The conference marked the nineteenth anniversary of the Hiroshima and Nagasaki bombings. Jones reported on it for the *WIG* and sent her article to Manu from the International Hotel in Kyoto. For the diasporic community, the use of atomic weaponry, especially against a nation of color, revealed the dangers of militarized nuclear white nations. The conference committed itself to the elimination of nuclear weaponry and extended its support for liberation struggles in Asia, Africa, and Latin America. Jones also noted a special resolution condemning the US's growing intervention in Vietnam. She wrote that the conference issued a demand for the immediate withdrawal of US troops and military advisors and the reunification of Vietnam under terms agreeable to its people. Jones singled out the US as the "chief enemy of peace," arguing that its recent bombings in the country threatened "the peace everywhere." Not all the attendees agreed that the US and its imperialist ambitions were the problem, but Jones argued that atomic weaponry alone was not the issue – those who wielded it were. She made space for support of some of the atomic powers, like China. She also briefly noted the women's panel she had attended and spoke at, and reiterated her commitment to the belief that women were and had to be leaders in the peace movement.[85]

After the conference, at the invitation of a Chinese peace group, Jones traveled to China, where she spent seven weeks with other delegates. She visited five cities and praised the "massive socialist achievements of the past 15 years." She met and interviewed Madame Soong Ching Ling, the widow of Chinese statesman Sun Yat-Sen. The interview was featured in the November 1964 *WIG*. The two discussed the improvements made in agriculture as well as the lives of Chinese peasants. Soong Ching Ling mentioned her husband Sun Yat-Sen's work for orphaned children and the work of his organization the China Welfare League during the revolution against the "reactionary Kuomintang" backed by "US imperialism." Jones wrote that Soong Ching Ling, who was serving as the Vice-Chairman of the People's Republic, supported and continued his work and had contributed to the defeat of US imperialists, the Nationalists, and, during World War II, the Japanese. Jones noted that Soong Ching Ling came to Marxist Leninism during the war years. They discussed the people's communes and Jones expressed disappointment at Soong Ching Ling's refusal to discuss her own accomplishments.[86] As Liu argues, Jones's anti-imperialist politics were now aligned with Mao's "theory of world revolution." She praised Mao's statement on Black liberation and linked the Black Freedom movement to China's "anti-imperialist struggle."[87]

Jones's trip to China, like her visit to the Soviet Union, was organized by the hosts to avoid revealing the country's problems and contradictions. She was part of a delegation that met Mao himself and was included in a photo with him and the other delegates. Jones's reports, according to Liu, enhanced her claims that China was a world leader in the revolutionary struggle. But in ignoring the highly curated nature of her visit, she ended up "downplaying the brutality and violence of China's radical project." Ultimately, Jones did not "challenge" her hosts, but produced "hagiographies of Chinese Revolutionaries."[88] In the process of aligning with China and its nuclear weapons program, she "ignored China's geopolitical ambitions" and helped form a "hierarchical solidarity that served Beijing's foreign policy goals." Nevertheless, Liu does not believe that Jones's expressions of solidarity with China and her belief in its anti-imperialist leadership meant that she was providing an "unqualified endorsement of revolutionary violence." Her belief in peace was not pacifist, since she "endorsed" the use of force by "national liberation movements." She was, however, rightfully concerned about US militarism and its new commitment to perpetual war through its policing of postcolonial states, and she was increasingly disillusioned by the Soviet Union's deference to US might for the sake of détente.[89]

Jones was also mindful of the movements throughout Africa, and would frequently feature their liberation struggles in the *WIG*. South Africa, with its violent opposition to freedom struggles, was a particular concern. Jones was a central organizer for demonstrations against the infamous Rivonia trial. Conducted between October 1963 and June 1964, the trial included Nelson Mandela and nine other defendants charged under the Sabotage Act, which had widened what could be considered sabotage to include trade union strikes and graffiti, increased penalties, and put the burden of proof on defendants. The men were accused of planning to overthrow the South African government, and their conviction could lead to a death sentence. Jones planned a hunger strike against the trial in April 1964, worked with the Afro Asian Caribbean organization to plan a "massive demonstration," and was involved in "every protest" across London.[90]

Jones's new political alignments marked not just her constantly evolving political understanding, but also her commitment to national liberation movements, the people of the diaspora, and her anti-imperialist convictions. After her expulsion from the United States, she remained devoted to her belief that a socialist world order would usher in peace and equity. Though she still focused on interracial solidarity and alignment with white leftists, her politics shifted toward supporting national liberation movements and resistance to the global white supremacist order backed by the US military behemoth.

Jones's true legacy is one of a committed communist. Her memory has been sanitized and neutralized in the UK, a country that downplays its own racist past and present. The egregious expression of racism in the US has given other Western nations a pass, enabling them to divert attention away from their own problems and claim moral superiority. Jones recognized that Britain had its own racism problem, which included blaming West Indians for the violence against them, reversing course by stripping Commonwealth citizens of their British citizenship, and ignoring the fascist elements within its own borders. The KKK openly operated in Britain and attacked Jones and her colleagues; riots were incited by homegrown fascists, and Parliament reacted by punishing the oppressed. There was no qualitative difference between the UK and the US, but it is simpler to claim Jones as a benign activist rather than a radical communist because it prevents the UK from having to acknowledge its own racism.

# Conclusion

*A Friend*
(To Claudia, June 1956)

The longer you are gone, my dearest friend,
The harder are the lonely days to bear,
Eight months have passed – and you so far away;
I have no one my thoughts and dreams to share,
I long to hear your laughter, ringing free,
I long to see your warm and pleasant smile,
To hear your words of comradeship to me
As your swift hands flew at the loom, the while.

Your days are marred by sorrow at my fate,
My days are solitary and they harder grow,
But we can hope – the dawn is never late,
And we will meet again, dear friend, I know.
                              Elizabeth Gurley Flynn[1]

In June 1964, Jones wrote a reflection on what she imagined the future would be. She wrote that she was "certain" that humans would take the "high road to a socialist future." For Jones, "togetherness" was essential despite "human limitations." She reflected on her own characteristics that presented some limitations, but also seemed to fuel her strength and dogged determination for justice. She bemoaned weaknesses in herself and others that prevented progress, and scolded her own "harshness" toward personal weakness. She noted that she had been praised for her "single-mindedness of purpose," and she worried about the "disappointment of non-togetherness." The introspective essay sounded like an attempt to come to terms with her own limitations in personal relationships and political work. But throughout she reiterated her confidence and "faith in the future." She believed in the "Loom of Language" and in "the Family of Man!" Despite overwhelming odds, Jones remained optimistic that the future would be one of equality and justice.[2]

Five months later, Jones was found dead in her flat. She was not yet fifty years old. Eric Levi, a CPGB member and Jones's neighbor, broke into her apartment the day after Christmas 1964. After trying to contact her on Christmas Day with no response, and trying again, Levi began to worry. He broke a window, climbed inside and found Claudia "lying in bed, dead," having suffered a massive heart attack. That year, Jones's good friends, fellow defendants, and leading communists Elizabeth Gurley Flynn and Ben Davis also died. The year before, W.E.B. Du Bois passed. Some of the most outspoken advocates against oppression were passing on, while a new generation was left to mourn and take up their legacy.[3]

## Funeral

Manu was in China at the time, and he later complained that people who did not associate with Jones during her life had tried to arrange the funeral without permission. He claimed that, after returning from China, it was he who had bought the plot in Highgate Cemetery and arranged the funeral. On January 9, 1965, a procession of Jones's friends and comrades went to the Golders Green Crematorium where they held a celebration of her life. Jones's diverse and impressive array of friends either attended the funeral or sent their condolences. Her friend Pearl Prescod sang the old spiritual "Lift Every Voice and Sing." The "chief mourner" George Lamming spoke, along with the Algerian Ambassador L. Khelifa. Her American comrades sent their own condolences. Paul and Essie Robeson sent statements to be read, and Paul sent a recording to be played. Paul also agreed to chair the Claudia Jones Memorial Committee. Manchanda's tribute was reprinted in the December–January issue of the *WIG*. In it he recounted Jones's many years of activism, her belief in communism and peace, and her leadership in revolutionary movements. He closed by saying that her "shining example" would inspire people in the "struggle against imperialism, colonialism, neo-colonialism, against racialism and for peace." Nadia Catouse closed the event by singing "We Shall Overcome."[4]

Over a month later, on February 27, Jones's ashes were interred at Highgate Cemetery. Manchanda spoke at her grave, noting that Jones had been a "loyal pupil" of Karl Marx, who she was buried next to, and that it was the "revolutionary ideas of Marxism–Leninism" that had inspired much of her work. He said that she had given her life for the movement, and suggested that, as they interred her ashes, they should rededicate themselves to "the cause for which she died." Flowers and wreathes were left at the gravesite by organizations and friends. That same day a public memorial was held at St. Pancras town hall. Actress Ruby Dee sent a recording of her reading Jones's statement to the US court that had convicted her in 1953; a recording of Paul Robeson was also played. Speeches were given by Lord Fenner Brockway, George Lamming, L. Khelif, Kwesi Armah, Oliver Tambo, and others. Nadia Catouse sang, poems were read, and a film of the funeral was played.[5]

The December–January 1965 *WIG* issue featured Jones's final editorial, which was on Martin Luther King Jr.'s stop in London on his way to Oslo to accept the Nobel Peace Prize. The February edition was a memorial issue, and included the announcement that Carnival would not happen in 1965 because of Jones's unexpected death. Several of her colleagues and comrades wrote about the impact she had on their lives. Alphaeus Hunton, a US comrade and one of the leaders of the Council on African Affairs, noted that Jones spent her lifetime "warring against the decadent old order" that had bolstered prejudice and oppression. Hunton called her a "twentieth-century Harriet Tubman" leading people to freedom, and described her "deep, unshakable conviction" that racism, colonialism, and imperialism would be destroyed. Shirley Graham Du Bois wrote that she was overwhelmed with grief at Jones's passing, adding that she had hoped to bring Jones to Ghana, where she had lived with her late husband W.E.B. Du Bois, and expressed regret that this would not happen.[6]

The paper printed Robeson's recorded message for her funeral in which he noted that Jones's death was a "great loss to us on this side of the Atlantic" as well as to those in England. He spoke of her importance in the struggle to create unity in the working class and for the liberation of women and people of color. Eslanda Robeson noted how "saddened" women were by her passing, as a powerful voice for women was now lost, and that her work and all she had accomplished in her lifetime would be remembered. Actors and activists Ruby Dee and Ossie Davis sent a message lamenting Jones's death and the loss of such an important leader. Gus Hall and Henry Winston, CPUSA leaders, sent their condolences, noting that a "Progressive America will always cherish the memory of Claudia Jones."[7]

Jones's American friends shared their grief with a worldwide community. Condolences poured in from London City Council, the Chinese Peace Committee, the Cuban ambassador to the UK Louis Recardo Alanzo, and Japanese activists. Friends from Belgium who had worked with Jones at the anti-nuclear conference in Japan called for a movement for "Action for Peace and the Liberation of all Peoples" to be inaugurated in Jones's memory. The Soviet women's committee offered their "profound sympathy" and said they dipped "their banner to a gallant fighter." Despite the tense relationship between Jones and the CPGB, Reginald Birch, an "Executive Member," sent his condolences.[8]

Barney Desai of the Coloured People's Congress of South Africa wrote that Jones was the "driving spirit" behind the hunger strike during the Rivonia Trials. She had showed true solidarity in her actions and protests against the trials and other injustices in apartheid South Africa, and would be remembered as a rebel against "injustice and oppression."[9] Raymond Kunene of the African National Congress sent a note expressing his grief that the liberation movement had lost "one of the most dynamic and . . . militant fighters." He wrote that it was hard to think of anyone who had remained as "incorruptible" as Jones in the face of resistance. She "belonged at the forefront" of the movement against "imperialism, colonialism, and fascism." Kunene said that Jones had a special place in the South African anti-apartheid movement, as she had stood by it throughout every phase, and that while her death felt like a "great political deprivation," her life was the "life of the revolution!"[10]

Kwesi Armah, the High Commissioner for Ghana, wrote of his "deepest sorrow" on hearing about Jones's death, noting that she was "endowed with a formidable courage and wisdom." Armah offered his financial support to the Claudia Jones Memorial Committee and spoke of his pride in mourning a "great sister and comrade." The British Guianese newspaper *Mirror* published a eulogy that was reprinted in the *WIG*. Calling Jones the "doughty Trinidadian," the eulogy said that she would be deeply missed because she devoted her life to others. The *Mirror* editors retained hope that the "cause for which her life was devoted" would continue.[11]

Lord Fenner Brockway and Lord Charles Royle from the Labour Party both sent letters expressing their grief. Brockway wrote that during her time in England Claudia would always be there whenever anyone spoke out for human rights. When she spoke to trade unionists and factory workers she had moved them with her appeals for unity, and they often asked for her to return to speak. Royle noted that she was of great service in improving the lives of West Indians in Britain, and hoped that her "great spirit" would go on to inspire future struggles.[12]

Her closest collaborators in London also expressed grief at her passing. George Lamming wrote that he would remember Jones as a "superior person" – not superior to other people but in how she lived. Despite the difficulties in her life, including her illness, she found "a reason to live" through her work. Politics, he wrote, "resided in every nerve of Claudia's body"; she was gracious with those she disagreed with because the "lioness could disagree like an angel." She had a "certain flexibility of mind" and a "generous heart." She left her mark on all who knew her. Andrew Salkey, a West Indian leader in London, wrote that despite sometimes lukewarm support from the community, they always needed her. She had died "without a country" and "without the comfort of knowing we cared."[13]

David Pitt, who had worked with Jones on several campaigns, lauded her ability to bring West Indian culture to a wider audience through the *WIG* and Carnival. He said that when she arrived in London, she realized that the West Indian community there needed a voice, that it needed to express itself and articulate its demands for rights and respect. She created institutions to do that, and did so while constantly suffering from illness. Pitt would remember her with pride and admiration as a woman who "lived for others and whose life was shorter than it might have been because she refused to live selfishly and lazily."

The *WIG* memorial issue included an appeal for subscribers to keep Jones's paper alive, but because it was in regular financial straits and had been held together mostly by Jones, it was only able to produce one more issue. Its last issue included an article on the assassination of the American Black Nationalist Malcolm X on February 21, 1965. Only a few weeks earlier, a picture had been taken of Malcolm X holding the *WIG* issue announcing Jones's death.[14]

## Manchanda and Jones's Memory

Jones's conflict with the CPGB would continue to reverberate even after her death. In October 1965, Manchanda was suspended from the Party for three months. The charge was that in the final issue of the *WIG* he had accused the Soviet Union of being a partner in imperialism with the United States. The CPGB claimed that this was in violation of the Party's policy, and that Manu had ignored its calls for a meeting and failed to respond to the charge. What this reflected was Jones's and the *WIG*'s movement away from Soviet communism and toward China as the anti-imperialist, socialist leader. In his letter of protest, Manu noted the injustice of his suspension and said that his time had been spent organizing Jones's funeral and memorials and working on the *WIG*. He was unable to deal with the charge because of the burdens left after Jones's unexpected death. He countered that the Party had been negligent during Jones's life, and that it had ignored her death. He wrote that the treatment of Jones by the Party after her deportation was a "betrayal of the sacred trust" of the CPUSA and of the "oppressed Negro people" for whom she was a representative and leader. Upon her death the CPGB's behavior had been "inhuman and vindictive" owing to their disagreements with her, and had left Manu with "heavy financial commitments," which he felt was "uncomradely and inglorious." Manu was expelled from the Party.[15]

In 1967, Manu married Diane Langford. The two had a daughter in 1970 who they named after Claudia (and nicknamed Chu Chu). The apartment in which both Jones and Manu lived contained most of her things, including her passport, papers, cosmetics, and clothes. Langford wrote about Manu's care of many of her possessions and about her own interest in preserving some of Jones's papers, among them letters from her American friends, many of whom had also passed away. Langford kept the documents in good order and purchased a filing cabinet to keep them safe.[16]

One issue that Manu and the Claudia Jones Memorial Committee faced immediately after her death was that there was not enough money to pay for a headstone at the burial site, so it remained unmarked. Starting in 1969, pensioner and communist Bill Fairman and his friend Bill Ellis began tending to Jones's gravesite as well as Marx's, which had also been neglected. Fairman told the *Camden New Journal* that he had come across her grave by accident, but when he later learned of her importance, he took it upon himself to care for it. He was also determined to raise funds for an appropriate headstone, as "People from all over the world" came to visit her grave "only to find nothing." Despite his good intentions, Fairman set off a controversy about who had the rights to Jones's memory and who could take credit for caring for her in life.[17]

Manu met Fairman at the grave and the two discussed a headstone. Fairman had contacted the Afro Caribbean Organization (ACO) to help secure funds. The group created the Claudia Jones Memorial Fund and issued a flyer to raise money. The flyer noted that her grave had gone untended until Fairman and Ellis decided to care for it. Winston Pinder of the ACO had been a friend of Claudia's and had admired her dedication to socialism and the cause of Black people; he was eager to see her grave marked. The group raised the funds, ordered the headstone, and planned a ceremony for September 26, 1982.

Manu, however, objected to both the headstone and the ceremony; he obtained solicitors and prevented the event from proceeding.[18] His objection was that people with no claim to either Claudia's life or memory had taken it upon themselves to organize the event and the headstone without contacting either him or the Claudia Jones Memorial Committee. He was, it seemed, angry that people with links to the CPGB belatedly wanted to care for Claudia and lay claim to her memory. He told Fairman that in her life Jones had struggled with landlords and income but that these old "comrades" had been nowhere to be seen when she needed help. "Those people," he wrote, never lifted a finger to "help her or afford any comfort in her suffering." When she unexpectedly and "prematurely" died, the "fake friends and comrades" moved in to profit from her legacy.[19]

Winston Pinder argues quite the opposite of Manchanda. He stated that Jones had purchased the gravesite before her death; therefore, when she died, there was no living owner. After Fairman drew attention to the unkempt gravesite, Jones's cousin Trevor Carter, as her only relative in London and the head of the Claudia Jones Memorial Committee, tried to arrange for a headstone with the help of Jones's circle of friends, including several Afro Caribbeans from the Party, but faced hostility from Manu. Pinder worked with Carter and spent time raising funds and working with others to organize the headstone, only to find themselves embroiled in a controversy that he blames on Manu. Pinder argues that Manu laid claim to Jones's memory, and it was his claims that have been preserved and not those of her close friends in the Party. While the Party hierarchy might not have gone out of its way to memorialize Jones, she had friends in the Party who did.[20]

Manu was in poor health in 1982. He engaged solicitor F.H. Myles Hickey, who took up some of the correspondence and dealings with both the ACO and Fairman. In January 1983, Pinder, representing the ACO, contacted Manchanda stating that they had met with Trevor Carter and he had outlined the conditions on which they could unveil the headstone. Pinder said that if they failed to obtain permission to place the headstone on Jones's grave, they would place it elsewhere instead. By August, Fairman was expressing frustration with Manchanda's intransigence and was urging Hickey to allow the unveiling ceremony to proceed. In September, Manu wrote the Highgate Cemetery's superintendent claiming that he was the sole owner of Jones's gravesite and reminding them that he had not given permission to any organization to place a headstone at the site.[21]

Pinder had also secured a lawyer, who told him to place the headstone anyway, given that Manu's claims to ownership were insubstantial and had no legal standing. Later that year Pinder and friends placed it near her grave with the inscription "Claudia Vera Jones, Born Trinidad 1915, Died London 25. 12. 64. Valiant Fighter against racism and imperialism who dedicated her life to the progress of socialism and the liberation of her own black people." Manu at this point had separated from his wife and his health was in serious decline. On October 25, 1985, he had a massive heart attack. He was taken to hospital, and Langford was told not to expect him to recover. He died two days later with Langford and Chu Chu by his side.[22]

For his part, Pinder argues that Manu and Langford co-opted Jones's memory, foregrounding Manu and vilifying the Party. It was true that Manu had problems with the Party and that it had not elevated many of its Black members to leadership in the same way that the CPUSA had. But, as Pinder remembers it, the Afro Caribbean CPGB members made up a social and political group that worked hard to strengthen the Party's anti-colonialism. They socialized, partied, and played dominos together every Friday, and organized against racism both within and outside the Party. They worked alongside Jones in distributing the *WIG* – Pinder himself sold it to Black industrial workers – and organized against British racists. The story of Manu as the guardian of Jones's memory has elided many of her good friends and compatriots in her memorializing, and has left behind bitterness.[23]

## Jones's Legacy

Jones's ideas and activism offer a way forward. Her vision of emancipation was global; she worked with freedom fighters across the world to resist racist, capitalist imperialism. She wrote about the devastation caused by imperialism and capitalism, and participated in boycotts, hunger strikes, and demonstrations in support of the oppressed everywhere.

Jones articulated an emancipatory ethos that insisted the most vulnerable and the most oppressed had to be the leaders in liberation struggles. She argued that freedom meant freedom for all, not just industrial workers, as some Marxists and labor organizers emphasized, and not just white women, as feminism foregrounded. Civil rights did not just mean integration – how could integration ameliorate centuries of economic exploitation? Most importantly, emancipation could not happen under capitalism. Capitalism ensured inequality, exploitation, and the hoarding of wealth and privilege. How could a country reform its way to liberation?

Jones's activism and writings offer many lessons for understanding our present historical moment. For her, fascism was not some aberration that afflicted Europe for a short period; it was an endemic part of Western capitalist nations. In the United States, segregation, racist violence, sexism, and monopoly capitalism evidenced the persistence of fascist sentiment. In the years after World War II, she witnessed the rise of fascism as a permanent component of US foreign and domestic policy. The US committed itself to military expansion and interference in liberation movements, all in the interests of corporate dominance. Meanwhile, in the US itself, racial fascism persisted with segregation, illegitimate elections that prevented people of color from voting, women's oppression, and law enforcement violence. Police acted as fascist agents who deployed racist violence and ignored racist actions against people of color. The rise of right-wing fascism today and the continuance of police violence are not an aberration – they are part of the long history that Jones observed, recorded, and struggled against.

This history is also not absent in Britain. Jones challenged the notion that the UK was somehow above reproach, and noted that its policies mirrored those in the United States. Even while its empire was in decline, Britain retained its imperialist commitments by marginalizing Commonwealth citizens, excusing racist attacks on immigrant communities, and adopting fascist immigration restrictions. The UK would also be the US's most committed ally in its policing of liberation movements abroad and in the endless wars it entered into.

Jones argued that the Cold War commitment to permanent war would marginalize the most vulnerable communities in both the US and the UK and in the postcolonial states. She was also concerned that women would remain targets of the war state as their reproductive labor would be co-opted and they would remain exploited in the home and in industry. She warned that war not only prevented social justice but was also used to excuse the harassment and punishment of activists like herself. The Cold War state had justified her imprisonment and deportation as a matter of national security.

Jones advanced the idea of Black women's triple oppression, and argued that women had to take the lead in all emancipatory struggles. She pointed to the historical mistreatment of Black Americans, immigrants, women, and others and insisted that it had to be confronted. She believed that well-meaning liberals were just as often guilty of oppression as others. She argued against the growing military-industrial complex and insisted that freedom required peace. Jones's vision was that of a future in which capitalists could not determine the fate of others and all could enjoy liberation. The way ahead was not to keep trying to fix the same institutions that repeatedly proved to be incompetent; rather, the future required "togetherness." Liberation could not occur when selfish interests reigned; Jones believed until her last days in the "Family of Man!"[24] For her, the answer was socialism. The oppressed could not reform their way to liberation; liberation required the destruction of all the institutions responsible for oppression, especially capitalism.

This is her legacy for today's activists confronting some of the same problems Jones struggled against. Right-wing leaders in both the US and the UK have continued to red-bait their opponents and silence those who challenge them, all the while working to uphold capitalism's power. To be sure we face different challenges as well, particularly a global climate catastrophe and the recognition of different expressions of sexuality and gender. But capitalism's power has only grown in the years since Jones's death, and it continues to wreak havoc on the planet while undermining labor rights and fomenting division among the oppressed. The growth of right-wing power demonstrates that fascism remains virulent and that it feeds on divisions. Fascists attack those who seek gender and race equality, sow doubt about the climate emergency, accuse their enemies of undermining tradition, blame immigrants for the social ills wrought by capitalist exploitation, and thrive on obfuscating the reality behind social problems.

What Jones would say today is hard to determine, but piecemeal reform has failed to secure social justice and the US commitment to militarism has compromised freedom struggles globally. As her example demonstrates, collective action by the people is needed to undermine capitalism's power. Jones, who spent her entire adult life as an advocate for others, working to the point of illness and exhaustion for the oppressed, remained optimistic in the face of oppression. Confronting what seemed to be insurmountable obstacles, she believed that change required struggle, sacrifice and solidarity, and that ultimately, despite so many setbacks, freedom was possible. That freedom would be achieved through solidarity across race, class, and gender lines, and in mass struggle against monopoly capitalism. For Jones, socialism would destroy the institutions that divide us, and usher in our liberation.

# Notes

*Abbreviations used*

AMC    Abhimanyu Manchanda Collection, Marx Memorial Library, London
CJMC    Claudia Jones Memorial Collection, Schomburg Center for Research in Black Culture, Harlem, New York
DBP    W.E.B. Du Bois Papers, University of Massachusetts, Amherst, Massachusetts
MMKP    Mary Metlay Kaufmann Papers, Sophia Smith Collection, Smith College, Northampton, Massachusetts
TL    Tamiment Library and Robert F. Wagner Labor Archive, New York University, New York

Introduction

1 Edith Segal, "For Claudia Jones," *Daily Worker*, January 2, 1956, 6. Text appears courtesy of International Publishers.
2 "Happy Birthday, One Year Old, Claudia Jones Club," *People's World*, July 19, 1969, 11; "Claudia Jones: Heroine from Harlem," *World Magazine*, February 9, 1974, Box 113, Folder 49, Communist Party Papers, TL; "In Memoriam – Black Communists," *Daily World*, February 15, 1969, M-9; Alva Buxenbaum, "USA: Wider Level of Struggle," *Daily World*, 1974, Communist Party of Great Britain Papers, The National Archives, Kew, Richmond.
3 Angela Davis, *Women, Race, and Class* (New York: Vintage Books, 1981), 168–9.
4 Buzz Johnson, *"I Think of My Mother": Notes on the Life and Times of Claudia Jones* (London: Karia Press, 1985); Margaret

Busby and Nia Reynolds, "Obituary of Buzz Johnson," *The Guardian*, March 5, 2014, https://www.theguardian.com/books/2014/mar/05/buzz-johnson; Buzz Johnson, "Black Woman's Struggle," *Morning Star*, February 21, 1985, Box 113, Folder 49, Communist Party Papers, TL.

5 Claudia Jones Organization, "History," at https://www.claudiajones.org; interview with Amandla Thomas-Johnson, February 9, 2023.

6 Pauline de Soza, "Camden Black Sisters," in *Companion to Contemporary Black British Culture*, ed. Alison Donnell (London: Routledge, 2002), 62; Jennifer Tyson to Comrades, June 9, 1987, Box 113, Folder 49, Communist Party Papers, TL; Jennifer Tyson and the Camden Black Sisters, *Claudia Jones, 1915–1964: A Woman of Our Times* (London: Spider Web, 1988).

7 Donna Langston, "Claudia Jones: Valiant Fighter against Racism and Imperialism," 1–3, Box 113, Folder 49, Communist Party Papers, TL; Donna Langston, "The Legacy of Claudia Jones," *Nature, Society, and Thought* 2:1 (1989), 76–96.

8 Tim Gibney, "Poignant Story of a Fight for Rights," *Kensington Post*, January 26, 1989, 15; "Profile: Claudia Jones," *People's Daily World*, February 13, 1988, Ron Johnson, "A Fighting Caribbean-American Leader," *People's Daily World*, February 10, 1989, Box 113, Folder 49, Communist Party Papers, TL.

9 Marika Sherwood, *Claudia Jones: A Life in Exile* (London: Lawrence & Wishart, 1999). The book was reprinted in 2021 (https://roarmag.org/essays/claudia-jones-olufemi/).

10 Rebecca Hill, "Fosterites and Feminists, Or 1950s Ultra-Leftists and the Invention of AmeriKKKa," *New Left Review* 228 (1998), 34; Kate Weigand, *Red Feminism: American Communism and the Making of Women's Liberation* (Baltimore: Johns Hopkins University Press, 2001); Charisse Burden-Stelly, "Carole Boyce Davies and Claudia Jones: Radical Black Female Subjectivity, Mutual Comradeship, and Alternative Epistemology," *Journal of the African Literature Association* (2022), 3, DOI: 10.1080/21674736.2022.2067740

11 Robin D.G. Kelley, *Freedom Dreams: The Black Radical Imagination* (Boston: Beacon Press, 2002), 55; Burden-Stelly, "Carole Boyce

Davies and Claudia Jones," 3; John McClendon, "Claudia Jones," in *Notable Black American Women* (Detroit: Gale Research, 2006), 343–6.

12 Carole Boyce Davies, *Left of Karl Marx: The Political life of Black Communist Claudia Jones* (Durham, NC: Duke University Press, 2007), 1; Burden-Stelly, "Carole Boyce Davies and Claudia Jones," 6.

13 Julia Manchester, "Majority of Young Adults Hold Negative View of Capitalism: Poll," *The Hill*, June 28, 2021, https://thehill.com/homenews/campaign/560493-majority-of-young-adults-in-us-hold-negative-view-of-capitalism-poll; Lydia Saad, "Socialism as Popular as Capitalism among Young Adults in US," *Gallup*, November 25, 2019, https://news.gallup.com/poll/268766/socialism-popular-capitalism-among-young-adults.aspx; "Majority of Young Brits Want a Socialist System," politics.co.uk, July 6, 2021, https://www.politics.co.uk/news/2021/07/06/majority-of-young-brits-want-a-socialist-economic-system/; Ellen Berry, "Austerity, That's What I Know: The Making of a Young UK Socialist," *New York Times*, February 24, 2019, https://www.nytimes.com/2019/02/24/world/europe/britain-austerity-socialism.html; Mona Chalabi, "Trump's Angry White Men," *The Guardian*, January 8, 2016, https://www.theguardian.com/us-news/2016/jan/08/angry-white-men-love-donald-trump.

14 Lydia Lyndsey, "Black Lives Matter: Grace P. Campbell and Claudia Jones – An Analysis of the Negro Question, Self-Determination, Black Belt Thesis," *Africology: Journal of Pan-African Studies* 12:10 (2019), 110–11.

15 "Black Lives Matter Might Be the Largest Movement in US History," *Carr Center*, June 3, 2020, https://carrcenter.hks.harvard.edu/news/black-lives-matter-may-be-largest-movement-us-history; "How Statues Are Falling around the World," *New York Times*, September 12, 2020, https://www.nytimes.com/2020/06/24/us/confederate-statues-photos.html,

16 Graham Lanktree, "What MLK Said about Advertising after Dodge Criticized for Using His Words to Sell Trucks," *Time*, February 5, 2018, https://www.newsweek.com/martin-luther-king-advertising-dodge-super-bowl-799355; interview with Amandla Thomas-Johnson, February 9, 2023.

17 Lola Olufemi, "Claudia Jones: A Life in Search of the Communist Horizon," *Roar*, September 25, 2021, https://roarmag.org/essays/claudia-jones-olufemi/.
18 "Claudia Jones Blue Plaque Unveiled," *Caribbean*, August 22, 2008, https://www.itzcaribbean.com/uk/carnival-uk/claudia-jones-blue-plaque-unveiled/ As of this writing in 2022 the documentary was available to view on YouTube at https://www.youtube.com/watch?v=VUMTOwrzgzs; Harriet Sherwood, "Notting Hill Carnival's 'Founding Spirit' to Be Honoured with Blue Plaque," *The Guardian*, January 26, 2023, https://www.theguardian.com/culture/2023/jan/26/claudia-jones-founding-spirit-notting-hill-carnival-blue-plaque-london-home-english-heritage
19 Ellen E. Jones, "Small Axe: The Black British Culture behind Steve McQueen's Stunning New Series," *The Guardian*, November 14, 2020, https://www.theguardian.com/tv-and-radio/2020/nov/14/small-axe-the-black-british-culture-behind-steve-mcqueens-stunning-new-series; Ben Travers, "Steve McQueen on 5 Integral Moments That Connect His 'Small Axe' Series," *Indie Wire*, June 3, 2021, https://www.indiewire.com/2021/06/small-axe-connections-series-steve-mcqueen-interview-1234641368/
20 Olufemi, "Claudia Jones: A Life in Search of the Communist Horizon."

1 Jones's Early Years (1915–1936)

1 Claudia Jones, "Change the Mind of Man," August 28, 1964; written on the plane returning from two-day visit to Yenan; Box 1, Folder 5, CJMC.
2 "The Weather," *New York Times*, February 10, 1924, 1. Though her surname was Cumberbatch, for the sake of consistency and ease for the reader I will use her pen name, Claudia Jones.
3 Claudia Jones to Comrade Foster, December 6, 1955, CJMC.
4 Glenroy Taitt, "Three Residents' Perspectives: St. Joseph, Trinidad and Tobago, in the First Half of the Twentieth Century," *The Journal of Caribbean Studies* 51:1 (2017), 58, 60–1; Eric Williams, *History of the People of Trinidad and Tobago* (New York: Frederick E. Praeger Publishing, 1962), chap. 3, Kindle.

5 Charisse Burden-Stelly, "Modern U.S. Racial Capitalism: Some Theoretical Insights," *Monthly Review* 72:3 (2020); Hilary McD. Beckles, *How Britain Underdeveloped the Caribbean: A Reparation Response to Europe's Legacy of Plunder and Poverty* (Kingston: University of West Indies Press, 2021), xi–xii.
6 Williams, *History of the People of Trinidad and Tobago*, chapters 3 and 4; Paula Prescod, "Introducing Entanglements and Interdependencies in the Americas: Perspectives from the Carib-Kalinago-Garifuna People," *Forum for Inter-American Research* 15:1 (2022), 8.
7 Williams, *History of the People of Trinidad and Tobago*, chapters 3 and 4.
8 Staff writer, "The Commonwealth Caribbean" (1989), Library of Congress, USA; Beckles, *How Britain Underdeveloped the Caribbean*, 218.
9 Beckles, *How Britain Underdeveloped the Caribbean*, 218; Williams, *History of the People of Trinidad and Tobago*, chap. 5; Gelien Matthews, "Presbyterian Homes for Indian Girls in Trinidad, 1890–1912: Continuity and Change," *Journal of Caribbean Studies* 52:2 (2018), 158.
10 Winston James, *Holding Aloft the Banner of Ethiopia: Caribbean Radicalism in Early Twentieth-Century America* (London: Verso, 1998), 14–15; Charisse Burden-Stelly and Gerald Horne, "Third World Internationalism and the Global Color Line," in *The Cambridge History of America and the World, Volume IV, 1945 to the Present*, ed. David C. Engerman, Max Paul Friedman, and Melanie McAlister (Cambridge: Cambridge University Press, 2021), 370–96.
11 Williams, *History of the People of Trinidad and Tobago*, chapters 9 and 10; James, *Holding Aloft the Banner of Ethiopia*, 59, 64–5.
12 Colin A. Palmer, *Eric Williams and the Making of the Modern Caribbean* (Chapel Hill: University of North Carolina Press, 2006); interview with Amandla Thomas-Johnson, February 9, 2023.
13 Williams, *History of the People of Trinidad and Tobago*, chapters 9 and 10; James, *Holding Aloft the Banner of Ethiopia*, 59, 64–5.
14 Charles Cumberbatch, Declaration of Intent, *New York, U.S., State and Federal Naturalization Records, 1794–1943* [database online]. Provo, UT, USA: Ancestry.com Operations, Inc., 2013;

Sybil Cumberbatch death record, November 19, 1928, certificate number 28654, New York, New York Extracted Death Index, 1862–1948. "Voltaire, Ship Manifest," February 9, 1924, *New York, U.S., Arriving Passenger and Crew Lists (including Castle Garden and Ellis Island), 1820–1957* [database online]. Lehi, UT, USA: Ancestry.com Operations, Inc., 2010; Boyce Davies, *Left of Karl Marx*, 26; Sylvia Cumberbatch Naturalization, 1946, *New York, U.S., Index to Petitions for Naturalization filed in New York City, 1792–1989* [database online]. Provo, UT, USA: Ancestry.com Operations, Inc., 2007.

15 Charles Cumberbatch, Declaration of Intent, *New York, U.S., State and Federal Naturalization Records, 1794–1943* [database online]. Provo, UT, USA: Ancestry.com Operations, Inc., 2013; Claudia Jones to Comrade Foster, December 6, 1955, CJMC.

16 Stephen Robertson, Shane White, Stephen Garton, and Graham White, "The Harlem Life: Black Families and Everyday Life in Harlem in the 1920s and 1930s," *Journal of Social History* 44:1 (2010), 98–9.

17 Robertson et al., "The Harlem Life," 99; Sarah Dunstan and Patricia Owens, "Claudia Jones, International Thinker," *Modern Intellectual History* (April 2021), 6; James, *Holding Aloft the Banner of Ethiopia*, 64–5; Langston, "The Legacy of Claudia Jones," 76–7.

18 "Voltaire, Ship Manifest," February 9, 1924, *New York, U.S., Arriving Passenger and Crew Lists (including Castle Garden and Ellis Island), 1820–1957* [database online]. Lehi, UT, USA: Ancestry.com Operations, Inc., 2010. Meta is listed with the other Cumberbatch children, and all the children listed an Aunt named Mrs. Robinson as their contact in Trinidad. Meta's father is listed as F. Cumberbatch.

19 Andy McCarthy, "Class Act: Researching New York City Schools with Local History Collections," nypl.org, October 20, 2014, https://www.nypl.org/blog/2014/10/20/researching-nyc-schools; Claudia Jones to Comrade Foster, December 6, 1955, Box 1, Folder 8, CJMC.

20 Sybil Cumberbatch death record, November 19, 1928, certificate number 28654, *New York Extracted Death Index, 1862–1948*; Joseph Doane, M.D., "Cerebrospinal Meningitis," *The American Journal of Nursing* 27:4 (1927), 247, 249–50.

21 Johnson, "*I Think of My Mother*"; Abner Berry, "Birthday Party in Harlem," *Daily Worker*, March 3, 1952, 7; New York State Census, 1925, *New York, U.S., State Census, 1925* [database online]. Provo, UT, USA: Ancestry.com Operations, Inc., 2012; Federal Census, 1930, *1930 United States Federal Census* [database online]. Provo, UT, USA: Ancestry.com Operations Inc., 2002. The 1930 census only records Claudia and Evon (*sic*) living with Charles. The census takers might have missed that Sybil, then only sixteen, and Lindsay, the youngest, were not home, or the two could have gone to live with a relative to ease the pressure on Charles; interview with Winston Pinder, May 7, 2022.

22 Claudia Jones, "Claudia Jones Writes about Her Father," *Daily Worker*, June 26, 1956, 4; Claudia Jones to Comrade Foster, December 6, 1955, CJMC.

23 Claudia Jones to Comrade Foster, December 6, 1955, Box 1, Folder 8, CJMC; "Harriet Beecher Stowe Junior High loses 236 students to Graduation," *The New York Amsterdam News*, January 29, 1930, 4; "Jones: FBI Used Trickery for Midnight Raid," *The Worker*, January 25, 1948, 11.

24 Landmark Preservation Commission (LPC), Abyssinian Baptist Church and Community House Designation Report (LP-1851), prepared by Christopher Moore and Andrew S. Dolkart (New York: City of New York, 1993); LPC, Mount Morris Park Historic District Designation Report (LP-0452), (New York: City of New York, 1971); LPC, Washington Apartments Designation Report (LP-1842), prepared by Virginia Kurshan (New York: City of New York, 1993); Claudia Jones to Comrade Foster, December 6, 1955, Box 1, Folder 8, CJMC.

25 Mark Naison, *Communists in Harlem during the Depression* (Urbana: University of Illinois Press, 1983), 200; Boyce Davies, *Left of Karl Marx*, xxiii; "An Open Letter," *New York Age*, October 21, 1933, 9; interview with Winston Pinder, May 7, 2022.

26 Claudia Jones to Comrade Foster, December 6, 1955, Box 1, Folder 8, CJMC; Louis Miller, M.D., To Whom It May Concern, December 19, 1952, Box 14, Folder 7, MMKP; Barron Lerner, "New York City's Tuberculosis Control Efforts: The Historical Limitations of the 'War on Consumption,'" *American Journal of Public Health* 83:5 (1993), 758–9.

27 Lerner, "New York City's Tuberculosis Control Efforts," 789–90; "Lay Hospital Cornerstone," *New York Times*, October 12, 1917, 11; Christopher Gray, "Seaview Hospital: A TB Patients' Haven Now Afflicted with Neglect," *New York Times*, July 16, 1989, 6.
28 Claudia Jones to Comrade Foster, December 6, 1955, Box 1, Folder 8, CJMC; "An Open Letter," *New York Age*, October 21, 1933, 9.
29 Louis Miller, M.D., To Whom It May Concern, December 19, 1952, Box 14, Folder 7, MMKP.
30 Claudia Jones to Comrade Foster, December 6, 1955, Box 1, Folder 8, CJMC.
31 "Negro WPA Editor to Speak at Fete," *New York Age*, June 13, 1936, 3; Baxter R. Leach, "The Negroes Contribution to Radio Broadcasting," Box 2, Folder 36, Federal Writers' Project Negro Group Papers, Beinecke Rare Book and Manuscript Collection, Yale University Library, New Haven, Connecticut.
32 Baxter R. Leach, "Newspaperman to Tell Story of W.P.A. Writer's Project Here," *New York Age*, September 24, 1938, 1.
33 Baxter R. Leach, "Says Federal Writers' Project to "give revolutionary slant" to Book Negroes of New York," *New York Age*, October 8, 1938, 3; "10,000 Stop Work on WPA Projects," *New York Times*, May 28, 1937, 1.
34 Leach, "Says Federal Writers' Project," 3; "Writers' Project Called Red Nest," *New York Times*, November 2, 1936, 8; "Allsberg Denies He Is Red," *New York Times*, November 2, 1936, 8.
35 "Testimony Cited on WPA book bias," *New York Times*, November 27, 1938, 31; Charisse Burden-Stelly, "Constructing Deportable Subjectivity: Antiforeigness, Antiradicalism, and Antiblackness during the McCarthyist Structure of Feeling," *Souls* 19:3 (2017), 342–3, 345.
36 Abner Berry, "Birthday Party in Harlem," *Daily Worker*, March 3, 1952, 7; Charles Bertramb (*sic*) Cumberbatch, Draft Registration Card, 1942, The National Archives at St. Louis; St. Louis, Missouri. Record Group Title: *Records of the Selective Service System*. Record Group Number: 147.

## 2 Communist Party, USA (1936–1946)

1. Claudia Jones, "Clay Sculpture," Box 1, Folder 5, CJMC.
2. Claudia Jones to Comrade Foster, December 6, 1955, Box 1, Folder 8, CJMC.
3. Erik McDuffie, "For a New Anti-fascist, Anti-imperialist People's Coalition: Claudia Jones, Black Left Feminism, and the Politics of Possibility in the Era of Trump," in *Post-Cold War Revelations and the American Communist Party*, ed. Vernon L. Pedersen, James G. Ryan, and Katherine A.S. Sibley (London: Bloomsbury Academic, 2021), 188–9; Erik McDuffie, *Sojourning for Freedom: Black Women, American Communism, and the Making of Black Left Feminism* (Durham, NC: Duke University Press, 2011), 48.
4. Alberto Toscano, "Incipient Fascism: Black Radical Perspectives," *CLCWeb: Comparative Literature and Culture* 23:1 (2021), https://doi.org/10.7771/1481-4374.4015
5. Alberto Toscano, "The Long Shadow of Racial Fascism," *Boston Review*, October 28, 2020, https://bostonreview.net/race-politics/alberto-toscano-long-shadow-racial-fascism; Bill V. Mullen and Christopher Vials (eds.), *The U.S. Anti-Fascism Reader* (London: Verso, 2020), 7; Sarah Dunstan, *Race, Rights, and Reform: Black Activism in the French Empire and the United States from World War I to the Cold War* (Cambridge: Cambridge University Press, 2021), 190–1; Toscano, "Incipient Fascism: Black Radical Perspectives."
6. McDuffie, *Sojourning for Freedom*, 59–60; Claudia Jones to Comrade Foster, December 6, 1955, Box 1, Folder 8, CJMC; Sarah Dunstan and Patricia Owens, "Claudia Jones, International Thinker," *Modern Intellectual History* (April 2021), 8.
7. Lindsey, "Black Lives Matter: Grace P. Campbell and Claudia," 113–14; Cheryl Higashida, *Black Internationalist Feminism: Women Writers of the Black Left, 1945–1995* (Urbana: University of Illinois Press, 2011), 33.
8. Lindsey, "Black Lives Matter," 113, 116, 119.
9. Higashida, *Black Internationalist Feminism*, 36–7; Lindsey, "Black Lives Matter," 119.
10. James Goodman, *Stories of Scottsboro* (New York: Vintage Books, 1994).

11 Claudia Jones to Comrade Foster, December 6, 1955, Box 1, Folder 8, CJMC.
12 "Harlem Rallies for Scottsboro Tomorrow," *Daily Worker*, April 7, 1939, 5; "Harlem Rallies for Scottsboro Today," *Daily Worker*, April 8, 1939, 3; McDuffie, *Sojourning for Freedom*, 59–60.
13 "Harlem Rallies for Scottsboro Tomorrow," *Daily Worker*, April 7, 1939, 5; "Harlem Rallies for Scottsboro Today," *Daily Worker*, April 8, 1939, 3; McDuffie, *Sojourning for Freedom*, 59–60; Erik McDuffie and Komozie Woodard, "'If you're in a country that's progressive, the woman is progressive': Black Women Radicals and the Making of the Politics and Legacy of Malcolm X," *Biography* 36:3 (2013), 516; Ashley Farmer, "Mothers of Pan-Africanism: Audley Moore and Dara Abubakari," *Women, Gender, and Families of Color* 4:2 (2016), 278–80.
14 Jocelyn Jurich, "Pettis Perry and the 'Negro Question,'" *American Communist History* 16:3–4 (2017), 148–9.
15 McDuffie, *Sojourning for Freedom*, 92; Mary Helen Washington, "Alice Childress, Lorraine Hansberry, and Claudia Jones: Black Women Write the Popular Front," in *Left of the Color Line: Race, Radicalism, and Twentieth-Century Literature of the United States*, ed. Bill Mullen and James Smethurst (Chapel Hill: University of North Carolina Press, 2003), 183–204.
16 Denise Lynn, "Fascism and the Family: American Communist Women's Antifascism During the Ethiopian Invasion and Spanish Civil War," *American Communist History* 15:2 (2016), 184.
17 Lynn, "Fascism and the Family," 184.
18 Claudia Jones to Comrade Foster, December 6, 1955, Box 1, Folder 8, CJMC.
19 Lydia Lindsey, "Red Monday: The Silencing of Claudia Jones in 20th Century Feminist Revolutionary Thought," *Journal of Intersectionality* 3:1 (2019), 13.
20 Boyce Davies, *Left of Karl Marx*, 33, 36; Lindsey, "Red Monday," 12–13; Louise Thompson, "Toward a Brighter Dawn," *Woman Today* (April 1936), 14, 30.
21 Claudia Cumberbatch, "Negro Congress Youth Aid Domestic Workers," *Daily Worker*, March 30, 1936, 8; Gerald Cook, "C.P. Board Hits Arrest of Claudia Jones," *Daily Worker*, January 21, 1948, 2; Boyce Davies, *Left of Karl Marx*, 5.

22 Henry Winston, *Life Begins with Freedom* (New York: New Age Publishers, 1937); Lindsey, "Black Lives Matter," 119.
23 Manning Marable, *Let Nobody Turn Us Around: Voices of Resistance, Reform, and Renewal. An African-American Anthology* (Lanham, MD: Rowan & Littlefield, 2009), 366; Art Shields, "Old Glory, Hammer and Sickle Raised High as Communist Party Marks 18th Anniversary," *Daily Worker*, September 15, 1937, 5.
24 Angelo Herndon, *Let Me Live* (Ann Arbor: University of Michigan Press, 2006), xvi.
25 Lindsey, "Black Lives Matter," 119; Jonetta Richards, "Fundamentally Determined: James E. Jackson and Esther Cooper Jackson and the Southern Negro Youth Congress, 1937–1946," *American Communist History* 7:2 (2008), 191–2; Lindsey R. Swindall, *The Path to the Greater, Freer, Truer World: Southern Civil Rights and Anticolonialism, 1937–1955* (Gainesville: University Press of Florida, 2014), 30.
26 Swindall, *The Path to the Greater, Freer, Truer World*, 30; Claudia Jones, "NAACP Youth Delegates Map Program," *Daily Worker*, July 2, 1937, 3.
27 Richards, "Fundamentally Determined," 193; Claudia Jones, "Negro Youth Pamphlet," *Daily Worker*, June 17, 1938, 7; Higashida, *Black Internationalist Feminism*, 39–40.
28 "Demonstrate on Anti-Lynch Bill," *Daily Worker*, April 4, 1939, 4; "Changes Suggested by Members for Draft of YCL Constitution," *Daily Worker*, April 30, 1937, 6; Esther Cantor, "East Harlem, Italian, Negro YCL Clubs Meet Together to Plan Joint Social Program," *Sunday Worker*, May 7, 1939, 5.
29 Denise Lynn, *Where is Juliet Stuart Poyntz? Gender, Spycraft, and Anti-Stalinism in the Early Cold War* (Amherst: University of Massachusetts Press, 2021).
30 Gerald Horne, *Black Liberation/Red Scare: Ben Davis and the Communist Party* (New York: International Publishers, 2021), 78–81.
31 "Anti-War Rally!" *Daily Worker*, October 21, 1940; Claudia Jones, *Jim Crow in Uniform* (New York: New Age Publishers, 1940), 1–2; Donna T. Haverty-Stacke, "Punishment of Mere Political Advocacy: The FBI, Teamsters Local 544, and the Origins of the 1941 Smith Act Case," *The Journal of American History* 100:1 (2013), 68–71.

32 Jones, *Jim Crow in Uniform*, 6–8; Claudia Jones, "Jim Crow in Uniform," *Weekly Review*, July 27, 1940, 1.
33 Jones, *Jim Crow in Uniform*, 13.
34 Jones, *Jim Crow in Uniform*, 16–19.
35 "YCL Launches Statewide Antidraft Drive," *Daily Worker*, August 19, 1940, 3; "Lend-Lease Bill Will Send Men, Foster Warns," *Daily Worker*, February 14, 1941, 2.
36 Lara Vapnek, *Elizabeth Gurley Flynn: Modern American Revolutionary* (New York: Routledge, 2015); "Women to Hold Dramatic City Peace Rally," *Daily Worker*, May 9, 1941, 5.
37 "Women to Hold Dramatic City Peace Rally," *Daily Worker*, May 9, 1941, 5; Denise Lynn, "Anti-Nazism and the Fear of Pronatalism in the American Popular Front," *Radical Americas* 1:1 (2016), 34.
38 Claudia Jones, "International Women's Day and the Struggle for Peace," *Political Affairs*, March 1950.
39 Christina Mislán, "The Imperial 'We': Racial Justice, Nationhood, and Global War in Claudia Jones's *Weekly Review* Editorials, 1938–1943," *Journalism* 18:10 (2017), 1415; Sarah Dunstan and Patricia Owens, "Claudia Jones, International Thinker," *Modern Intellectual History*, April 20, 2021, https://doi.org/10.1017/S1479244321000093
40 Mislán, "The Imperial 'We,'" 1416–17.
41 Boyce Davies, *Left of Karl Marx*, 73–4; Dunstan and Owens, "Claudia Jones, International Thinker," 3.
42 Mislán, "The Imperial 'We,'" 1420–21.
43 Mislán, "The Imperial 'We,'" 1420–4.
44 Mislán, "The Imperial 'We,'" 1424–6.
45 Claudia Jones, "Quiz: Why Not Negotiate with Hitler?" *Weekly Review*, September 9, 1941, 13; Dunstan and Owens, "Claudia Jones, International Thinker," 13.
46 Claudia Jones, "Quiz: Since Great Britain and the United States Are Imperialist Powers, How Can We Support Them?" *Weekly Review*, September 16, 1941, 13.
47 Claudia Jones, "Quiz: Is Not the Question for the Struggle for Negro Rights Equally an Important Issue as the Defeat of Hitler?" *Weekly Review*, November 18, 1941, 13; Dunstan and Owens, "Claudia Jones, International Thinker," 14.

48 "Marriage Certificate," Abraham Scholnick and Claudia Cumberbatch, September 15, 1940, Bureau of Vital Statistics, New York, New York; 1910; Census Place: Manhattan Ward 11, New York, New York; Roll: T624_1012; Page: 22A; Enumeration District: 0256; 1920; Census Place: Manhattan Assembly District 8, New York, New York; Roll: T625_1200; Page: 4A; Enumeration District: 644; "Brooklyn Assembly Candidates seeking Mandate of the People," *The Brooklyn Eagle*, November 6, 1938, 14.
49 U.S., *World War II Draft Cards Young Men, 1940–1947* [database online]. Lehi, UT, USA: Ancestry.com Operations, Inc., 2011; "On the Home Front," *Brooklyn Eagle*, October 14, 1942, 11; Boyce Davies, *Left of Karl Marx*, 147.
50 Declaration of Intent, Yvonne Cumberbatch, May 20, 1941; Minnie Cumberbatch, July 20, 1927; Charles Cumberbatch, November 19, 1936, *New York, U.S., State and Federal Naturalization Records, 1794–1943* [database online]. Provo, UT, USA: Ancestry.com Operations, Inc., 2013; Yvonne Cumberbatch Naturalization, December 16, 1943; Sylvia Berthel Cumberbatch, April 15, 1946; and Lyndsay Cumberbatch, August 17, 1959, *New York, Index to Petitions for Naturalization Filed in Federal, State, and Local Courts Located in New York City, 1792–1989*. New York, NY, USA: The National Archives at New York City; Yvonne Cumberbatch, *U.S., Department of Veterans Affairs BIRLS Death File, 1850–2010* [database online]. Provo, UT, USA: Ancestry.com Operations, Inc., 2011.
51 Louis Miller, M.D., To Whom it May Concern, December 19, 1952, Box 14, Folder 7, MMKP.
52 Claudia Jones, *Lift Every Voice for Victory* (New York: New Age Publishers, 1942), 3–4.
53 Jones, *Lift Every Voice for Victory*, 7–8.
54 Dorothy Hunton, *Alphaeus Hunton: The Unsung Valiant* (New York, International Publishers, 2021), 51–2, 91; Higashida, *Black Internationalist Feminism*, 40.
55 Claudia Jones, "Paul Robeson – Man and Artist," *Weekly Review*, June 22, 1943, 4.
56 "New Unit Replaces Communist League," *New York Times*, October 18, 1943, 17; Robert McCarthy, "Something New Has Been Added," *Spotlight*, October 1943, 3.

57 Dorothy McConnell, "Gold Stars and Carnations," *Woman Today*, May 1937, 4; "Women to Hold Dramatic City Peace Rally," *Daily Worker*, May 9, 1941, 5; Claudia Jones, "From the Editor," *Spotlight*, May 1944, 2.
58 Claudia Jones, "From the Editor," *Spotlight*, June 1944, 2; Claudia Jones, "From the Editor," *Spotlight*, July 1944, 2.
59 Claudia Jones, "6 Months of Spotlight," July 1944, 1–2. United States Politics and Serials Collection, Box 15, Folder 15, TL.
60 "Focus on AYD," *Spotlight*, February 1945, 26; Jones, "6 Months of Spotlight," 5–7; "We Suspend Publication," *Spotlight*, May 1945, 2.
61 Rhodri Jeffreys-Jones, *The FBI: A History* (New Haven: Yale University Press, 2007), 88–92; Haverty-Stacke, "Punishment of Mere Political Advocacy," 68–71.
62 Athan G. Theoharis, "FBI Surveillance During the Cold War: A Constitutional Crisis," *The Public Historian* 3:1 (1981), 5–6; Athan G. Theoharis, *Chasing Spies: How the FBI Failed in Counterintelligence But Promoted the Politics of McCarthyism in the Cold War Years* (Chicago: Ivan R. Dee, 2002), 11.
63 Federal Bureau of Investigation, Claudia Jones File, Part 1, Volume 1, 5–7.
64 Federal Bureau of Investigation, Claudia Jones File, Part 1, Volume 1, 10–13,
65 Federal Bureau of Investigation, Claudia Jones File, Part 1, Volume 1, 19, 23.
66 Athan G. Theoharis, *Abuse of Power: How Cold War Surveillance and Secrecy Policy Shaped the Response to 9/11* (Philadelphia: Temple University Press, 2011), 9, 12.
67 Beverly Gage, *G-Man: J. Edgar Hoover and the Making of the American Century* (New York: Viking, 2022), 645–6, 649, 651, 680–6; Federal Bureau of Investigation, Claudia Jones File, Part 5, Volume 5, 1–111.
68 Trevor Aaronson, "The Snitch in the Silver Hearse," *The Intercept*, February 7, 2023, https://theintercept.com/2023/02/07/fbi-denver-racial-justice-protests-informant; Ed Pilkington, "FBI Failing to Address White Supremacist Violence, Warns Former Special Agent," *The Guardian*, May 20, 2022, https://www.theguardian.com/us-news/2022/may/20/fbi-white

-supremacist-violence-michael-german; Lerone Martin, *The Gospel of J. Edgar Hoover: How the FBI Aided and Abetted the Rise of Christian Nationalism* (Princeton: Princeton University Press, 2023), 4–5.
69 Theoharis, *Abuse of Power*, 11–12; Federal Bureau of Investigation, Claudia Jones File, Part 1, Volume 1, 33, 34.
70 Horne, *Black Liberation/Red Scare*, 119, 122, 128; Dunstan and Owens, "Claudia Jones, International Thinker," 9–10.
71 Claudia Jones, "Concord at Crimea," *Spotlight*, March 1945, 8, 10.
72 Horne, *Black Liberation/Red Scare*, 130–1; Howard Eugene Johnson and Wendy Johnson, *A Dancer in the Revolution: Stretch Johnson, Harlem Communist at the Cotton Club* (New York: Fordham University Press, 2014), 99–101.
73 Horne, *Black Liberation/Red Scare*, 137–9, 143.
74 Claudia Jones, "Discussion Article by Claudia Jones," *Political Affairs*, August 1945, 717–19.
75 Jones, "Discussion Article by Claudia Jones," 719–20.
76 Claudia Jones, "On the Right to Self-Determination for the Negro People in the Black Belt," *Political Affairs*, January 1946, 67; Higashida, *Black Internationalist Feminism*, 44.
77 Jones, "On the Right to Self-Determination for the Negro People in the Black Belt," 69; Boyce Davies, *Left of Karl Marx*, 220.
78 Jones, "On the Right to Self-Determination for the Negro People in the Black Belt," 70–1.
79 Higashida, *Black Internationalist Feminism*, 42; Weigand, *Red Feminism*, 156.
80 Harry Haywood, *Black Bolshevik: Autobiography of an Afro-American Communist* (Chicago: Liberator Press, 1978), 543; Lindsey, "Black Lives Matter," 122.

## 3 The Early Cold War (1945–1950)

1 Claudia Jones, "To Elizabeth Gurley Flynn," Box 1, Folder 5, CJMC.
2 Vincent D. Intondi, *African Americans against the Bomb: Nuclear Weapons, Colonialism, and the Black Freedom Movement* (Stanford: Stanford University Press, 2015), 9–10.

3 Nick Fischer, *Spider Web: The Birth of American Anticommunism* (Urbana: University of Illinois Press, 2016); Burden-Stelly, "Modern U.S. Racial Capitalism."
4 Fischer, *Spider Web*, 251; Burden-Stelly, "Modern U.S. Racial Capitalism." Liberals are defined as those who want to reform the existing system; radicals in the case of Jones and her fellow communists wanted to create a new system.
5 Christopher Vials and Bill Mullen, "Fascism, Racial Capitalism, and Police Violence: Antifascist Reflections from the 1930s to the Black Panthers," Verso, June 23, 2020, https://www.versobooks.com/blogs/4767-fascism-racial-capitalism-and-police-violence-antifascist-reflections-from-the-1930s-to-the-black-panthers; Ruth Wilson Gilmore, *Abolition Geography: Essays Toward Liberation* (London: Verso, 2022), 252, 338, 458.
6 Horne, *Black Liberation/Red Scare*, 13; Gerald Horne, *Race Woman: The Lives of Shirley Graham Du Bois* (New York: New York University Press, 2000), 112; Erik McDuffie, "Black and Red: Black Liberation, the Cold War, and the Horne thesis," *Journal of African American History* 96:2 (2011), 236–7.
7 Charisse Burden-Stelly, "Claudia Jones, the Longue Durée of McCarthyism, and the Threat of US Fascism," *Journal of Intersectionality* 3:1 (2019), 45, 48.
8 Burden-Stelly, "Claudia Jones, the Longue Durée of McCarthyism," 63; Mullen and Vials (eds.), *The U.S. Anti-Fascism Reader*, 7.
9 "Brothers Describe Freeport Shooting," *New York Times*, July 18, 1946, 27; Claudia Jones, "Army's Exoneration of Slain Negro Puts Ferguson Case Up to Dewey," *Daily Worker*, April 17, 1946, 1.
10 Claudia Jones, "Lawyers Ask US Probe in Freeport," *Worker*, March 10, 1946, 5.
11 Claudia Jones, "The Freeport Murder Case Won't Be Buried, Gov Dewey," *Worker*, July 7, 1946, 7; William L. Patterson (ed.), *We Charge Genocide: The Crime of Government against the Negro People* (New York: International Publishers, 1971), 61.
12 "Announce New Editors of the Worker," *The Worker*, December 30, 1945, 2; Claudia Jones, "Negro People Learn the Union Way is the Road to Liberation," *Daily Worker*, April 28, 1946, 2; Claudia Jones, "Shrewd Racial Strategy or Negro-White

Unity," *The Worker*, June 16, 1946, 13; Claudia Jones, "Negro Congress Labor Delegates Score Truman," *Daily Worker*, May 31, 1946, 3.

13 Claudia Jones, "CIO, AFL Unions already Endorse Negro Congress," *Daily Worker*, May 26, 1946, 12.

14 Jones, "CIO, AFL Unions already Endorse Negro Congress," 12; "Call Truman Doctrine Threat to Negro People," *Daily Worker*, April 4, 1947, 3.

15 Erik S. Gellman, *Death Blow to Jim Crow: The National Negro Congress and the Rise of Militant Civil Rights* (Chapel Hill: University of North Carolina Press, 2012), 155–6, 255; Claudia Jones, "How Randolph Aided Filibuster," *Daily Worker*, February 23, 1946, 9.

16 Claudia Jones, "Negro Reaction to Churchill: No!" *Daily Worker*, March 18, 1946, 2.

17 Federal Bureau of Investigation, Claudia Jones File, Part 2, Volume 1, 10, 15.

18 Mislán, "The Imperial 'We'"; Federal Bureau of Investigation, Claudia Jones File, Part 3, Volume 2, 7–19.

19 Claudia Jones, "A Hot Radio Debate on Military Training," *Daily Worker*, August 4, 1947, 11.

20 Hill, "Fosterites and Feminists," 34; Denise Lynn, "Socialist Feminism and Triple Oppression: Claudia Jones and African American Women in American Communism," *Journal for the Study of Radicalism* 8:2 (2014), 14; Lindsey, "Black Lives Matter," 117.

21 Weigand, *Red Feminism*, 46–7.

22 Weigand, *Red Feminism*, 48–9, 55.

23 Weigand, *Red Feminism*, 63.

24 House Committee on Un-American Activities, "Report on the Congress of American Women," United States Government Printing Office, 1949, 69–71, 73, 83, 91–2, 98, 107, 115.

25 "Divorce Decree," 1947, Box 1, Folder 1, CJMC; "The Perils of Mexican Divorce," *Time*, December 27, 1963.

26 Boyce Davies, *Left of Karl Marx*; Claudia Jones, "For New Approaches to Our Work among Women," *Political Affairs*, August 1948, 738.

27 Jones, "For New Approaches to Our Work among Women," 738–40.

28 Jones, "For New Approaches to Our Work among Women," 738–40.
29 Jones, "For New Approaches to Our Work among Women," 741; Higashida, *Black Internationalist Feminism*, 42.
30 Federal Bureau of Investigation, Claudia Jones File, Part 2, Volume 1, 16, 22, 26, 48.
31 Federal Bureau of Investigation, Claudia Jones File, Part 2, Volume 1, 48–9, 62; Part 3, Volume 2, 3, 36; Theoharis, "FBI Surveillance During the Cold War," 5–6.
32 Federal Bureau of Investigation, Claudia Jones File, Part 3, Volume 2, 36, 43–6.
33 Gerald Cook, "C.P. Board Hits Arrest of Claudia Jones," *Daily Worker*, January 21, 1948, 2.
34 "Claudia Jones Dramatizes Communist Fight for Negroes," *Daily Worker*, February 8, 1948, 5; Charisse Burden-Stelly, "In Battle for Peace during 'Scoundrel Time': W.E.B. Du Bois and United States Repression of Radical Black Peace Activism," *Du Bois Review* 16:2 (2019), 555–6.
35 Ben Davis, "Face to Face," *Daily Worker*, March 28, 1948, 2; Federal Bureau of Investigation, Charlotta Bass File, Part 1a, 20.
36 Davis, "Face to Face," 2.
37 Barbara Ransby, *Eslanda: The Large and Unconventional Life of Mrs. Paul Robeson* (New Haven: Yale University Press, 2013), 184; Mary Hamilton, "A Pennsylvania Newspaper Publisher in 'Gideon's Army': J.W. Gitt, Henry Wallace, and the Progressive Party of 1948," *Pennsylvania History: A Journal of Mid-Atlantic States* 61:1 (1994), 18, 21–2; "Throngs Cheer Wallace at Garment Area Rally," *Daily Worker*, October 29, 1948, 11.
38 "CP Convention Adopts '48 Election Platform of Peace and Freedom," *Daily Worker*, August 9, 1948, 15; "Communists Offer a Program for Peace and Security," *Daily Worker*, August 15, 1948, 4.
39 Timothy Johnston, "Peace or Pacifism: The Soviet Struggle for Peace, 1948–1954," *Seer* 86:2 (2008), 260–61; Burden-Stelly, "In Battle for Peace during 'Scoundrel Time,'" 557–9; Intondi, *African Americans against the Bomb*, 9–10.
40 "Demonstration Sparks Fight for Claudia Jones, Bittelman," *Daily Worker*, February 8, 1948, 10; "Harlem Rally to Protest

Claudia Jones Deportation," *Daily Worker*, February 9, 1948, 6; Federal Bureau of Investigation, "Claudia Vera Scholnick, Internal Security-C," January 31, 1948, Claudia Jones File, Part 3, Volume 2, 61; Federal Bureau of Investigation, "Claudia Vera Scholnick, Internal Security-C," April 4, 1948, Claudia Jones File, Part 4, Volume 2, 4; John Munro, *The Anticolonial Front: The African American Freedom Struggle and Global Decolonization, 1945–1960* (Cambridge: Cambridge University Press, 2017), 178; Farmer, "Mothers of Pan-Africanism," 278; Claudia Jones Defense Committee (New York, N.Y.). Letter from Claudia Jones Defense Committee to W.E.B. Du Bois, February 19, 1948, MS 312, DBP.

41 "Picket Claudia Jones Hearing Today," *Daily Worker*, September 30, 1948, 4; Elizabeth Gurley Flynn, "Life of the Party," *Daily Worker*, September 13, 1948, 10; Claudia Jones to William Foster, December 6, 1955. Claudia Jones Vertical File, TL; Carole Boyce Davies, "Deportable Subjects: U.S. Immigration Laws and the Criminalizing of Communism," *South Atlantic Quarterly* 100:4 (2001), 980–5; Michael G. Hanchard, *The Spectre of Race: How Discrimination Haunts Western Democracy* (Princeton: Princeton University Press, 2018), 112–13.

42 "Miss Jones Statement," *Daily Worker*, September 14, 1948, 11; Elizabeth Gurley Flynn, "Life of the Party," *Daily Worker*, September 17, 1948, 10; "Witness Missing, Alien Case Halts," *New York Times*, September 14, 1948, 11.

43 "Hewitt Testifies at New Hearing," *New York Times*, September 16, 1948, 6; "Stachel," *Daily Worker*, September 15, 1948, 11; "Rotten to the Core," *Daily Worker*, September 15, 1948, 2. Art Shields, "Angelo Herndon Refused to Be Government Stoolie," *Daily Worker*, October 1, 1948, 3.

44 "Ouster Ordered of Claudia Jones," *New York Times*, December 22, 1950, 13; "Rotten to the Core," *Daily Worker*, September 15, 1948, 2; John Gate, "Claudia Jones Writes from Ellis Island," *Daily Worker*, November 8, 1950, 2, 9; Elizabeth Gurley Flynn, "A Better World," *Daily Worker*, October 31, 1950, 8.

45 "Rotten to the Core," *Daily Worker*, September 15, 1948, 2; John Gate, "Claudia Jones Writes from Ellis Island," *Daily*

*Worker*, November 8, 1950, 2, 9; "A Letter from Ellis Island," *Daily Worker*, November 12, 1950, 7.

46 Elizabeth Gurley Flynn, "Lady Liberty's Torch Grows Dim," *Daily Worker*, November 9, 1950, 8; "McCarran Victims Urge Intensified Repeal Drive," *Daily Worker*, December 4, 1950, 4;

47 Federal Bureau of Investigation, "Air Tel," November 10, 1952, Claudia Jones File, Part 7, Volume 7; "Challenges Legality of Deportation Proceeding," *Daily Worker*, November 28, 1950, 2; "6 Deportation Proceedings Today in 4 Cities," *Daily Worker*, December 21, 1950, 2; Harry Raymond, "Order Claudia Jones Deported under McCarran Law," *Daily Worker*, December 22, 1950, 2; "Claudia Jones Ordered to Ellis Island," *Daily Worker*, November 10, 1952, 3; "Justice Department Cancels Order of Justice Department," *Daily Worker*, November 14, 1952; American Committee for the Protection of the Foreign Born, "Defeat Police-State Conditions of Walter-McCarran Law," Box 39, Civil Rights Congress Papers, Schomburg Center, Harlem, New York.

48 Carole Boyce Davies (ed.), *Claudia Jones: Beyond Containment* (Oxfordshire: Ayebia Clarke Publishing Limited, 2011), 73.

49 Boyce Davies, *Left of Karl Marx*, 50; Weigand, *Red Feminism*, 101.

50 Weigand, *Red Feminism*, 101; McDuffie, "For a New Anti-fascist, Anti-imperialist People's Coalition," 186; Carole Boyce Davies and Charisse Burden-Stelly, "Claudia Jones Research and Collections: Questions of Process and Knowledge Construction," *Journal of Intersectionality* 3:1 (2019), 6.

51 McDuffie, *Sojourning for Freedom*, 51; Lynn, "Socialist Feminism and Triple Oppression," 2–5; Claudia Jones, "An End to the Neglect of the Problems of Negro Women!" *Political Affairs* [reprint] 1949, 4.

52 Boyce Davies, *Left of Karl Marx*, 39; Jones, "An End to the Neglect," 13.

53 Boyce Davies, *Left of Karl Marx*, 34; Jones, "An End to the Neglect," 15–17.

54 Munro, *The Anticolonial Front*, 123–4; Jones, "An End to the Neglect," 15–17.

55 Weigand, *Red Feminism*, 102; Boyce Davies, *Left of Karl Marx*, 37; Higashida, *Black Internationalist Feminism*, 44, 47.
56 Claudia Jones, "We Seek Full Equality for Women," *Daily Worker*, September 4, 1949, 11.
57 Jones, "We Seek Full Equality for Women," 11.
58 "To Hold Parley on Woman Question," *The Daily Worker*, May 27, 1949, 5; Denise Lynn, "Enlightening the Working Class: W.E.B. Du Bois and the Jefferson School of Social Science," *Socialism and Democracy* 32:2 (2018), 165–6; Jones, "We Seek Full Equality for Women," 11.
59 Jefferson School of Social Science, "Marxism and the Woman Question," Jefferson School of Social Science Collection, Box 3, Folder 11, TL.
60 Jones, "We Seek Full Equality for Women," 11.
61 Ted Morgan, *Reds: McCarthyism in America* (New York: Random House, 2004), 314; Ellen Schrecker, *Many Are the Crimes: McCarthyism in America* (Princeton: Princeton University Press, 1998), 196.
62 Claudia Jones, "Un-American Committee and the Negro People," *Daily Worker*, August 1, 1949, 2.
63 Jones, "Un-American Committee and the Negro People," 2.
64 Claudia Jones, "Henry Winston: Prisoner of Wall Street's Cold War," *Daily Worker*, June 27, 1949, 2.
65 Claudia Jones, "Un-American Committee and the Negro People," *Daily Worker*, August 2, 1949, 2; Claudia Jones, "Un-American Committee and the Negro People," *Daily Worker*, August 3, 1949; Gerald Horne, *Paul Robeson: The Artist as Revolutionary* (London: Pluto Press, 2016), 117, 140.
66 Horne, *Paul Robeson*, 121–4; Claudia Jones, "Heroines of Peekskill Made Stirring History," *Daily Worker*, September 15, 1949, 2.
67 Schrecker, *Many Are the Crimes*, 190; Russell Porter, "11 Communists Convicted of Plot," *New York Times*, October 15, 1949, 1; McDuffie, "Black and Red," 236.
68 Vials and Mullen, "Fascism, Racial Capitalism, and Police Violence"; Gage, *G-Man: J. Edgar Hoover*, 384, 690–2.
69 Vials and Mullen, "Fascism, Racial Capitalism, and Police Violence."

## 4 Anti-Cold War and Deportation (1950–1955)

1. Elizabeth Gurley Flynn, *My Life as a Political Prisoner: The Rebel Girl Becomes "No. 11710"* (New York: International Publishers, 2019), 211. Text appears courtesy of International Publishers.
2. Boyce Davies, *Left of Karl Marx*, 78; Christina Mislán, "Claudia Jones Speaks to 'Half the World': Gendering Cold War Politics in the *Daily Worker*, 1950–1953," *Feminist Media Studies* 17:2 (2017), 283–5.
3. "Equality for Women," *Woman Worker*, August 1935, 7.
4. Weigand, *Red Feminism*, 91–3; Claudia Jones, "Half the World," *Daily Worker*, April 23, 1950, 11.
5. Intondi, *African Americans against the Bomb*, 32; Mislán, "Claudia Jones Speaks to 'Half the World,'" 285; Claudia Jones, "Half the World," *Daily Worker*, April 2, 1950, 11.
6. David Vine, *The United States of War: A Global History of America's Endless Conflicts, From Columbus to the Islamic State* (Oakland: University of California Press, 2020), 220–1; Mark Phillip Bradley and Mary L. Dudziak, *Making the Forever War: Marlyn B. Young on the Culture and Politics of American Militarism* (Amherst: University of Massachusetts Press, 2021), 40; Mary Dudziak, *Wartime: An Idea, its History, its Consequences* (Oxford: Oxford University Press, 2012), 8.
7. Claudia Jones, "International Women's Day and the Struggle for Peace," *Political Affairs*, March 1950, 32–4.
8. Hill, "Fosterites and Feminists," 34; Jones, "International Women's Day and the Struggle for Peace," 34–5.
9. Jones, "International Women's Day and the Struggle for Peace," 39–42.
10. Jones, "International Women's Day and the Struggle for Peace," 44–5.
11. Bill Mullen, *Un-American: W.E.B. Du Bois and the Century of World Revolution* (Philadelphia: Temple University Press, 2015), 167–8; Denise Lynn, "Reproductive Sovereignty in Soviet and American Socialism During the Great Depression," *American Communist History* 17:3 (2018), 269–81.
12. Claudia Jones, "America's Women Rally to the Peace Struggle," *Daily Worker*, June 12, 1950, 1, 9; Boyce Davies, *Left of Karl Marx*, 151.

13 Mullen, *Un-American*, 164.
14 Peace Information Center, "Peace-gram," 1, MS 312, DBP; W.E.B. Du Bois to Secretary of State Dean Acheson, July 14, 1950, DBP; Intondi, *African Americans against the Bomb*, 32–3; Burden-Stelly, "In Battle for Peace during 'Scoundrel Time,'" 555–6: Shirley Graham Du Bois, *His Day is Marching On: A Memoir of W.E.B. Du Bois* (Philadelphia: Lippencott, 1971), 90.
15 Burden-Stelly, "In Battle for Peace during 'Scoundrel Time,'" 557–8; Michael Brenes, *For Might and Right: Cold War Defense Spending and the Remaking of American Democracy* (Amherst: University of Massachusetts Press, 2020).
16 Burden-Stelly, "In Battle for Peace during 'Scoundrel Time,'" 559.
17 Claudia Jones, "For the Unity of Women in the Cause of Peace," *Political Affairs*, February 1949, 151–3.
18 Jones, "For the Unity of Women in the Cause of Peace," 159; "Midwest College Students Hear Jones on McGee Case," *Daily Worker*, May 25, 1951, 2; "Willie McGee," *Daily Worker*, May 20, 1952, 8.
19 Claudia Jones, "Half the World," *The Worker*, June 17, 1951, 8; "Police Eject 20 Students Who Boo Red's Talk," *Chicago Tribune*, May 24, 1951, 7.
20 Claudia Jones, "Half the World," *The Worker*, 17 June 1951, 8; "Police Eject 20 Students Who Boo Red's Talk," *Chicago Tribune*, May 24, 1951, 7.
21 "A Call to Negro Women," Louise Thomson Patterson Papers, Box 15, Folder 26, Emory University Archives, Atlanta, Georgia; Charlotta Bass, "Why We're Going to Washington," *Daily Worker*, September 27, 1951, 2; Erik McDuffie, "A 'New Freedom Movement of Negro Women': Sojourning for Truth, Justice, and Human Rights during the Cold War," *Radical History Review* 101 (2008), 86; McDuffie, *Sojourning for Freedom*, 173; Boyce Davies, *Left of Karl Marx*, 36–7.
22 McDuffie, *Sojourning for Freedom*, 183.
23 Claudia Jones, "Half the World," *The Worker*, November 25, 1951, 11.
24 Jones, "Half the World," 11.
25 Claudia Jones, "Negro Women in the Fight for Peace," 1952,

9, Vertical Files, Claudia Jones, TL; "A Petition to the Human Rights Commission of the Social and Economic Council of the United Nations; and to the General Assembly of the United Nations; and to the Several Delegations of the Member States of the United Nations," National Committee to Free the Ingram Family, 1948–1954, Mary Church Terrell Papers, Library of Congress; Claudia Jones, "Sojourners for Truth and Justice," *The Worker*, February 10, 1952, 8; Jones, "An End to the Neglect," 15.

26 Jones, "Sojourners for Truth and Justice," 8.
27 William Patterson, *The Man Who Cried Genocide* (New York: International Publishers, 2017), 164–5; Gerald Horne, *Black Revolutionary: William Patterson and the Globalization of the Black Freedom Struggle* (Urbana: University of Illinois Press, 2013), 114–17; Charles H. Martin, "Internationalizing the American Dilemma: The Civil Rights Congress and the 1951 Genocide Petition to the United Nations," *Journal of American Ethnic History* 16:4 (1997), 37–8; Patterson (ed.), *We Charge Genocide*.
28 McDuffie, "A 'New Freedom Movement of Negro Women,'" 95–7; Horne, *Black Revolutionary*, 138–9; "LYL Rally to Hear Claudia Jones," *Daily Worker*, March 7, 1952, 2; "Students Hear Claudia Jones," *Daily Worker*, March 12, 1952, 4.
29 Joseph Keith, *Unbecoming Americans: Writing Race and Nation in the Shadows of Citizenship, 1945–1960* (New Brunswick: Rutgers University Press, 2013), 166.
30 Federal Bureau of Investigation, Claudia Jones File, Part 5, Volume 3, 1; Claudia Jones, "Claudia Jones Discusses the Tobacco Habit," *The Worker*, January 10, 1954, 12.
31 Claudia Jones, "Henry Winston: Prisoner of Wall Street's Cold War," *Daily Worker*, June 27, 1949, 2.
32 Michael Singer, "FBI Seizes 17," *Daily Worker*, June 21, 1951, 1, 9; "Claudia Jones, Betty Gannett, Freed on Bail," *Daily Worker*, June 24, 1951, 1; Claudia Jones, "Half the World," *The Worker*, February 3, 1952, 8.
33 Michael Singer, "FBI Seizes 17," *Daily Worker*, June 21, 1951, 1, 9; "Claudia Jones, Betty Gannett, Freed on Bail," *Daily Worker*, June 24, 1951, 1; Claudia Jones, "Half the World," *The Worker*,

February 3, 1952, 8; Claudia Jones, "Half the World," *The Worker*, July 8, 1951, 8.
34 Federal Bureau of Investigation, Claudia Jones File, Part 5, Volume 5, 1–111.
35 Schrecker, *Many Are the Crimes*, 120–1.
36 Federal Bureau of Investigation, Claudia Jones File, Part 5, Volume 5, 86–7; "Claudia Jones: From List Submitted by the Government 3/10/52," Box 14, Folder 11, MMKP.
37 Families of the Smith Act Victims, "The People Take Care of Their Own," 1952, 2, Smith Act Box, 1951–1963 Folder, James Jackson and Esther Cooper Jackson Papers, TL; Albert Kahn, *Vengeance of the Young: The Story of the Smith Act Children* (New York: The Hour Publishers, 1952), 8–9.
38 Claudia Jones, "Half the World," *The Worker*, October 14, 1951, 8; Deborah Gerson, "Is Family Devotion Now Subversive? Familialism against McCarthyism," in *Not June Cleaver: Women and Gender in Postwar America, 1945–1980*, ed. Joanne Meyerowitz (Philadelphia: Temple University Press, 1994), 151–76.
39 "Abner Berry, Journalist & Activist, Dies at 85," *People's Daily World*, July 3, 1987, 10-A; Abner Berry, "Birthday Party in Harlem," *Daily Worker*, March 2, 1952, 7.
40 Harry Raymond, "Harvey Matusow Is Third Stoolpigeon Called by Government in Foley Square Trials," *Daily Worker*, July 22, 1952, 3; William Foster, "Matusow Confesses Perjury," *Daily Worker*, February 1, 1955, 3.
41 Milton Howard and Art Shields, "13 Fight Excessive Bail after 1–3 Year Sentences," *Daily Worker*, February 4, 1953, 1. In Jones's autobiographical letter to William Foster in 1955 she mentions three arrests. This number has been repeated by several scholars, while others have identified four arrests including her October 1950 detention on Ellis Island. It appears that Jones got the details wrong in her letter. She was first arrested in 1948 for deportation, and then again in October 1950 when she was held in the "McCarran wing." Her letter claims this was October 1951 and the wing was called the "Walter McCarran wing." She was referring to the McCarran-Walter Act, which was not passed until the summer of 1952. There is no extant evidence to suggest she was taken into custody in October 1951, and she could not

have been under a law that had not yet been passed. This suggests that Jones got the date and the law wrong in her autobiographical letter. In fact, she was arrested in January 1948, October 1950, and July 1951. She was taken into custody in February 1953 while out on appeal after conviction, and was remanded to prison in January 1955. "Claudia Jones Ill, Trial of 16 Postponed," *Daily Worker*, June 17, 1952, 1; Denise Lynn, "Claudia Jones in Exile: Deportation and Policing Blackness in the Cold War," *Twentieth-Century Communism: A Journal of International History* 18 (2020), 39–63; Federal Bureau of Investigation, Claudia Jones File, Part 8, Volume 7, 60–1, 63, 78. The FBI notes two separate hospitalizations during the appeals, and a car accident in which Jones was not injured; Sherwood, *Claudia Jones*, 21; Claudia Jones to Comrade Foster, December 6, 1955, CJMC.

42 Claudia Jones, *13 Communists Speak to the Court* (New York: New Century Publishers, 1953), 19–26.

43 Michael Singer, "Ben Davis – More Than Ever Before, He's Needed Home," *Daily Worker*, December 5, 1954, 7.

44 Claudia Jones, "The Precious Charters of Liberty," *Party Voice*, Bulletin issued by the New York Communist Party, Special Issue, Negro History Week, February 1954, 7–8, Box 46, Civil Rights Congress Papers, Schomburg Center for Research in Black Culture, Harlem, New York.

45 Virginia Gardner, "Will Send 3 Women Leaders to West Virginia Jail," *Daily Worker*, January 21, 1955, 2; "3 Women Prisoners Due in Alderson Today," *Daily Worker*, January 25, 1955, 2; Mary Kaufmann, "Motion," and Louis Miller, M.D., To Whom It May Concern, December 15, 1952, Box 14, Folder 7, MMKP.

46 Louis Miller, M.D., To Whom It May Concern, December 19, 1952, and John Wood, "Echocardiogram," Box 14, Folder 7, MMKP. Nurse practitioner Erin Dupree examined Jones's medical records and told me that if she was reading the graphs of her heart activity correctly, it appeared Jones was having a heart attack; her blood pressure numbers were also extremely elevated. Virginia Gardner, "Will Send 3 Women Leaders to West Virginia Jail," *Daily Worker*, January 21, 1955, 2; "3 Women Prisoners Due in Alderson Today," *Daily Worker*, January 25, 1955, 2

47 Flynn, *My Life as a Political Prisoner*, 25–41; Jones, "Claudia Jones Discusses the Tobacco Habit," 12.
48 Mary Kaufmann to Warden, January 26, 1955; Mary Kaufmann to Claudia Jones, February 22, 1955, Box 9, Folder 12, MMKP.
49 Claudia Jones to Charles Cumberbatch, February 2, 1955, Box 9, Folder 12, MMKP.
50 Claudia Jones to Mary Kaufman, February 5, 1955; Claudia Jones to Mary Kaufmann, February 24, 1955, Box 9, Folder 12, MMKP.
51 Boyce Davies (ed.), *Claudia Jones: Beyond Containment*, 189–90.
52 Flynn, *My Life as a Political Prisoner*, iii, 25, 95, 140, 178.
53 Gerson, "Is Family Devotion Now Subversive?"; Flynn, *My Life as a Political Prisoner*, iii, 77; Claudia Jones to Mary Kaufmann, February 13, 1955; Mary Kaufmann to Claudia Jones, February 22, 1955, Box 9, Folder 12, MMKP.
54 Claudia Jones to Mary Kaufmann, March 6, 1955, Box 9, Folder 12, MMKP.
55 "Mrs. Bass Urges Support to Move to Free Claudia Jones," *Daily Worker*, April 3, 1955, 13; "Ben Davis Writes Our Readers," *Daily Worker*, April 14, 1955, 4; "Claudia Jones Denied Diet Prescribed for Heart Illness," *Daily Worker*, March 7, 1955, 6; "Hear Health Plea Monday by Claudia Jones, Jacob Mandel," *Daily Worker*, January 23, 1955, 2; "An Appeal in Defense of Negro Leadership," pamphlet, 1952, DBP; Sherwood, *Claudia Jones*, 23.
56 "Claudia Jones's Neighbors Plead with Parole Board: Give Back Our Friend," *Daily Worker*, May 11, 1955, 3; "Jamaica Union Asks Claudia Jones Pardon," *Daily Worker*, July 6, 1955, 4; "Claudia Jones in Prison Hospital a Week; Urge Renewed Parole Plea," *Daily Worker*, August 12, 1955, 3; "Trinidad Independence Party Urges Release of Claudia Jones," *Daily Worker*, September 1, 1955, 2; Federal Bureau of Investigation, Claudia Jones File, Part 9, Volume 8, 21, 30; Flynn, *My Life as a Political Prisoner*, 103–5, 107.
57 Claudia Jones, "Lament for Emmett Till," Box 1, Folder 5, CJMC.
58 Flynn, *My Life as a Political Prisoner*, 77–80, 100–1.
59 Claudia Jones to Mary Kaufmann, August 7, 1955, Box 9, Folder 12, MMKP.

60 Flynn, *My Life as a Political Prisoner*, 103–5, 107; Claudia Jones to Mary Kaufmann, August 28, 1955, Box 9, Folder 12, MMKP.
61 Flynn, *My Life as a Political Prisoner*, 116–17.
62 Flynn, *My Life as a Political Prisoner*, 117–18.
63 Federal Bureau of Investigation, Claudia Jones File, Part 8, Volume 7, 21; Part 9, Volume 8, 78, 99–105; "Claudia Jones Here 10:55 AM," *Daily Worker*, October 24, 1955, 1; "Greet Claudia Jones Today," *Daily Worker*, October 24, 1955, 5.
64 James Ford, "Renew Effort to Save Claudia Jones," *Daily Worker*, October 28, 1955, 8; John Hudson Jones, "1,000 Vow Fight to Free Roosevelt Ward Jr.," *Daily Worker*, October 1, 1951, 7; Roosevelt Ward, "Claudia Jones Enters Hospital; Faces Court Hearing on Monday," *Daily Worker*, October 27, 1955.
65 "Claudia Jones Here 10:55 AM," *Daily Worker*, October 24, 1955, 1; "Greet Claudia Jones Today," *Daily Worker*, October 24, 1955, 5.
66 James Ford to W.E.B. Du Bois, November 12, 1955, DBP; Bill V. Mullen, *W.E.B. Du Bois: Revolutionary across the Color Line* (London: Pluto Press, 2016), 141.
67 William Foster, "Defend Claudia Jones!" *Daily Worker*, November 10, 1955, 3; William Foster, "Statement of National Committee of Communist Party on Claudia Jones," November 1955, Box 1, Folder 12, CJMC.
68 "Ask Stay for Claudia Jones to Testify at Smith Trial," *Daily Worker*, November 4, 1955, 3; Virginia Gardner, "Claudia Jones Granted Stay to Give Deposition," *Daily Worker*, November 10, 1955, 1; "Claudia Jones Will Go to London; Too Ill to Fight Deportation," *Daily Worker*, November 21, 1955, 1; "Claudia Jones Loses," *New York Times*, November 10, 1955, 39; "Red Agrees to Leave the Country," *New York Times*, November 18, 1955, 10; Lynn, "Claudia Jones in Exile: Deportation and Policing Blackness in the Cold War"; "Memorandum in Opposition to Defendants Application for an Order Staying the Deportation of Claudia Jones," Box 14, Folder 8, MMKP. Flynn, *My Life as a Political Prisoner*, 116–17.
69 William Foster, National Chairman, Communist Party, USA to Harry Pollitt, General Secretary, Communist Party of Great Britain, December 9, 1955, Box 1, Folder 12, CJMC; Claudia

Jones to William Foster, December 6, 1955, Claudia Jones Vertical File, TL.
70 William Foster, "Statement of National Committee Communist Party on Claudia Jones," Box 1, Folder 12, CJMC; "CP Hits Deportation of Claudia Jones," *Daily Worker*, December 2, 1955, 2.
71 Augusta Strong, "Hundreds Say Last Goodbye to Claudia Jones, Who Sails Today," *Daily Worker*, December 9, 1955, 3; Sherwood, *Claudia Jones*, 26; William Patterson, "Remarks on the Eve of the Deportation of Claudia Jones," Box 113, Folder 49, Communist Party Papers, TL.
72 Strong, "Hundreds Say Last Goodbye to Claudia Jones," 3; Paul Robeson, "Statement," December 7, 1955, Box 1, Folder 2, CJMC; Sherwood, *Claudia Jones*, 26.
73 "200 at Pier Bid Farewell to Claudia Jones," *Daily Worker*, December 12, 1955, 3; Federal Bureau of Investigation, Claudia Jones File, Part 10, Volume 8, 25–6, 34.

## 5 London (1955–1964)

1 Claudia Jones, "Storm at Sea," October 8, 1962, Yalta, Sanitorium, Box 1, Folder 5, CJMC.
2 McDuffie, "For a New Anti-fascist, Anti-imperialist People's Coalition," 186.
3 "You're Welcome Here Claudia," *Daily Worker*, December 14, 1955, 3; "Welcome Claudia! A Brave Woman is Deported," January 1956, Box 1, Folder 22, CJMC.
4 Claudia Jones, "Claudia Jones Tells Dreary Round of Life in Prison," *Daily Worker*, February 5, 1956, 11.
5 Claudia Jones to Stretch Johnson, April 21, 1956, Box 1, Folder 9, CJMC; Flynn, *My Life as a Political Prisoner*, 118; Sherwood, *Claudia Jones*, 37.
6 Sherwood, *Claudia Jones*, 37, 39; Claudia Jones to Stretch Johnson, April 21, 1956, Box 1, Folder 9, CJMC.
7 Claudia Jones to "Comrade Foster," December 6, 1955, Box 1, Folder 12, CJMC; Heloise Robinson to Claudia Jones, December 21, 1957, Box 1, Folder 14, CJMC.
8 Sherwood, *Claudia Jones*, 38; "Families of McCarran Victims Place Protests before UN," *Worker*, November 19, 1950, 5; "To

Honor Father of Claudia Jones," *Daily Worker*, June 17, 1955, 2; "Funeral Services Tonight for Charles Cumberbatch," *Daily Worker*, June 11, 1956, 3; Claudia Jones to "Daddy," Box 1, Folder 5, CJMC.
9 Claudia Jones, "Claudia Jones Writes about Her Father," *Daily Worker*, June 26, 1956, 4.
10 Passenger Manifest, KLM Royal Dutch Airlines, July 12, 1956, Depart New York, Arrive London, England, Passenger and Crew Lists of People Departing from New York, National Archives; Heloise Robinson to Claudia Jones, September 16 [year is illegible], Box 1, Folder 14, CJMC; interview with Winston Pinder, May 7, 2022.
11 Boyce Davies, *Left of Karl Marx*, 142–3.
12 Claudia Jones, "I Was Deported Because...," an interview with Claudia Jones by George Bowrin," in Boyce Davies (ed.), *Claudia Jones: Beyond Containment*, 16–19.
13 Jones, "I Was Deported Because...," 17.
14 Jones, "I Was Deported Because...," 18.
15 Heloise Robinson to Lorraine Hansberry, July 7, 1960, Box 2 Folder 15, Lorraine Hansberry Papers, Schomburg Center for Research in Black Culture, Harlem, New York; Sherwood, *Claudia Jones*, 41, 52, 73.
16 Sherwood, *Claudia Jones*, 41, 52, 73; Claudia Jones, "Statement," Box 2, Folder 2, CJMC.
17 Sherwood, *Claudia Jones*, 43, 72; Claudia Jones to Stretch Johnson, April 21, 1956, Box 1, Folder 9, CJMC; Claudia Jones to Dr. Eric Williams, July 23, 1957, Box 1, Folder 6, CJMC; Canadian Peace Congress to Shirley Graham Du Bois, June 10, 1952, DBP.
18 Sherwood, *Claudia Jones*, 64–5; Susan Pennybacker, *From Scottsboro to Munich: Race and Political Culture in 1930s Britain* (Princeton: Princeton University Press, 2009), 28, 49.
19 Sherwood, *Claudia Jones*, 64–5, 70; Evan Smith, "National Liberation for Whom? The Postcolonial Question, the Communist Party of Great Britain, and the Party's African and Caribbean membership," *International Review of Social History* 61:2 (2016), 283–4.
20 Sherwood, *Claudia Jones*, 70; Smith, "National Liberation for Whom?" 283–4; Johnson, "*I Think of My Mother*," 76–7.

21 Sherwood, *Claudia Jones*, 74.
22 Smith, "National Liberation for Whom?" 284–5.
23 Claudia Jones, "Sunday Morning, No. 14," 1957, 1–2, Box 1, Folder 26, CJMC.
24 Sherwood, *Claudia Jones*, 68; Jones, "Sunday Morning, No. 14," 2–3.
25 Jones, "Sunday Morning, No. 14," 3–5; Smith, "National Liberation for Whom?" 306.
26 Sherwood, *Claudia Jones*, 76; Claudia Jones, "West Indians in Britain," *World News*, June 29, 1957, 412.
27 Jones, "West Indians in Britain," 412.
28 Jones, "West Indians in Britain," 412, 416.
29 Boyce Davies, *Left of Karl Marx*, 225.
30 Claudia Jones, "Clamor Grows in Britain: Let Robeson Sing!" *Worker*, July 8, 1956, 8; Sherwood, *Claudia Jones*, 77.
31 Ransby, *Eslanda*, 240, 262–3.
32 Donald Hines, "The West Indian Gazette," in Sherwood, *Claudia Jones*, 125–9; Donald Hines, "The West Indian Gazette: Claudia Jones and the Black Press in Britain," *Race & Class* 50:1 (2008), 89–90; Boyce Davies, *Left of Karl Marx*, 172–3; Tony Martin, *Amy Ashwood Garvey: Pan-Africanist, Feminist, and Mrs. Marcus Garvey No. 1, or a Tale of Two Amies* (Dover, DE: The Majority Press, 2007), 271.
33 Claudia Jones, "The Caribbean Community in Britain," *Freedomways* 4:3 (1964): 354–5.
34 Hines, "The West Indian Gazette," 131–4; Rochelle Rowe, "'Colonisation in Reverse': Claudia Jones, the West Indian Gazette and the 'Carnival Queen' Beauty Contest in London, 1959–64," in *Imagining Caribbean Womanhood: Race, Nation, and Beauty Contests, 1929–1970*, ed. Pamela Sharpe, Lynn Abrams, Penny Summerfield, and Cordelia Beattie (Manchester: Manchester University Press, 2013), 164.
35 Sherwood, *Claudia Jones*, 50–5.
36 Martin, *Amy Ashwood Garvey*, 256–7, 272.
37 Hines, "The West Indian Gazette," 134, 140; Rowe, "'Colonisation in Reverse,'" 165.
38 Elizabeth Gurley Flynn, "With Claudia Jones in London," *Sunday Worker*, November 16, 1938, 9.

39 Claudia Jones to Delegations of the Leeward and Windward Islands, Commission in the UK British Guiana and British Honduras, June 22, 1959; Claudia Jones to Essie Robeson, June 6, 1959; Claudia Jones, "Opening Speech," July 18, 1959, Box 1, Folder 20, CJMC.
40 Paul Robeson, "Meet Paul Robeson: West Indian Gazette, 'one of my favorite newspapers,'" *West Indian Gazette*, September 1959, 4; "West Indian Gazette Presents Paul Robeson," September 28, 1960, Box 1, Folder 20, CJMC.
41 Kennetta Hammond Perry, "'Little Rock' in Britain: Jim Crow's Transatlantic Topographies," *Journal of British Studies* 51 (2012), 155–6; Camilla Schofield and Ben Jones, "'Whatever Community Is, This Is Not It': Notting Hill and the Reconstruction of 'Race' in Britain after 1958," *Journal of British Studies* 58 (2019), 142–4; Kennetta Hammond Perry, *London is the Place for Me: Black Britons, Citizenship, and the Politics of Race* (Oxford: Oxford University Press, 2016), 90.
42 Hammond Perry, *London is the Place for Me*, 91–2, 108.
43 Hines, "The West Indian Gazette," 142; Hines, "The West Indian Gazette: Claudia Jones and the Black Press in Britain," 92; Hammond Perry, *London is the Place for Me*, 108–10.
44 A. Whiteman to B. Ape, August 18, 1958, Box 1, Folder 28, CJMC; Hines, "The West Indian Gazette," 134, 140; "Racist Poison in Britain," *Sunday Worker*, September 7, 1958, 16; Flynn, "With Claudia Jones in London," 9.
45 Bill Schwarz, "Claudia Jones and the *West Indian Gazette*: Reflections on the Emergence of Post-colonial Britain," *Twentieth Century British History* 14:3 (2003), 264, 269–70.
46 Schwarz, "Claudia Jones and the *West Indian Gazette*," 272–3; Hines, "The West Indian Gazette: Claudia Jones and the Black Press in Britain," 91.
47 Colin Prescod, "Carnival," in Sherwood, *Claudia Jones*, 150, 156–8; Edward Pilkington, *Beyond the Mother Country: West Indians and the Notting Hill Riots* (London: I.B. Tauris, 1990), 143.
48 Schwarz, "Claudia Jones and the *West Indian Gazette*," 274; Prescod, "Carnival," 150–1.
49 Prescod, "Carnival," 158; Rowe, "'Colonisation in Reverse,'" 152.

50 Rowe, "'Colonisation in Reverse,'" 150–8.
51 Rowe, "'Colonisation in Reverse,'" 167–8.
52 Rowe, "'Colonisation in Reverse,'" 151, 170–4.
53 Schwarz, "Claudia Jones and the *West Indian Gazette*," 276–7, 279.
54 Martin, *Amy Ashwood Garvey*, 273–5.
55 Hammond Perry, *London is the Place for Me*, 130–1.
56 Hammond Perry, *London is the Place for Me*, 127.
57 Hammond Perry, *London is the Place for Me*, 128; Sherwood, *Claudia Jones*, 95; "Kelso Cochrane Memorial Meeting," May 28, 1959, Box 14, Eslanda Robeson Papers, Moorland-Spingarn Research Center, Howard University, Washington, DC.
58 Hines, "The West Indian Gazette," 141–3.
59 Hammond Perry, *London is the Place for Me*, 137–8; Sherwood, *Claudia Jones*, 97.
60 Hammond Perry, *London is the Place for Me*, 143.
61 Hammond Perry, *London is the Place for Me*, 97, 135; Sherwood, *Claudia Jones*, 97.
62 Maddalena Marinari, "Divided and Conquered: Immigration Reform Advocates and the Passage of the 1952 Immigration and Nationality Act," *Journal of Ethnic History* 35:3 (2016), 13; Hammond Perry, *London is the Place for Me*, 153.
63 Hammond Perry, *London is the Place for Me*, 153–4; Claudia Jones, "Butler's Bill Mocks Commonwealth," *Race & Class* 58:1 (2016), 119. The article originally appeared in the *Gazette* and was reprinted in *Race & Class*.
64 Jones, "Butler's Bill Mocks Commonwealth," 199; Beverley Bryan, Stella Dadzie, and Suzanne Scafe, *The Heart of the Race: Black Women's Lives in Britain* (London: Verso, 2018), 139; Hammond Perry, *London is the Place for Me*, 154.
65 Jones, "Butler's Bill Mocks Commonwealth," 120; Smith, "National Liberation for Whom?" 309.
66 Jones, "Butler's Bill Mocks Commonwealth," 120–1; Sherwood, *Claudia Jones*, 98.
67 Hammond Perry, *London is the Place for Me*, 173, 176.
68 Hammond Perry, *London is the Place for Me*, 172–3, 177–81; Sherwood, *Claudia Jones*, 99.
69 Jones, "The Caribbean Community in Britain," 341–57; David Killingray, "The West Indian Federation and Decolonization

in the British Caribbean," *The Journal of Caribbean History* 34:1 (2000), 71–88; "New Immigration Rules," *West Indian Gazette*, July 1962, 5.
70 Jones, "The Caribbean Community in Britain," 343–4, 346–7.
71 Jones, "The Caribbean Community in Britain," 347–8, 350.
72 Jones, "The Caribbean Community in Britain," 356–7.
73 Sherwood, *Claudia Jones*, 109, 137; Claudia Jones to Abhimanyu Manchanda, August 21, 1962, MM 59739, AMC.
74 Claudia Jones to Abhimanyu Manchanda, August 21, 1962, October 26, 1962, MM 59739, AMC; Claudia Jones, "Visit to the USSR," *West Indian Gazette and Afro-Asian Caribbean News*, October 1962, 5.
75 Jones, "Visit to the USSR," 5.
76 Sherwood, *Claudia Jones*, 110, 147, 162; "Review of the World Congress of Women in Moscow," Reproduced from the *Hsinhua News Agency* correspondent, Moscow, July 4 and 5, 1963; Claudia Jones to Abhimanyu Manchanda, October 26, 1962, MM 59739, AMC.
77 Sherwood, *Claudia Jones*, 110, 147, 162; "Review of the World Congress of Women in Moscow," Reproduced from the *Hsinhua News Agency* correspondent, Moscow, July 4 and 5, 1963.
78 Sherwood, *Claudia Jones*, 108; Claudia Jones, "Dirty War: Negro Americans Oppose Intervention in Indochina War," *Negro Affairs Quarterly*, 1954, 2; Dr. Rinjana Sidhant, "Vietnam War May Spread," *West Indian Gazette*, May 1964, 10.
79 Sherwood, *Claudia Jones*, 48, 100–1; Claudia Jones to Shirley Graham Du Bois, Telegram, August 29, 1963, DBP; Claudia Jones to Stretch Johnson, April 21, 1956, 3, Box 1, Folder 9, CJMC.
80 Claudia Jones, "Dr. Luther King's Warning," *West Indian Gazette and Afro-Asian Caribbean News*, December–January 1965, 1, 4.
81 Sherwood, *Claudia Jones*, 81–2; Claudia Jones to George Matthews, May 7, 1963, Box 2, Folder 1, CJMC.
82 Zifeng Liu, "Decolonization Is Not a Dinner Party: Claudia Jones, China's Nuclear Weapons, and Anti-Imperialist Solidarity," *The Journal of Intersectionality* 3:2 (2019), 21.
83 "WIG Editor Hails Chinese A. Bomb Test," *West Indian Gazette and Afro-Asian Caribbean News*, November 1964, 2.

84 Liu, "Decolonization Is Not a Dinner Party," 22–3.
85 Claudia Jones to West Indian Gazette and Afro-Asian Caribbean News, August 7, 1964, Box 2, Folder 14, CJMC.
86 Claudia Jones, "First Lady of the World, I Talk with Mme Sun Yat-Sen," *West Indian Gazette and Afro-Asian Caribbean News*, November 1964, 7.
87 Liu, "Decolonization Is Not a Dinner Party," 25–6, 30; Intondi, *African Americans against the Bomb*, 32.
88 Sherwood, *Claudia Jones*, 112–14; Liu, "Decolonization Is Not a Dinner Party," 36, 38.
89 Liu, "Decolonization Is Not a Dinner Party," 26–8, 30.
90 Barney Desai, President, Coloured People's Congress of South Africa, "Rebel Against Injustice," *West Indian Gazette and Afro-Asian Caribbean News*, February 1965, 4; Raymond Kumene, African National Congress, "World Liberation Movement's Loss," *West Indian Gazette and Afro-Asian Caribbean News*, February 1965, 5.

Conclusion

1 Flynn, *My Life as a Political Prisoner*, 212. Text appears courtesy of International Publishers.
2 Claudia Jones, "Tonight I Tried to Imagine What Life Would Be Like in the Future," June 18, 1964, in Boyce Davies (ed.), *Claudia Jones: Beyond Containment*, 19–20.
3 Sherwood, *Claudia Jones*, 163–5; Telegram from West Indian Gazette to Shirley Graham Du Bois, August 29, 1963, MS 312, DBP.
4 Sherwood, *Claudia Jones*, 165–9; A. Manchanda, "Dear Claudia! We Shall Hold High Your Banner of Anti-Imperialism," *West Indian Gazette and Afro-Asian Caribbean News*, December–January 1965, 5, 7; Funeral Program, Box 113, Folder 49, Communist Party Papers, TL; A. Manchanda to E. Herman, September 8, 1983, Box 12, Folder 19, CJMC.
5 A. Manchanda, Claudia Jones Memorial Committee, February 18, 1965, Box 1, Folder 18; "In Memory of Claudia Jones," Box 2, Folder 15, CJMC; "Claudia Jones Left Indelible Impact on Liberation History," *West Indian Gazette and Afro-Asian Caribbean News*, April–May 1965, 8.

6 "May We Remain Faithful to the Cause for Which She Died," and "Mrs. Du Bois Overwhelmed with Grief," *West Indian Gazette and Afro-Asian Caribbean News*, February 1965, 1, 4.

7 "Robeson's Grief," and "GIANT Officer in Struggle – Ruby Dee Negro Artist," and "Tribute from America," *West Indian Gazette and Afro-Asian Caribbean News*, February 1965, 3, 7, 9; Penny von Eschen, *Race against Empire: Black Americans and Anticolonialism, 1937–1957* (Ithaca: Cornell University Press, 1997), 185.

8 "British Leaders Homage," and "Belgian Friends Lament Claudia," and "Soviet Women's Sympathy," *West Indian Gazette and Afro-Asian Caribbean News*, February 1965, 1–3.

9 "Rebel against Injustice," *West Indian Gazette and Afro-Asian Caribbean News*, February 1965, 4.

10 "World Liberation Movement's Loss," *West Indian Gazette and Afro-Asian Caribbean News*, February 1965, 5.

11 "Symbol of Inspiration – Kwesi Armah," and "World Mourns Says PPP," *West Indian Gazette and Afro-Asian Caribbean News*, February 1965, 8–9.

12 "Outlaw Racial Discrimination," *West Indian Gazette and Afro-Asian Caribbean News*, February 1965, 5.

13 George Lamming, "We Mourn Her to Celebrate Her Example," and "West Indians Were Proud of Her," *West Indian Gazette and Afro-Asian Caribbean News*, February 1965, 8.

14 "Dr. Pitt's Pride and Sorrow," *West Indian Gazette and Afro-Asian Caribbean News*, February 1965, 9.

15 A. Manchanda to the Members of the Executive Committee, October 29, 1965, Communist Party of Great Britain Papers, National Archive, London, England.

16 Diane Langford, *The Manchanda Connection: A Political Memoir by Diane Langford*, July 2015, 18, 24, 26, http://abhimanyumanchandaremembered.weebly.com/#sthash.zg4Gca4a.dpuf

17 Sherwood, *Claudia Jones*, 170; "Now He Wants a Mark for a Remarkable Woman," *Camden New Journal*, June 17, 1982, Box 2, Folder 19, CJMC.

18 A. Manchanda to Bill Fairman, August 2, 1982; "A Grave for Claudia," *Afro Caribbean News*, Box 12, Folder 19, CJMC; Sherwood, *Claudia Jones*, 170.

19 A. Manchanda to Bill Fairman, August 2, 1982, Box 12, Folder 19, CJMC.

20 Interview with Winston Pinder, May 7, 2022.
21 Bill Fairman to F.H. Myles Hickey, August 14, 1983; Winston Pinder to A. Manchanda, April 4, 1983; A. Manchanda to E. Herman, September 8, 1983, Box 12, Folder 19, CJMC.
22 A. Manchanda to June J. Marriot, January 10, 1984, Box 12, Folder 19, CJMC; Langford, *The Manchanda Connection*, 25–7; Boyce Davies (ed.), *Claudia Jones: Beyond Containment*, xvi; interview with Winston Pinder, May 7, 2022.
23 Interview with Winston Pinder, May 7, 2022.
24 Jones, "Tonight I Tried to Imagine What Life Would Be Like in the Future," 19–20.

# Index

AACC (Afro Asian Caribbean Conference) 198–9
AACP (Association for the Advancement of Colored People) 191–2
ABB (African Black Brotherhood) 40
abortion 97
Acheson, Dean 126, 129
ACLU (American Civil Liberties Union) 86
ACO (Afro-Caribbean Organization) 220, 221
ACPFB (American Committee for the Protection of Foreign Born) 99, 107
actors, Black 34–5
Africa
    Pan-African politics 171, 182, 182–3, 185, 208
African National Congress 216
African Women's Day 180
African Women's Freedom Movement 180
Alanzo, Louis Recardo 216
Alcantara, Theophilus 61
Alderson Prison, West Virginia 148–57, 166
Alexander, Charles 33
Alfrey, Phyllis 186
*Amsterdam News* 33

Amter, Israel 139
anticommunism
    and racism 34, 115–16, 146–7, 170–1
    in the United States 5, 9, 12–13, 34, 81–3, 84, 85, 114–19, 146, 170
    and CPUSA members 99–100, 103, 115–16, 118–19, 139, 140–7
Armah, Kwesi 215, 217
Atlantic Charter 80
atomic weapons 81, 103, 125, 129, 207–9
AYD (American Youth for Democracy) 65, 66, 67

Baker, Ella 46
Bass, Charlotta 100, 153
Bates, Ruby 43
Beans, Everett 33
Bennett, Louise 199
Berry, Abner 60–1, 73, 143
Biddle, Francis 69, 71
Biden, Joe 130
Birch, Reginald 216
birth control 97
Bittelman, Alexander 74, 99, 139
Black Americans
    activists and the FBI 70–1
    and the Black Belt Thesis 41

Black Americans (*cont.*)
   and Browderism 74–5
   and civil rights 84
   and communism 72
   and fascism 38
   liberals 101, 116–17
   lynching of Black men 75–6, 131–2, 131–3, 134–5, 154–5
   and police violence 83, 85, 86–7, 91, 122, 223
   soldiers 53, 54, 55, 130
   and the Soviet Union 90
   and the Vietnam War 204
   and the *We Charge Genocide* petition 136–7
   and World War II 53–61, 63, 80
   *see also* Black women
Black Belt Thesis 40–1, 43, 72, 74, 75–6, 77, 115
Black families, Jones on 97
Black Freedom Struggle 8, 12–13, 14, 39, 43, 44, 46, 74, 76, 85, 159
   and China 207, 209
   and the FBI 69, 70
   and US fascism 87, 91
   and US military anticommunism 81
Black history week (later month) 3
Black Left feminism 44
Black Lives Matter 10, 38, 70–1, 119
Black Nationalists 39, 40, 43, 45
Black Panther Party 71
Black Popular Front 44–5
Black women
   African Women's Freedom Movement 180
   and beauty culture 189–91
   and the "Black Sash movement" 190
   and the CAW 93
   in the CPUSA 37, 41, 45–6
   and double jeopardy 110
   Ingram case and lynch law 135–6
   Jones on 3, 7, 8, 14, 15, 19, 101, 108–14, 192
   New York street corner "slave markets" 46, 47
   superexploitation of 37, 47, 109–11
   triple oppression of 15, 46, 47, 77, 109–11, 113, 224
   West Indian women in Britain 171
BLM *see* Black Lives Matter
Bloor, Mother Ella Reeve 55
Bowrin, George 170, 171, 181
Britain
   antiracism mystique 185–6
   and the Caribbean 21–2, 23
   Commonwealth Immigration Act 195–201, 205
   Jones's deportation to 160–3
   Labour Party 174, 195, 197, 217
   memory of Jones in 12, 13
   racism in 192–5, 205–6, 211, 224
   West Indian immigrants 175, 176–9, 177–8, 183–4, 185–6, 195, 196–8, 201
   *see also* London
Brockway, Fenner (later Lord) 178, 192, 198, 215, 217
Browder, Earl 50, 72, 74
Browderism 71–8
Brownell, Herbert 153, 154, 161
Burnham, Louis 179
Butler, Rab 196
Buxenbaum, Alva 3

CAA (Council on African Affairs) 64
*Californian Eagle* 100, 152
*Camden New Journal* 219–20
Campbell, Grace 37, 40
CAO (Council of African Organizations) 193
capitalism 223, 224, 225
    abolitionists of 83
    and Browderism 72
    capitalist imperialism 85
    and democracy 122
    Jones's critique of monopoly capitalism 14–15, 19
    and labor unions 16
    late-stage 9–11, 17
    racial capitalism 20–1, 83, 200–1
    and racial fascism 78
    in the US south 40
    and war 126, 127, 130–1
    and women 96–7
Carew, Jan 181, 190
Caribbean diaspora
    and Jones's life in London 165
Caribbean Labor Congress (CLC) 175
*Caribbean News* 180
    Jones's interview in 170–1
Carter, Trevor 221
Cattouse, Nadia 183, 214
CAW (Congress of American Women) 93–5
CBS (Camden Black Sisters) 5
CPPA (Coloured People's Progressive Association) 194–5
Charney, Charles 160
Chicago
    Claudia Jones Club 3
*Chicago Tribune* 132–3
China 203, 207–8, 209–10, 213–14

Churchill, Winston 72
    "Iron Curtain" speech 90, 91
CIO (Congress of Industrial Organizations) 88
citizenship
    and racial fascism 78
Civil Rights Congress 87
CJO (Claudia Jones Organization) 4–5
class
    and Browderism 74–5
    and the CPGB 176
    and the CPUSA 37, 40
    Jones on class and racism in Britain 178
    and labor unions 15–16
    racism and sexism 15
    and women's issues 97–8, 111–12
*Claudia Jones: A Woman of Her Time* (BBC documentary) 6
Claudia Jones Memorial Committee 219, 220, 221
Claudia Jones Memorial Fund 220
CLC (Caribbean Labor Congress) 175
Cochrane, Kelso 192–3, 195, 200
Cold War 5–6, 16–17, 59, 121–2, 224
    and Black Americans 137
    and the Black Popular Front 44–5
    and China 207
    containment policy 122
    the early Cold War (1945–1950) 79–119
    Jones and CPUSA's opposition to 125–7
    and Jones's deportation 165, 170
    and the Smith Act 67
    *see also* United States

# INDEX

colonialism 16
  and the Commonwealth Immigration Act 199–200
  and the CPGB 174–5, 175–7, 222
  *see also* imperialism
Colston, Edward 11
Columbus, Christopher 20
Comintern (Communist International) 41, 44, 174
Commonwealth Immigration Act 195–201
communism
  American communists 67, 80
  and Browderism 71–8
  Hoover's obsession with 69–71
  and the New York FWP 33–4
  US anticommunism 5, 9, 12–13
  *see also* CPGB (Communist Party of Great Britain); CPUSA (American Communist Party)
Congress of American Women 203
Connor, Edric 183, 194
Connor, Pearl 183, 194, 198
Constantine, Sir Leary 206
Cooke, Marvel 6, 46
Cooper, Anna Julia 110
Coppock, Richard 179
Cornejo, Judge Jesus Barba 95
Coughlin, Charles 66
Covid-19 pandemic 9–10, 10–11
CPA (Communist Political Association) 72
CPGB (Communist Party of Great Britain) 12, 160–1
  African and Caribbean membership 175–6, 222
  *The British Road to Socialism* 175–6

  Charter of Rights for Coloured Workers in Britain 174
  and the Commonwealth Immigration Act 197, 206
  and Jones's death 207, 216, 218–19, 220, 222
  Jones's relations with 166, 169, 172, 173–80, 185, 201, 206–7
  and racism 173–80
CPUSA (American Communist Party) 2, 9, 26, 33
  and anticommunist US policy 121–2
  purges of party members 115–16, 118–19, 139–47
  antifascism 37–8, 38–9, 44–5, 51–2, 64, 86–7, 92
  antiwar politics 37, 51–5
  Black Belt Thesis 40–1, 43, 72, 74, 75–6, 115
  Black membership 40–6
  Browderism 71–8
  and the Cold War state 83–4
  and the fascist triple K 55, 92–3, 126–7
  and FBI surveillance 70, 98–9
  Harlem branch 40, 42–3, 104
  histories of 7
  and Jones in London 166, 167, 171, 172
  and Jones's death 219
  and Jones's deportation 159, 161, 165
  and Jones's father (Charles Cumberbatch) 168
  Jones elected to National Board 67
  Jones's membership of 35, 37, 38, 39, 42–6, 140
  letter-writing campaigns 42
  and lynch law 42, 132
  and the NAACP 49–50

INDEX

name change to Communist
  Political Association (CPA)
  72, 74
National Convention (1948)
  101–3
National Peace Commission
  145
National Training School 48
and the "Negro Question"
  39–41, 77
peace initiatives 103
Popular Front platform 44–6,
  47, 56, 92
and racism 76–7, 171, 173–4
and Robeson 64–5
and the Scottsboro campaign
  41–4, 50, 104
*Sunday Worker* newspaper 183
Unemployed Councils 48
Women's Commission 3, 93,
  95, 97
and women's rights 77, 95–8,
  113
  Black women 109, 110, 112
*see also Daily Worker* newspaper
  (CPUSA)
CRC (Civil Rights Congress)
  89–90, 117, 136
Cuba 201
Cullors, Patrisse 10
Cumberbatch, Charles Bertrand
  19, 24, 25, 26, 28, 143
  death 168–9
  and the FWP (Federal
    Writers' Project) 32–5
  and Jones's imprisonment
    152, 153, 158
  "Negro Actors, Past and
    Present" 34–5
  *Negroes of New York* 32, 35
  US citizenship 62
Cumberbatch, Claudia *see* Jones,
  Claudia

Cumberbatch, Lindsay 24, 62,
  169
Cumberbatch, Sybil Logan
  (Minnie) 19, 24, 25, 26,
  27–8, 62
Cumberbatch, Sylvia 24, 62, 99
Cumberbatch, Yvonne 24, 62, 98,
  99, 169

*Daily Worker* newspaper (CPGB)
  166, 179–80, 206–7
*Daily Worker* newspaper (CPUSA)
  44, 67, 84–5, 100, 107,
  145–6, 159–60, 187
  Jones's articles for 47–8, 50,
    52
  on the Cold War state 91–2
  from London 166
  "Half the World" column
    122–5, 132–3, 134–7,
    139–40
  "Negro Affairs" articles 85–6
  on peace activism 128–9
  on smoking 138–9
  on US fascism 84–92
  "We Seek Full Equality for
    Women" 108, 113–14
  and Jones's deportation 158,
    159–60
  letters from Jones on Ellis
    Island 106–7
  Lowenfels's article 124
*Daily World* newspaper 3
Dale, Thelma 75
David, Prudhomme 23
Davis, Almena 100
Davis, Angela 5, 49, 213
  *Women, Race, and Class* 3
Davis, Ben 72, 74, 89, 100, 101,
  104, 138, 153, 162, 166–7,
  173
  arrest, trial and conviction
    115, 116, 118, 145–6

267

Davis, Ossie 205, 215–16
Davis, Sallye 49
Dee, Ruby 214–15, 215–16
Delaine, Reverend Joseph A. 158–9
democracy
  and anticommunism 137–8
  and capitalism 122
Democratic Centralism 8
Dennis, Eugene 115, 142
Dennis, Peggy 142
Desai, Barney 216
Dewey, Thomas 86
Dies, Martin 34
Dimock, Judge Edward 145
Doane, Dr. Joseph 27
Doyle, Charlie and Mikki 167
Draper, Muriel 94
Du Bois, Shirley Graham 173, 179, 205, 215
Du Bois, W.E.B. 3, 33, 57–8, 64, 102, 113, 136, 179, 215
  death 205, 213
  and Jones's deportation 159, 161
  peace activism 129, 130
  and the US State Department 173
Duclos, Jacques 74
Dulles, John Foster 161, 204
Dumbarton Oaks conference 73

Edelman, Mildred 162
Ellington, Olivia 193
Ellis, Bill 219, 220
Engels, Friedrich 113
English Heritage 13
Ethiopia, Italian invasion of 39, 45
Eustache, Catherine 24
Evers, Medgar 205
Ezzrecco, Donald 198
Ezzrecco, Frances 194, 198–9

Fairman, Bill 219–20, 221
fascism 6, 37, 37–9, 56–7, 225
  in Britain 185
  European 37–8, 85
  the fascist triple K 55, 92–3, 126–7
  Jones's antifascism 65–6, 84–92, 92–3, 223
  in the United States 37–9, 41–2, 63–4, 81, 84–92, 122, 223
  the CPUSA and antifascism 37–8, 38–9, 44–5, 51–2, 64, 86–7, 92
  racial fascism 77–8, 119, 223
FBI (Federal Bureau of Investigation)
  and deportation attempts 105, 106, 108
  and families of CPUSA members 142
  and former communists 105
  and Jones's arrest and trial 141
  and Jones's deportation 157–8, 160, 162–3
  and the STJ (Sojourners for Truth and Justice) 137
  surveillance of Jones 67–71, 77, 98–9, 100, 103, 104, 139, 140
FCSAV (Family Committee of the Smith Act Victims) 142–3, 152
Federated Youth Clubs of Harlem 39
feminism 8, 123, 223
  anti-imperialist 171
  Black Left feminism 44, 77, 134
  Marxist 121
  *see also* Black women; women

Ferguson brothers, police killing of 85, 86–7, 91
Fisher, Nigel 190
Floyd, George 11
Flynn, Elizabeth Gurley 6, 55, 74, 94, 102, 105, 107
   *The Alderson Story* 148
   arrest and trial 139–40, 143, 147
   death 213
   *Farewell to Claudia* 120–1, 157
   *A Friend* (To Claudia) 212
   imprisonment 148, 150, 151, 155, 156, 157, 166
   Jones's poem to 79–80, 162
   and the *West Indian Gazette* 183, 184
Ford, James 3, 52–3, 153, 158, 159
Foster, William 54, 74, 77, 113, 159–60, 172
   Jones's autobiographical letter to 160, 166, 168
Fraenkel, Osmond K. 86
France
   and Trinidad 20
Francisco, Slinger 189
Franco, Francisco 45
freedom 223, 224, 225
*Freedomways* 179, 199

Gannett, Betty 106, 107
   arrest and trial 139–40, 144, 147
   imprisonment 148, 150, 151, 166
Garvey, Amy 110, 181, 182–3, 191–2, 194
Garvey, Marcus 26, 43, 110, 192
Garza, Alicia 10
Gates, John 55

gender
   and the Black Belt Thesis 41
   and the CPUSA 37
Geneva Accords 161
Germany 102, 139
   and the Second World War 51, 55–6, 58–60, 73
Ghana 182, 215, 217
Gilpin, Charles 35
Glasgow, Alice 26
Gollobin, Ira 99
Graham, Shirley 102

Haitian revolution 20
Hall, Gus 138, 216
Hamm, Jeffrey 185
Hansberry, Lorraine 113, 171–2
Harding, Gilbert 179
Harlem Renaissance 25
Hawkins, Wiletta 131–2
Hays, Arthur Garfield 86
Haywood, Harry 77
Herndon, Angelo 48–9, 106
Hewitt, George 105, 106
Hickey, F.H. Myles 221
Hines, Donald 4, 7, 181, 188
Hitler, Adolf 37, 59–60, 64, 90, 115
Ho Chi Minh 41, 204
Hoover, J. Edgar 68, 69–71, 114–15, 118, 162–3
Hungary 38
Hunton, Alphaeus 64, 87, 215

ICAA (International Committee on African Affairs) 64
ILD (International Labor Defense) 43, 49, 74
imperialism 16–17, 222
   anti-imperialism and CPUSA members 37, 45, 51
   in Britain 223–4
   and the CPGB 174–8

imperialism (*cont.*)
  race and gender 112
  and US wars 58
  *see also* colonialism
Indian Workers' Association 197
Indochina 204
Ingram, Rosa Lee 135–6, 137
intersectionality 109, 121, 163
Ireland
  Easter Rebellion (1916) 55
IRFCC (Inter-Racial Friendship Coordinating Council) 194, 195
Italian invasion of Ethiopia 39, 45
IWA (Indian Workers' Association) 182
IWW (International Workers of the World) 55

Jackson, Esther Cooper 6, 45, 49, 50, 142, 143
Jackson, James 6, 49, 50, 142
Jamaica Federation of Trade Unions 153
James, C.L.R. 179, 183
Japan 81, 208, 216
  World Conference Against the Hydrogen and Atomic bombs 208–9
Jefferson School of Social Science 113–14, 144
Johnson, Buzz 23
  "*I Think of My Mother*": Notes on the Life and Times of Claudia Jones 4, 7
Johnson, Howard "Stretch" 73, 167, 173, 205
Johnson, Reverend Hewlett 171
Jones, Claudia
  antifascism 65–6, 84–92, 92–3
  antiwar views 55, 124–9
  arrests 48, 99–100, 103–4, 138
  and trial 139–47
  articles
    on the Black Belt Thesis 75–6, 77
    "For the Unity of Women in the Cause of Peace" 131–2
    "Heroines of Peekskill" 117–18
    Neglect 7, 108–12, 124, 133, 141, 175, 192
    "New Approaches" 95–8, 141
    on racism and anticommunism 115–17
    on the Soviet Union 202–3
    *Weekly Review* 53, 56, 59, 63, 64–5, 65
    "West Indians in Britain" 175, 176–7
    *see also Daily Worker* newspaper
  birth (as Claudia Cumberbatch) 24
  and Black socialist feminism 81
  and Browderism 71–8
  in China 209–10
  and the CPUSA 35, 37, 38, 39–51, 67, 219
  and World War II 51–61
  death 3, 165, 207, 213
  deportation 2, 99, 128, 157–63, 224
    failed attempts at 103–6, 107–8
    and Jones's life in England 165, 169
  divorce 95
  early years 18–35
    arrival in the US 19
    schooling 26–9, 31–2

tuberculosis 29–31
work 32
essay on a socialist future 212–13
FBI surveillance of 67–71, 77, 98–9, 100, 103, 104, 139, 140
funeral 213–18
grave 219–22
health issues 12, 29–31, 62, 107, 138, 147–9, 152–4, 155, 156–7, 160–1
  in London 167–8
  in prison 147–9, 152–4, 155, 156–7, 160–1
  and travel 202
imprisonment 106–7, 144, 147–57, 166, 224
and intersectionality 109, 121
on the Korean War 53
legacy 222–5
Leninism 76
in London *see* London
Manchanda and Jones's memory 218–22
marriage to Abraham Scholnick 61–2
Marxism–Leninism 76–7
pamphlets
  *Ben Davis: Fighter for Freedom* 145–6
  *Jim Crow in Uniform* 52–3
  *Lift Every Voice* 63
peace activism 14, 15–16, 124–31
as pen name 47–8, 68, 69, 105
poetry 157, 158
  *Change the Mind of Man* 18
  *Clay Sculpture* 36
  "For Consuela - Anti-Fascista" 150–1
  *Lament for Emmitt Till* 154–5

*Storm at Sea* 164
*To Elizabeth Gurley Flynn* 79–80
radicalization 37, 45, 145
radio broadcast on military training 91
Roosevelt College (Chicago) talk 132–3
scholarly treatments of 5–9
smoking habit 62, 138–9
and South Africa 210–11
in the Soviet Union 201–2
speeches
  "I think of my mother" 27–8
  "International Women's Day and the Struggle for Peace" 126
  Mother's Day (1941) 65–6
and *Spotlight* magazine 65–7
and US citizenship 61–2, 68, 138
on the "Woman Question" 95–8, 108–14
and world communism 201–11
and World War II 16, 51–66
*see also Daily Worker* newspaper
Joseph, Yvonne 5

Kane, Lee 5
Kaufmann, Mary 147, 148–9, 152, 158, 160
Keith, Joseph 138
Kelly, Ken 181
Kennedy, John F. 204, 205
Kenyatta, Jomo 41
Kerr, Sir Hamilton 182–3
Khelifa, L. 215
Khrushchev, Nikita 175, 177
King, Carol 105, 106, 107
King, Martin Luther Jr. 71, 198, 205–6, 215
Kleeck, Mary van 94

# INDEX

Korean War 53, 121, 123, 125, 128, 133, 134, 137, 140, 145, 204
Krupskaya, Nadezhda 123
Ku Klux Klan 178, 186–7, 211
Kunene, Raymond 216

labor movement (US) 87–8
labor unions 15–16
Lamming, George 183, 190, 214, 215, 217–18
Langford, Diane 9, 219, 222
Leach, Baxter R. 32–4
Leninism 8, 76, 77, 177
  *see also* Marxism–Leninism
Levi, Eric 213
liberals 34, 37, 101
liberation movements 16, 28, 223, 224
Lincoln, Abraham 166
Lindbergh, Charles 60, 65
Lipton, Marcus 190
Logan, Thomas 24
London
  Afro People's Centre 190
  CBS (Camden Black Sisters) 5
  Chelsea Royal Court Young People's Theater 6
  Jones in 164–211
  adjustment to life in England 166–73
  and the Commonwealth Immigration Bill 197–201
  and the CPGB 166, 169, 172, 173–80, 185, 201
  housing issues 167–8, 171–2, 182, 203
  and Pan-African politics 171, 182–3, 185, 208
  passport applications 172–3, 203
  and racist violence 194–5
  and world communism 201–11
  Notting Hill Carnival 5, 9, 11, 12, 13, 165, 188–95, 215, 218
  Notting Hill riots 185–8, 191–2, 200
  racist violence in 192–5
  West Indian community 5, 170, 183–4, 191–5, 218
  *see also* WIG (*West Indian Gazette*)
*Los Angeles Tribune* 100
Louis, Joe 63
Lowenfels, Walter 124
LYL (Labor Youth League) 132–3

McCarthy, Senator Joseph 118, 146
McGee, Willie 131–2, 135, 152
Mack, Joseph J. 106
McKay, Claude 32–3
Macmillan, Harold 193
McQueen, Steve 13
Malcolm X assassination 218
Manchanda, Abhimanyu (Manu) 4, 9, 208
  and the CPGB 218–19
  death 222
  and Jones's death 213–14
  and Jones's memory 219–22
  marriage 219
  and the *West Indian Gazette* 181, 182, 202
Mandela, Nelson 210
Manley, Norman 186, 199
Mao Tse Tung 207, 208, 210
Marshall Plan 126
Marshall, Thurgood 86
Marx, Karl 4, 214
Marxism 223
  and feminism 121

Marxism–Leninism 14–16, 76–7
  in China 209
  and the CPGB 176
  Jones's commitment to 145, 165, 169, 171, 177, 214
  and women's rights 109–14, 128
Matthews, George 206
Matusow, Harvey 144, 149
Maugham, Somerset 149
MCF (Movement for Colonial Freedom) 197
Millard, Betty 114
  *Woman against Myth* pamphlet 108–9
Miller, Dorie 63
Miller, Dr. Louis 31, 147–8
Moore, Audley 43–4, 89, 104
Moore, Richard B. 104
Morgan, J.P. 53
Mosley, Oswald 185
Mussolini, Benito 38
Myrdal, Gunnar 146–7

NAACP (National Association for the Advancement of Colored People) 26, 29, 86, 101, 146, 191, 205
  *Crisis* magazine 46
  Youth Council 49–50
National Council of Negro Women 93
NATO (North Atlantic Treaty Organization) 126
Nazi Germany 51, 55–6, 58–60, 80, 139
Nazi–Soviet pact 128
NCDNL (National Committee to Defend Negro Leadership) 153, 154, 158
*Negro Affairs Quarterly* 144–5, 204
Nelson, Rose 107

New Age Publishers 67
*New China News* 172, 182
New York
  Ellis Island 99, 105, 106–7, 108
  Harlem 19, 25–9
  Federated Youth Clubs 39
  Schomburg Center for Research in Black Culture 7
  street-corner speakers 42
  Seaview sanitorium, Staten Island 30–1
  WPA (Works Progress Administration), FWP (Federal Writers' Project) 32–5
*New York Age* newspaper 32–4
Nkrumah, Kwame 182
NNC (National Negro Congress) 47, 48, 49, 61, 64, 87–9
Norman, Bill 104
North, Joseph 138
*Notable Black American Women* (encyclopedia) 8
Notting Hill Carnival 5, 9, 11, 12, 13, 165, 188–91, 215, 218
  beauty culture and the Carnival Queen 189–91
Notting Hill riots 185–8, 191–2, 200
Nubian Jak Community Trust 13
nuclear weapons 81, 103, 125, 129, 207–9, 210

Offord, Irma 31
Ottley, Roi 33

Pan-African politics 171, 182, 182–3, 185, 208
Paris Peace Congress 129

Patterson, William  74, 90, 136, 153, 158, 168
  and Jones's deportation  161–2
peace activism  14, 16–17, 124–31, 136–7, 145
Permanent Committee of the Partisans of Peace  125
Perry, Pettis  3, 44, 139, 143, 144
PIC (Peace Information Center)  129
Pinder, Winston  220–2
Pinnock, Winsome
  *A Rock in the Water*  6
Pitt, David  218
*Pittsburgh Courier* newspaper  63
police and racial violence
  in the United States  83, 85, 86–7, 91, 122, 223
Pollitt, Harry  160–1
Popular Front  44–6, 47, 56, 92
Prescod, Colin  7, 189
Prescod, Pearl  189, 214
Puerto Rico  151, 183–4

racial capitalism  20–1, 83, 200–1
racial equality
  and CPUSA membership  37
racial fascism  38–9, 77–8, 85, 119, 223
racism  6, 14, 15, 35
  and anticommunism  34, 115–16, 146–7, 170–1
  in Britain  192–5, 205–6, 211, 224
  and the CPGB  12, 173–80
  and the CPUSA  76–7, 171, 173–4
  and fascism  38, 38–9, 85
  and Jones's schooldays  28–9, 31
  and right-wing politics today  10
  systemic racism  111, 178
  in the United States  19, 25, 34, 38, 82, 85, 86–7, 211
Randolph, A. Philip  87, 90
rape  42, 43, 131–2, 151–2
Reuther, Walter  88
revolutionary figures, attempts to mainstream  11–12
Reynolds, Nia  13
Richardson, Beulah  133–4
Robeson, Eslanda  65, 102, 145, 162, 180, 184, 192, 193, 214, 215
Robeson, Paul  5, 6, 35, 63, 87, 102, 116–17, 129, 168, 204, 206
  and Jones's death and funeral  214, 215
  and Jones's deportation  162
  and Jones's imprisonment  153
  Jones's interview with  64–5
  passport issues and move to London  179–80
  and the *West Indian Gazette*  184–5
Robinson, Heloise  168, 171–2
Robinson, Jackie  116–17
Rogers, George  195
Rogers, J.A.  32–3
Romeika, Joseph  86–7
Roosevelt, Eleanor  107
Roosevelt, Franklin  53–4, 65, 67, 69, 72, 75, 80, 88, 92, 101
Rosas Cevallos, Xavier  95
Royle, Lord Charles  217

Salkey, Andrew  217–18
Schmeling, Max  63
Scholnick, Abraham  61–2, 95
Schomburg Center for Research in Black Culture  7, 9
Schomburg, Arthur  33
Schwartz, Bill  187–8, 191

SCLC (Southern Christian Leadership Conference) 46
Scottsboro campaign 41–4, 50, 104, 174
Segal, Edith
*For Claudia Jones* 1
Seneca Falls Women's Convention 95
sexism 6, 14, 15, 35
Sidhant, Dr Rinjana 204
Simon, Joseph Dill 193–4
Skinner-Carter, Corrine 191
*Small Axe* films 13
Smith, Lawrence 71
SNCC (Student Nonviolent Coordinating Committee) 46
social justice 9, 225
socialism 10, 17, 224
socialist feminism 8
Sojourners for Truth and Justice (STJ) 133–7, 142, 143, 153
Soong Ching Ling, Madame 209
South Africa
　apartheid 176, 183, 199, 216
　Rivonia trials 210–11, 216
South America 74
Soviet Union 86, 210
　and American communists 67
　and China 207–8
　and the Cold War 92, 103
　and the CPUSA 51
　and Jones's death 216
　Jones's visits 201–2
　Nazi-Soviet pact 51–2, 90
　and nuclear weapons 207–8
　postwar hostility towards 90
　and Stalinism 128, 175, 177
　and US anticommunism 82–3, 126

and the US Progressive Party 102
and women's rights 128
and World War II 55–6, 59–60, 64, 80
the Yalta Conference and Browderism 72–3
*Soviet Woman* magazine 201
Spain and Trinidad 20
Spanish Civil War 45
Sparks, Fay 191
*Spotlight* magazine
　Jones's articles for 65–7, 72–3
Stalin, Joseph 72, 128, 175, 177, 179
Stalinism 128
STJ (Sojourners for Truth and Justice) 133–7, 142, 143, 153
Stockholm Peace Appeal 125
Strachan, Billy 4, 175
Strong, Edward 179
Sun Yat-Sen 209
*Sunday Worker* newspaper 183
SYNC (Southern Negro Youth Congress) 49, 50
systemic racism 111, 178

Tambo, Oliver 215
Thomas, Yvette 4
Thomas-Johnson, Amandla 4, 11–12, 23
Thompson Patterson, Louise 42–3, 45, 134
"Towards a Brighter Dawn" 46–7
Thurmond, Strom 102
Till, Emmitt 154–5, 158
Tometi, Opal 10
Torresola, Consuela 150–1
Trachtenberg, Alex 160
Trade Union Committee for Claudia Jones 143

trade unions 178–9, 201, 210
Trinidad and Tobago 19, 20–4, 26, 173
  European settlers 20–3
  hurricane relief for 182
  and Jones's deportation 108, 158
  Trinidad Independence Party 154
  World War I 23–4
Truman, Harry S. 67, 88–9, 102, 105, 125, 126
Trump, Donald 9, 39
Truth, Sojourner 5, 184
Tubman, Harriet 5, 184, 215
Tyson, Jennifer 5

UNIA (United Negro Improvement Association) 43
United Defense Committee Against Discrimination 192
United Nations 73, 107, 136–7, 168
United States
  Alien Friends Act (1918) 99
  anticommunism 5, 9, 12–13, 34, 81–3, 84, 85, 114–19, 146, 170
    CPUSA criticism of 121–2
    and CPUSA members 99–100, 103, 115–16, 118–19, 139, 140–7
    and racism 115–16, 146–7, 170–1
  antiradicalism 85
  Burke-Wadsworth conscription bill 54
  and the Caribbean 22
  civil rights movement 83–4, 204–5
  Civil War 40

Claudia Jones School for Political Education 13–14
COINTELPRO (Counterintelligence Program) 71
Cumberbatch family in Harlem 25–35
Democrats 102
Equal Rights Amendment (ERA) 127
Fair Employment Practices Committee (FEPC) 75, 80, 88
fascism 37–9, 41–2, 63–4, 81, 84–92, 122, 223
  racial fascism 38–9, 77–8, 85, 119, 223
Great Depression 28, 29, 37, 48, 123
House Dies Committee 34
House Un-American Activities Committee (HUAC) 34, 94–5, 102, 115
immigration laws 104
Internal Security Act (1950) 62
Jim Crow system 49, 52, 56–7, 57–8, 73, 186
Lend-Lease Bill 54
lynch law 42, 53–4, 87, 117, 130, 131–3, 134–7, 146
McCarran Internal Security Act 106, 159
McCarran–Walter Act (1952) 144, 146, 162, 166, 170, 193, 195–6, 200
memory of Jones in 12–14
militarism 16–17, 81–3, 102–3, 122, 210, 225
military-industrial complex 130, 224
National Origins Act (1924) 195–6

New Deal 47, 72, 75, 86, 88
and nuclear weapons 81, 103, 125, 129, 207–9
police and racial violence 83, 85, 86–7, 91, 122, 223
poverty 19, 25, 37
prison literature 49
prison population 122
Procedure Act 107
Progressive Party 102
and Puerto Rico 183–4
racial fascism 38–9, 77–8, 85, 119, 223
racism 19, 25, 34, 38, 82, 85, 86–7, 211
Republican National Committee 34
Smith Act 67, 108, 162, 169, 170
  arrests and trials 95, 139–47, 159–60
Socialist Party 41
Special War Policies Unit 71
Supreme Court, *Dennis v. United States* 139
Truman Doctrine 88–9
and Vietnam 204, 208
West Indian immigration 146, 193
women's suffrage movement 95
and World War II 51–66, 72–3, 80–1
*see also* Cold War; CPUSA (American Communist Party); white supremacy
UNIA (United Negro Improvement Association) 26
Urban League 29, 30
USSR *see* Soviet Union

Vietnam 161, 203–4, 208

Wallace, Henry 92, 101–2
war
  Jones's antiwar views 55, 124–9
  *see also* World War I; World War II
*We Charge Genocide* petition 136–7
*Weekly Review* magazine (later *Spotlight*) 68
  Jones's articles in 53, 56, 59, 63, 64–5, 65
Weinstock, Louise 6
*West Indian American News* 28, 33, 169
West Indian Federation 182, 186, 188, 201
*West Indian Gazette see WIG (West Indian Gazette)*
West Indian Workers and Students Association 180, 181
West Indians
  in Britain 175, 176–9, 177–8, 183–4, 185–6, 195, 196–8, 201
  immigration to the USA 146, 193
White, Maude 37, 41
white supremacy 10, 49, 57, 70–1, 84, 85
  and the anticommunist state 139
  apartheid 199
  and capitalism 122
  and Cold War policy 137
  and CPUSA members 44
  and fascism 93
White, Walter 146–7
Whittaker, Julie 6
WIDF (Women's International Democratic Federation) 94–5, 203

*WIG (West Indian Gazette)* 172, 180–5, 203, 210, 222
    and the civil rights movement 205
    and the Commonwealth Immigration Act 198, 199–201
    final issue 218
    and Jones's death 214, 215, 217, 218, 219
    and Manu 181, 182, 202
    on Martin Luther King Jr. 205–6, 215
    and the Notting Hill Carnival 188–91
    and the Notting Hill riots 186–8, 192
    and racist violence 193–4
    renamed *West Indian Gazette and Afro-Asian Caribbean News* 180, 198
Wilkerson, Doxey 73, 89, 113
Williams, Eric 173, 186
    *History of the People of Trinidad and Tobago* 21, 23
Williamson, John and Mae 166, 167
Winston, Henry 3, 48–9, 60–1, 73, 89, 201, 216
    arrest and trial 115, 116, 118

women
    and the CPUSA 37, 77
    Jones on women's rights 95–8, 108–14, 127–8, 170
    in Jones's "Half the World" column 123–4
    and the labor movement 15
    suffrage movement 95
    and war 80, 126–7, 130–2
    *see also* Black women
Wood, Dr John 147–8
*The Worker* 95
World Congress of Women 203, 203–4
*World Magazine* 3
*World News* 177
World Peace Congress 125
World War I 53
    and British West India 23–4
World War II 16, 51–66, 72–3, 80–1, 93
    and China 209
Wright, Ada 174
Wright, Roy 42, 174

Yalta Conference 72–3
YCL (Young Communist League) 42, 48–9, 50–1, 65, 67, 167
    anti-draft campaign 54
    *Weekly Review* articles 52, 57
Yergan, Max 64